ADRENALIN RUSH

ADRENALIN RUSH

THE COLLECTED WORKS OF E.J. RUSH

Hodder Moa Beckett

A catalogue record for this book is available from the National Library of New Zealand.

ISBN: 1-86971-005-3

Published in 2004 by Hodder Moa Beckett Publishers Ltd
[a member of the Hodder Headline Group]
4 Whetu Place, Mairangi Bay
Auckland, New Zealand

Front cover illustration by Murray Webb
Designed and produced by Hodder Moa Beckett Publishers Ltd
Printed by Griffin Press, Australia

For Dad

Acknowledgements

The publishers wish to thank Photosport, Fotopress and the Rush family for the use of the photographs in this book.

Contents

Foreword

SEVENS RUGBY WILL NEVER BE THE SAME AGAIN.

It's a massive statement but one that when it comes to Eric Rush is spot on. No single player has had as much impact on sevens in New Zealand as Rushie. Yes, Jonah Lomu and Christian Cullen have put in performances at tournaments that you had to see to believe but no one has had the longevity of Rushie.

He was there in 1994 when I first took charge of the New Zealand sevens team and he was there this year as we competed for, and won, our fifth consecutive World Series.

It says much for the contribution he has made to the game that to simply describe him as 'Mr Consistency' somehow doesn't seem enough.

Of course, in one sense that is the perfect description for him. He made his sevens debut in 1988 and has played in more than 60 tournaments for New Zealand.

He captained both of our Commonwealth Games gold medal-winning teams and was the captain of the side that won the World Cup in 2001 before injury struck him down midway through the tournament.

He has been there when we have won numerous tournaments around the world and was inspirational in our breakthrough year at Wellington and, of course, our tournament wins on sevens' biggest stage in Hong Kong.

But he is — and always will be — remembered for more than just his on-field contributions.

Rushie has been the key driving force behind the special sevens culture that has made the team the perfect launching pad for so many All Black careers.

Whether your name was Jonah, Christian, Mils or Joe, Rushie would have made you feel welcome at your first sevens camp. He would always go out of his way to talk to and encourage the young players. He would have a laugh with them — although usually at their expense — and take them under his wing.

Rushie's ability to take pressure off his team-mates is the stuff of legends. They watch and learn that it's okay to switch off at a tournament — as long as you switch on when the time comes.

They learn the value of leadership because he encourages them to stand up and be heard.

And they learn about winning.

Those are the things that will be hard to replace now that East Tamaki in Auckland is the only team reaping the benefits of his life in rugby.

My challenge now as the coach of the team is to make sure that the culture he and others like Dallas Seymour have been responsible for setting up in the sevens team survives.

I have no doubt it will because Rushie has passed on his skills and knowledge to the new breed of players. They know the things that Eric Rush stood for and now they want to pay homage to him by continuing his legacy by continuing to win.

When we finished off this year's World Series without an injured Rushie in the team it was strange. After 10 seasons together, not having him on board with us didn't feel right.

But if I have my way the NZRU will find a way to involve him in the next two years. I want him employed as a technical advisor to the team so he can remain involved and continue to inspire.

Rushie has had plenty of opportunities to leave New Zealand and play and coach overseas but he has always turned his back on those offers. That type of loyalty needs to be rewarded.

I plan on standing down as coach of the team after the 2006 Commonwealth Games.

There is only one man I'd like to see in charge of the side after I go and that's Rushie.

Gordon Tietjens
September 2004

Introduction

JUST WHEN YOU THOUGHT IT WAS SAFE to go on a rugby tour again, my publisher rang and asked me for a third book!

Now, before all you fellas that have played rugby with me reach for the speed dial and ring your lawyers, just remember that plenty of players have been jerked by me in the past and all have survived — some even still talk to me.

If the truth be known, the reality is that most of the complaints I get from team-mates come when I have left them *out* of the book.

Mils Muliaina was embarrassed that I didn't mention him in my second book, *Rushie* — even though he was a part of the gold medal-winning team in Manchester. He did appear in a picture on page 19 but admittedly he was in the background and only his mother would have recognised him.

So Mils will be pleased with this effort because he even gets a photo.

Other players claim never to have read the first two books and yet they know that I have jerked them. And that's the reason why this book includes the collected works of E.J. Rush. I want to make sure that all the players I have mentioned have another chance to read what I have said about them. They won't be able to buy the first two books now as they both sold out (mind you, we only printed 20 copies of each).

And I want those players who think their nicknames are in the past to know that they aren't in the past!

So you will read about Christian Cullen (Beer Bottle — because he's empty from the neck up), Willie Lose (Mirror Man — because he is always looking in one) and Tony Ward (99 — because he has 99 parts in his hair).

And you will read about — and be reminded of — some of the great characters in this game called rugby.

So, to all my fellow rugby players who have paid for, borrowed or stolen a copy of this book, enjoy.

Thanks for all the great memories.

Winning Wellington

SEVENS RUGBY AIN'T WHAT IT USED TO BE — that's what the so-called experts say anyway.

I realise there is a lot more rugby on these days — from February to December if you follow the All Blacks. So sevens rugby has suffered a little in terms of coverage.

But the point ought to be made that the coverage on TV is terrible. I really hope that TV3 or Sky TV get it because TVNZ has just been playing the World Series as a highlights package. When TV3 covered Hong Kong, they showed every game live. Rugby people loved it. They were able to watch the team progress through the tournament and as a result it meant a little more to them when they saw us play at the business end of the competition.

The truth is, around the world, sevens is growing every year. The tournaments are getting bigger and so are the crowds. The average fan might not hear as much about the team as they did in the so-called glory years when David Campese was playing for Australia and guys like Zinzan Brooke, Jonah Lomu and then Christian Cullen were turning out for New Zealand, but we know that rugby people are following us because the Wellington leg of the IRB World Series is now rivalling Hong Kong as the best sevens event in the world.

Winning the tournament for the first time in 2003 was a real relief. It felt like every year that we played down there all the other teams were ganging up on us to try to spoil the party. That's how we play overseas. When you run out in Argentina in front of their crowd the first goal is to quiet them down — the best way to do that is to score an early try. It's a different story when you aren't playing, though. **The crowd is full of beautiful South American women so we'll always emerge from our changing room if Argentina are playing. When the Pumas score the women start dancing in the stands — the boys love it.** One time we were watching the game (or so I thought) and I turned to Craig Newby to talk about one of the Pumas players and, not only was he not watching the game, he was actually facing in a completely opposite direction to the field!

When teams come to Wellington, it's like they grow another leg. The tournament is probably the most popular with all the players now. Everyone wants to beat us on our own turf. And, from the New Zealand team's point of view, it couldn't be better. The crowd is right up there with the best of them. I've played in places around the world where the passion of Wellington has been matched, but the difference is in Wellington people in the crowd don't throw firecrackers at you, they don't spit on you and they don't chuck bottles at you.

Wellington and Hong Kong — and even Dubai — have more of a party atmosphere. Everyone is there to have a good time. It's almost like a throwback to what rugby used to be about — it's good hard stuff on the field but it's about mates and having a laugh off the field. It's like our own little rugby time warp.

I have never seen a New Zealand crowd like the one in Wellington. It's almost as if you go to the sevens at Westpac Trust Stadium and don't dress up, people will look at you and say, 'What's your problem? Are you too good for us or something?' One of my mates, Brian Marsh, who teaches at my old school Tangaroa College, is a real Warriors fan. He never misses the sevens and started something of a trend when he showed up at the 2001 event dressed as a doctor. I'd broken my leg at the World Cup a couple of weeks earlier, so, obviously inspired by the TV show, he had the letters E.R. printed on his uniform, only the E.R. stood for *Eric Rush* as well as *Emergency Room*.

He spotted me on my crutches and told me that there was a little kid in the crowd who wanted to meet me. 'He really loves you, Rushie,' he said. 'It touched my heart when the little fella

After breaking my leg at the World Cup Sevens in 2001, I was a soft target for my mates in Wellington.

asked me if I could get you to meet him. I told him I would do everything I could to make it happen. Would you come meet him, bro?' Well, there was no way that I wouldn't so I worked my way across the field and finally made it to the part of the stadium where Dr Marsh was. I didn't realise it at the time but he had been cavorting with three bays full of people and when he saw me, he blew his whistle and everyone went quiet. *'Okay, ladies and gentlemen . . . when I say "Eric" you say "Rush". Eric! . . . Rush! . . . Eric! . . . Rush!'* I was shrinking. **There was no kid! He just wanted to embarrass the shit out of me! He succeeded. Now there are 30 people dressed up as doctors every year at the sevens. They became my support group.**

The stadium is unbelievable when the sevens is on. It's an event on its own in terms of the New Zealand sporting calendar. The only advantage Hong Kong has over it is that we have to travel to get there — so when we lose, it's not like the end of the world. And I should know because we have lost in Wellington too many times.

The first year, in 2000, we lost in the final to Fiji, even though we had Cully and Jonah in the team. In 2001 — a couple of weeks after winning the World Cup — we lost to Fiji again, in the quarterfinals. The next year wasn't any better when the South Africans stuffed us 26–10 in the semi-finals. Here we were, the best team in the world, and we couldn't win at our own tournament. It was as if there was a mental block — like we were trying too hard. It was frustrating because a few weeks after losing to the Springboks in Wellington we played them in China and won 43–14.

It doesn't matter what New Zealand team you are playing for — the sevens side, the Maori or the All Blacks — when you lose it's always the same feeling. You feel terrible. Rock bottom. New Zealand rugby is unique compared with any other sport in the country because if you have that black jersey on you are expected to win. No other sport has that expectation, although that's beginning to change a little. Ours does and it's tough, but there's no point complaining about it because that's part of the

Gloomy faces after losing to South Africa in the semis of the Wellington tournament in 2002. At least our heads are high.

mana of getting the chance to pull on a black jersey.

The worst thing you can do is think about the expectations of the public. You need to try to push it to the back of your mind. The only thing you should think about is the next training or the next game. Before we went to Manchester for the 2002 Commonwealth Games, I showed the boys my gold medal from 1998. Some of them refused to even look at it, let alone touch it. Brad Fleming was one of them — 'I want to win my own one.' **I told the team that this was what we were playing for but this was the last time we would talk about the medal. 'Don't think too far ahead.** You've seen the medal, now forget about it. Forget about all the expectation from the country. Just think about the 12 people in this room.' *Every* rugby team should think that way. You know about the expectations but you can't afford to let that pressure get on top of you.

Tab Baldwin — who secured his place in the history of New Zealand sport when he led the Tall Blacks to an unexpected fourth place at the World Championships in 2002 — talked to the team a couple of years back and stressed the importance of the process rather than the outcome. In other words, if you are preparing for a Commonwealth Games final, don't think about the gold medal. Instead, think about the warm-up. Make sure you do that right because if you don't, the chances are there will be no gold medal at the end of the night.

The guys are aware of the pressure when they come into the team. You just have to accept the situation and make sure you do everything you can to meet those expectations. We have a saying in the team: *It's not supposed to be easy — that's why we are here to do the job.*

The fact is the sevens team loses a lot more than it used to because the landscape has changed. We aren't just trying to peak for one or two tournaments a year any more. The World Series has changed that. The series is about consistency. It doesn't matter how good you are, no team is going to go through all those tournaments — in Chile, Argentina, Australia, New Zealand, Hong Kong, Wales, England, France, Singapore and the United Arab Emirates — undefeated. It's almost a physical impossibility. But that doesn't make losing any easier to take. **I guess the good thing about sport is that it teaches you to win and lose. You shouldn't like losing but you should learn how to accept it and, if you don't like it, well, there is only one group of people that can do something about that.**

The sevens team is like any other New Zealand rugby team — we play for New Zealand and our goal is always a simple one: to be the best team in the world. And there is no 'Plan B'. We don't talk about 'Plan B'; we never have and we never will. We aren't going to win every World Series, we aren't always going to win the Commonwealth Games and we're not always going to win the World Cup. It just happens that at the moment we have all those titles locked away, but it won't always be like that.

When we do lose a game and find ourselves out of the running for one of the World Series event titles, I always tell the boys to try to learn from it. Remember the feeling that we are feeling right now and make sure we don't feel this way again next week. I tell them: 'We have to forgive ourselves and move on. We didn't play well, but that's not us. We are better than that. Let's prove it.'

On a personal level I have learnt to deal with losing. I was introduced to something called the Cycle of Success. Imagine a diagram where everyone starts with the same potential. Then there is an arrow to 'self-belief'. Then an arrow to 'performance' and then 'results'. Each can affect the other. If you have strong self-belief then your performance will be better and so will your results. It works the other way, too — if your results are bad, your performance suffers and so does your self-belief. **The key is to be able to change things when the shit is hitting the fan — like when we lost that semi-final to the South Africans at Wellington.**

It's all about making a conscious choice to get a few wins on the board to improve your self-belief.

Normally, the day after a tournament we don't train, we just have a recovery session. But we decided to have our recovery session in the morning and train in the afternoon. *A win on the board because no one else trained.* Then when we were in China leading up to the tournament, we trained twice a day instead of just once. *Another win. No one else is doing that.* We went into the lunchroom and they only had greasy stuff. None of us had any. All the other teams tucked in. We all had salad instead. *Another win.* Titch was on a roll . . .

I knew things were going to be tough in China when all the teams were taken to see the Great Wall of China. It was an awesome sight. The boys were just about to head up the steps to get to the top of the thing when this voice came bellowing out from behind us: 'Hey, hey, hey. Bloody hell! What the f . . . are you boys doing?' I told Titch we were in China and we were going to go up the Great Wall of China.

'No, you f . . . ing aren't! Look at the ground; it's the same down here as it is up there. Look at all those other silly players from the other teams walking up there. It's the legs! The legs! Their legs will be gone . . .' **So there we were, the New Zealand sevens team in China for the first time, walking around the bottom of the Great Wall of China. We'd come all this way and we weren't allowed to walk up the bastard!** The other teams, if they'd looked back, would have seen a whole lot of brown boys looking pissed off. And if they could have heard us it would have been a symphony of '*Whatever! Great f . . .ing Wall of f . . .ing China!*'

The victory against the Springboks in China was in the final, and that title really belongs to Titch. He made some significant tactical changes to the way we approached things after bombing in Wellington. Sometimes coaches, when they have a dumb strategy and it's not working, just work longer and harder. But Titch isn't afraid to make changes. **In Wellington the Boks had a lot of pace on the outsides and that sort of nullified our attack. They also had a few backs playing as forwards so we decided we'd take the game to them and bash them.** At the beginning of the final in China Joe Rokocoko was under instructions not to even try to beat his opposite number on the outside but instead bring the ball up through the middle to set up a ruck. I followed him and set up the ruck and the ball was then passed to a steamrolling Chris Masoe and he smaaaaashed them. Masoe knocked the ball on but two Africans were left on the ground and you could see in their eyes that they just didn't want to be out there with us.

Sure enough, after we smashed the Boks in the final Titch was on form. 'I told you fellas. I told you. Don't go up the Wall.' Up the wall? Titch was driving us up the wall . . .

China proved to me that our failures in Wellington were down to a state of mind. So, during the week building up to the 2003 tournament we held a team meeting to try to figure out why we couldn't win it. One idea we came up with was to make a real effort to be more focused. Often, when we play around the world, we will only leave the changing shed to play our games. As soon as the game is over, we're back in the shed. **Some guys have their cards, others their music or books — whatever you need for the day you take with you.** But in Wellington, we'd be all over the place seeing the whanau and having a look at all the people in the crowd. So we decided to make a change — on the first day we could do the whanau thing but on the second day we would be in the shed.

Capital conquest at last . . . holding high the elusive winner's trophy at Wellington in 2003.

I've never seen a crowd quite like the one we get at the Wellington sevens. As far as a party atmosphere goes, only Hong Kong and Dubai match it.

Another thing we were doing overseas but not in Wellington was having a bit of a warm-up at the hotel. We'd use the hotel corridors and have 20 stride-outs just to get the body moving. Just because we were at home didn't mean we didn't have to do that so we brought that back as well.

Those changes didn't seem enough, though, so I told the guys to speak up — 'Don't hold back fellas. If you have something to say, say it now 'cause it will be too late on Sunday night if we've lost the bloody thing again.'

Amasio Valance spoke up and asked why we hadn't been to the local marae. Straight away all the heads of the Maori boys went down — none lower than mine. In Maori culture when you visit an area, you get welcomed first by the local tribe. If you haven't been welcomed you shouldn't be in the area, but if you have been welcomed you can go to the marae anytime. Amasio — a Fijian — said, **'Maybe it's a spiritual thing, bro. We haven't been welcomed by the locals. Maybe we're not supposed to be here . . .' All I could think of was that he was right . . . so I organised it. It was time to pay a visit to the Wharenui marae.**

It was only a couple of days before the tournament but Titch didn't mind the late change to our plans. He'd grown up in Rotorua and had played with Maori team-mates all his life so he understood the significance of it.

The old fella at the marae stood up and welcomed us in Maori and then spoke to us in English. 'Yep, it's good to see you fellas here. We have been waiting for you to come.' Straight away I felt about one foot tall. 'There's no secret as to why you fellas haven't won here. You know there is a big carving outside the front of that stadium, now I am going to tell you what it means . . .'

He went through the story of how the centrepiece carving represents Rua Taranaki (the mountain). He told us the mountain represents the challenge of reaching the pinnacle in achievement. How it symbolises the hurdle to be overcome by people as they strive to achieve their valued goals. He told us about Ruakura (The Feathers) and Ka Awatea (The Spirits).

'You can't go into that stadium and drive past that carving and expect to do well. You didn't even know what it represents. But that's not important because you are here now — and I'll tell you what, you are going to win now!'

All the boys were as happy as Larry. We'd been given the blessing.

'And you know what else? The Hurricanes . . . they haven't been here yet. **They ain't going to win until they come either. And don't you tell them to come. Let them come under their own steam.'**

We talked about that old fella before the final against England. I told the boys that we were playing for his people too now. We knew their story and we were playing on their turf. We won the tournament. We go to the marae every year now . . .

Then and now

IT'S NOT A TOUGH CHOICE: the old days when we played for fun — or the modern-day professional game? If I could have my career again, I'd play it in the amateur era. Forget about the television exposure, the increased profile and the big money contracts, I'd turn back the clock in a heartbeat.

In the amateur days you played for the pure adrenalin of it. The payment you got was the thrill of wearing your representative jersey — whether it was the North Auckland jersey, the Auckland jersey, the Harbour jersey, the New Zealand Maori jersey or the All Blacks jersey.

I certainly don't have anything against professional rugby and I can't be accused of being a bitter player from the amateur days because I have had nine years in the game as a professional. It's just that with money in the game, rugby doesn't seem as pure any more.

I hear a few people criticising today's players because of all the money they make, but that's ridiculous. It's not their fault they are being paid! **And let me give you a tip: when Jonah Lomu is running full steam at you the last thing on your mind is how much interest your long-term deposit is making at the bank . . .**

But I do feel sorry for the modern players in the sense that the purity is gone. The days when players finished work and went to training. The days when, if you had to do extras, you'd get up in the dark and go for a run and then head to the gym in your lunch hour. When you were making those sacrifices it just made it easier for teams to bond because you were all giving things up to be at training. **The coaches expected you to show up at training fit and ready to go. Today, players go to training to get fit!**

I must admit, though, that I enjoyed my footie in the last days of my career just as much as I did when I was first starting out. In 2004 you can't get away with half the things we used to get away with off the field, but at the end of the day a footie team is a footie team and there are always plenty of characters around to keep you laughing.

It was good to see that things haven't changed when I ran into a couple of All Blacks at the 2003 World Cup. I was over there doing some speaking engagements when I went into a nightclub and everyone was saying that Prince Harry was there. They shut off a room with a pool table and sure enough there was Harry surrounded by all his mates. They were all wearing their English rugby jerseys. I was with Ric Salizzo from *Sports Café* and we started up a conversation with one of the security guys. It would be fair to say that he wasn't the most professional fella in his trade — he was pissed. I told him that since we'd been talking to him he hadn't even checked on how Harry was doing but he didn't care. 'Don't worry,' he said. 'There are six other security boys on the job — it's called being undercover.'

He slurred and told us that 'Harry loves the All Blacks. Go and say hello . . . he'll be chuffed.' I told the guy that Ric was John Mitchell and off he went, stumbling across to see the prince.

'Harry, these are two former All Blacks — they wanted to say hello.' Harry couldn't have been happier to see us but before we could say anything he said, 'Anyone who comes in here can't talk to me unless they kiss the rose on my English jersey. Kiss it!'

I told him, in my best steely Richard Loe voice, that we wouldn't be kissing any f . . . ing rose — I was sure we were going to get kicked out, but young Harry was fine.

Playing for the pure adrenalin rush . . . wearing North Harbour colours and just happy to be out there.

Caleb Ralph: suitor to the nobles. He cut Dan Carter's lunch with royal aplomb.

'Oh, that's great! That's why you guys are the All Blacks! All these other dickheads have been kissing it!'

It was refreshing to see a guy like that having such a good time. Princess Zara is the same. They are just normal people.

Zara was at Harry's do that night. Ric and I were giving her shit about all the horsey people her parents, Captain Mark Phillips and Princess Anne, helped make famous. I am sure the equestrian lot are a good bunch but — let's be honest — they have a reputation. I remember watching an interview with one of the dressage guys and he actually said *I'm a little bit rusty around the ring* . . . Probably not a wise choice of words. Ric reminded her about all that.

A couple of the All Blacks reserves showed up — Caleb Ralph and Dan Carter. **I pointed out to Caleb that Prince Harry and Princess Zara were there. He wasn't too impressed . . . until he saw Zara: 'Shiiiiiit, she's alright, eh!' he said. 'Be great to get with her. What a story that would be . . .'**

Caleb disappeared to get a drink from the bar — probably to get a bit of Dutch courage up. Then Zara came over and made a comment about 'the good-looking young All Blacks'. She was looking in Dan Carter's direction so I introduced them and left them to it. They seemed to be getting along quite well but Caleb wasn't having any of that. In the All Blacks there is a hierarchy. Caleb first played for the ABs in 1998 and was something of a senior figure in the team for the young guys like DC to look up to.

When Zara was off in the toilet doing whatever girls do in there with their mates, Caleb went up to DC and told him to f-off. He pulled rank on him and DC had no choice but to give up any intentions he had with Zara — and hand them to Caleb! It was only a matter of weeks before the press found out about Caleb and Zara. It was all on there for a while. I wonder if it would have lasted longer if it had been DC that Zara walked off into the sunset with?

Hmmm.

It's always important to have a bit of a laugh because life on the road can be tough. Life in the sevens team is always tough — Titch makes sure of that.

Part of the team's culture, though, is mocking your mates. It's almost as though you aren't accepted into the team unless you have been mocked. And it's not just the players who are targeted.

Once in Hong Kong I introduced our manager Tony Ward by telling everyone that he is the only manager of the New Zealand sevens team to be in the exclusive Mile High Club — unfortunately he was sitting in business class by himself at the time he performed the deed.

Titch didn't escape that day either. I grabbed the mike and told the audience of sponsors and their hangers-on that Titch had spent the whole morning doing his hair . . . but, unfortunately, he forgot to bring it with him.

Mocking guys in public like that is probably the best thing about being captain. But in the last few years I have tried to give the other guys a go. I'll introduce the first player and then he'll

Titch — he had a full head of hair before he took on the sevens job.

introduce the next one. They all pinch my lines — one of the favourites is to introduce a player as the G-Man because he wears a G-string when he plays. After everyone stops laughing you add the best bit: 'Sometimes he puts it on backwards and it doesn't really matter.' I first used the line on Craig Newby.

Another one the boys like to use is this gem: 'We call him Horse and it's not because of his running style. He has a very long . . . face!'

I have been on the receiving end a couple of times. When Matua 'Muts' Parkinson was the captain he called me Vintage. 'We just call him Vintage because he rallies once a year and you have to start him by hand!'

Handing the mike to the young fellas in the team isn't always a great idea. One time Tafai Ioasa got up in front of an audience in Hong Kong and made a dick of himself. Telecom — one of the team's great sponsors — had done a deal with a fellow communications company in Hong Kong called Reach and the event we were at was organised to pay homage to staff of Telecom's new partners. After I finished my speech Tafai asked for the mike because he wanted to slay me in front of everyone. As soon as he got the mike in his hand he froze. He didn't jerk me at all. He thanked a few people and then at the end said, 'I want to thank all the Reach people. It's fair to say that Rushie needs a fair bit of your product.' You could have heard a pin drop. Everyone was just standing there with blank looks on their faces because no one in the audience was from New Zealand, so they had no idea that in New Zealand 'Reach' is a toothbrush brand! I took the mike back and explained and got the best laugh of the night. Tafai grabbed me a few minutes later and said, 'Don't ever give me the mike again. Please don't give it to me.'

The guy that probably gets jerked the most is our physio. I have given him about 10 different nicknames and then at Hong Kong I told the crowd that he was a bit of a drinker so we call him The Exorcist. He looked at me all puzzled and I said, 'Because whenever he leaves the room he takes all the spirits with him.'

One of the great characters from my recent time in the

Rua Tipoki — sometimes left a bad taste in team-mates' mouths.

Harbour NPC side was Rua Tipoki. He always liked to play tricks on our prop Tony Coughlan. Harbour's mascot was the Harbour Master and he used to hand out trumpets to the kids in the crowd. We had a good win one day and one of the boys had got hold of one of the trumpets and we were passing it around the room. **Eventually it was passed to Rua. He didn't know I was watching him but when he thought no one was looking at him, he took off his sock and rubbed the mouthpiece in between his toes and then nonchalantly passed the trumpet to poor old TC**. Rua had this innocent look on his face as TC took the trumpet and had about five blows. No one was laughing because no one knew. That was the day I knew Rua was a very sick man.

Rua liked to mix it up, too. He used to love one of Titch's drills that saw us split up into pairs, drop to our knees and try to throw the other guy to the ground using only your arms. He was good at it — he was deceptively strong for a little fella. He'd get frustrated, though, because he could beat everyone at it except me. Don't think he liked getting beaten by the old fella!!!

Rua is probably best known for his run-in with Harbour

CEO Doug Rollerson in 2002. All us Maori boys love getting back to our roots and playing for our tribes in the Pa Wars — something Rua did without permission from Harbour. **It turned out he injured his hands in a game and instead of fronting up to Rollerson — who needed him for Harbour's NPC campaign — he told Doug and coach Buck Shelford that he injured his hands when a weight fell on them at a gym session . . . I remember thinking at the time that was a little far-fetched. Poor guy — he'll never live that one down.**

There's always a good chance you are going to be injured at the Pa Wars. I played in my first one when I was 15. As soon as I started making some of the rep teams, everyone wanted to smash you over. Usually the fields you play on are a bit smaller and narrower and you learn pretty quickly that you can only run away from people for so long — sooner or later they are going to catch up with you. There were times when I played when I felt like the whole team was after me. But in the last five years I have worked out a strategy where I pick out a guy in the opposition and I give it to him before he gives it to me. That way I only have to worry about one guy coming after me for the remainder of the game — the rest of his team just look at me and think I am crazy and they leave me alone. I've also learnt to go after one of the bigger guys because they'll give up more easily. **The little fellas have small man's disease and will keep coming all day and I am too old for that stuff.** It makes me look like an arsehole, but at least I am able to walk off the field and not have to be carried off!

Muts was another of the great Harbour characters. He's Glen Osborne's cousin so he had a black mark against him from the get-go. I first met Muts when he was coming up through the lower grades at Harbour. Oz had told me all about his old man Ruben — one of the hardest men I would meet. He'd been in and out of jail a fair bit so he was as tough as nails. You either liked him or you hated him and it was the same for him — he either loved you or wanted to hit you. I remember going down to the East Coast with Harbour. Frano

Botica and I were in the team and when Ruben saw us he yelled, 'You fellas still playing? For f . . .'s sake — get the f . . . out of it and give the young fellas a chance!'

I didn't realise it at the time but Frano's uncle actually shot Ruben once. They were arguing over a crayfish pot! I guess they are a bit territorial about their fishing spots.

Ruben thought the world of his boys, even though he was hard on them. One of the last things he ever said to me — a couple of days before he died — was to look after Muts. He told me: 'If that young fella ever gets out of line, kick his f . . .ing arse.'

I've got a lot of time for Muts. He was never a dirty player — although sections of the media would tell you otherwise — but he'd never take a step backwards from anyone. It's a pity that he never got the break that he needed to go all the way because I reckon he is as good as someone like Marty Holah. Richie McCaw is probably out there on his own as far as No. 7s go, but Muts was never too far behind.

He was a tough bugger. At his first sevens training he got into a couple of scraps. I don't mind a bit of biff at training. And it's not always on the field either. One time Chris Masoe and Jarrod Going had a scrap on the bus after training. That stuff happens when tempers are a bit frayed and everyone is on edge after one of Titch's training sessions. **Amasio Valance is normally the one who starts things off at training. (He'll beg to differ and say I'm the one that starts the biff, but this is my book and I have the last say!) Plenty of the boys like to have a scrap at trainings — Dan Parkinson was never shy when it came to dishing it.**

At one camp the team was split up and I was leading the young fellas and Muts had the more experienced boys. Muts was getting stuck into my boys because they weren't doing anything, and I thought it was time to show them a bit of a lesson. So the next time Muts played it up I smacked him. He hit me back and we wrestled for a while — it was all on. All the young fellas were standing back until one of them pulled us apart and told Muts to settle down. He yelled back: 'What's wrong with you young bastards? This is what it's all about. You

Muts Parkinson — he'd never take a backwards step . . . not to anyone.

have to stand up for yourself. It's good for you.'

Between the two of us we showed the young fellas that you don't sit back and take that stuff — you have to be on the front foot at the international level because a lot of the game is about physical intimidation. You can talk about fair play until the cows come home — that's all right when you're playing non-contact sports like netball — but in sevens you can't let a guy get on top of you physically, otherwise you will be chasing him the whole day.

Amasio loves a good scrap, too. On his day he is the best sevens player in the world — right up there with Fiji's legendary Waisale Serevi. He is the most underrated talent in the country and doesn't get the credit he deserves from anyone. He was there in 1998 when we won gold at the Commonwealth Games, there at the World Cup when we won, there in Manchester for another gold, and he has been ever-present in the side during the World Series wins in 2000, 2001, 2002, 2003 and 2004.

Amasio can be one of the fiercest competitors on the field. That was evident in January 2002 when we played Fiji in the semi-final of the Chilean leg of the World Series.

Everyone loves the Fijian team because of the flair and pace they bring to the game, but they can be extremely physical and, at times, niggly if things aren't going their way. We were getting on top of them on the scoreboard (we won the game 19–17) and we were winning the physical battle too. Amasio — a Fijian — was giving them heaps of verbals when Serevi got through a gap and was heading for the line. Amasio clobbered him around the head as he scored the try and Marika Vunibaka ran 50 metres across the field to hit him — an act that saw him banned for 12 weeks. **The night before the semi, Fiji had a massive scrap with Samoa and Titch and I warned the players not to get involved in the dirty stuff but, when someone runs 50 metres to hit your mate, you're involved.**

I am probably not the best example for the boys to follow when it comes to on-field discipline. When I was a kid I never made the rep teams so I had to fight tooth and nail for everything that came my way. I am only a small fella so I have that small man's disease — I come up swinging every time. So, in that sense, I am probably not a very good role model. Having said that, at least the young guys know that the old fella doesn't take things lying down. If you can sort things out without smacking someone then that's great, because if you live by the sword, you will die by the sword. I've had to live by that mantra myself a couple of times.

Titch is always disappointed if we get involved in the aggro. Not as disappointed as manager Wardy, though. He hates anything that detracts from the reputation of New Zealand rugby. **He should have been a lawyer because in the judiciary hearings he is outstanding. He is probably the best brown-noser in New Zealand rugby as well. Hey, you don't work for the NZRU for as long as he has if you don't have to wipe off your nose every once in a while.** When we played South Africa in a semi-final in Durban later in the year, Tafai Ioasa was smacked in the mouth after he

Tony Ward (left) and Titch. A great management team and, in Wardy's case, a champion brown-noser.

scored a try. It was a shocker. I looked at the ref (Tappe Henning) and he shook his head at me and said he wouldn't take any action because we scored the try.

From the kick-off the same player ran straight at Tafai. Tafai hit him back and the ref sent him off. 'Hang on a minute,' I said to Tappe. 'You just let a head high go and said "Carry on" and now you are sending my boy off. Where's the consistency in that? If you leave him on, you have to leave our guy on.'

Tappe said: 'Do you want to follow your mate?'

I said: 'Yeah, I'll follow him — that's the only way you're going to beat us!'

I was shown the red card and when I got to the sideline Titch asked me what I had done. I looked at him and said, 'I don't know! It's Tappe. He's a dickhead.' When I went to sit down on the team bench one of the officials pulled my arm to direct me to the neutral bench. I lost it with him, too.

Luckily, Wardy was at his very best at the judiciary. I wanted to play in the final and Wardy was desperate to make sure I did. He stood up and said, 'Eric Rush would never swear at anyone. And as for the official who man-handled Eric — he should never have touched the player.'

I got off all charges and Wardy couldn't help himself — 'I'm good! I'm the man! My wife's a lucky lady!' I heard that for the rest of the night.

Wardy reckoned he was a QC. He likes to think it stands for Queen's Counsel. I told the boys it stands for Queer something else . . .

Muts really came of age in 2004 when he captained the sevens team to its World Series win. I was injured for a lot of the season and when Karl Te Nana left to play in Japan I was always supportive of Muts taking on the captaincy. It may have been a strange choice from the outside looking in, but anyone who has played with him knows that he's a 100 per cent man. He puts his body on the line every time he goes out to train — let alone play. Titch asked me what I thought about him becoming the captain and it didn't take me long to give him the thumbs up.

The captaincy was good for him. He became a lot more serious about things — especially about his life off the field. He led the team by example and, boy, he played well with the 'C' next to his name. His first tournament in charge was at Wellington in 2004 and he was outstanding.

KT was another who thrived with the captaincy. He took over the skipper's job after I was injured at the 2001 World Cup — and he never let me forget it either. **Every chance he got he would slag me on TV. One reporter asked him how my recovery was going and he called me a halfback. The reporter was confused and asked him to elaborate. 'He's past it,' said KT with a straight face.**

His style was pretty similar to mine. He was a real character. Whenever the manager or physio or someone was trying to get serious with us, they'd be talking away and all of a sudden KT would make a 'blaaaaaaah' sound. It was his way of saying 'shut up'. If there were young, impressionable players around at the time, you could always guarantee that a couple of days later at the next meeting there would be a chorus of

Karl Te Nana is a real character, although he often struggled with arithmetic. Here he tries to signal No. 1 to the crowd.

'blaaaaaaahs'. When I was out injured I knew I had to get back into the team as soon as possible — not so much because the team missed me on the field but because KT had all the young fellas listening to rap music and wearing baggie pants.

KT was real tight with Damian Karauna, who played in the side between 1996 and 2003. When DK had his twin daughters I was straight on the phone saying, **'Daughters, eh? My boys will be round soon to take them out.' Somehow I think he thought his greatest dream — twin sisters — had all of a sudden become his worst nightmare.**

The good thing about KT, though, was that when it was time to switch on, he did. He was a real proud guy and loved playing for New Zealand. People forget that he is the only New Zealander who has won two Players of the Tournament at Hong Kong.

Like KT, Muts enjoyed the captaincy, although I'm not sure if he likes all the media requirements that come with the job. One part of the job he struggled with was introducing the team at sponsor events. Before each tournament the captain normally gets up and tells a few tales about the boys on the team. **Muts got better at it the longer he had the job, even though he stole a lot of my lines. And he had no shame about it either.** He'd say, 'I'm going use them, brother. I'm gonna use all of them. And if I am ever asked to do a speech I'll use them in that as well!'

One time I travelled from a sevens camp to appear on *Sports Café* and I was asked about Muts being the captain. I knew the boys were watching so all I said was that Muts would do a good job. **But the *Sports Café* guys wanted a Muts story so I told them that I called him Chilly Bin — because once you fill him up with piss you have to carry him around for the rest of the night.**

Ric then started talking about how the biff had gone out of rugby and I agreed with him.

'Come on, Rushie, when was the last time you were involved in a fight on the rugby field?'

'After what I just said about Muts, probably about 10.30 a.m. tomorrow . . .' I was right!

In 2004 I played in the team when Muts was the captain. There were no worries there. We have a saying in the sevens team that all the captain does is the toss. After that job is done, all the boys have to step up to the plate and be leaders.

I was talking to Michael Jones about how Polynesian players don't like to step up and be heard — they prefer to be in the background. If they walk into a seminar room they'll fill up the back of the room first before even thinking about sitting in the front row. **Ice told me that there is an old Polynesian saying that it's better to walk into a room and sit at the back and be asked to go to the front than sit at the front and be told to get to the back.** When I thought about it, that's exactly what happens on the marae. You can be a star at home but once you set foot on that marae you go to the back of the place, keep your mouth shut and wait to be spoken to.

In a team situation you will often see all the brown boys at the back and all the Pakeha boys at the front. I would always make a point of telling the brownies, 'Don't be afraid of sitting at the front. I understand that at church or on the marae it is considered humble and respectful, but this ain't the marae and it sure as hell isn't church. You are now in the New Zealand sevens team. Being at the front of the room here isn't showing off. **Being at the front here is being the best player you can be and that's what we need you to be doing.** So get out the front!' It takes them a while but they get it eventually.

One of Titch's drills has helped get that message through. When we are in Palmerston North he likes us to run around the seven fields jogging for two minutes and then going hard for three minutes. Usually, we'd do three laps but sometimes — depending on whether Titch feels loved or not — we'd have to do four or five laps. During the drill I'd break up the run by getting the different groups in the team to lead us — I'd start with the black arses, then the bongos and then the milky bars. After a few times doing that, anyone who was shy or reluctant to lead would be over it.

I enjoy leading — it's not just about being 'the captain', it's about helping guys feel comfortable because the quicker they feel like they belong the better it is for the team. I have always tried to treat everyone the same. I always make an effort to talk to the young fellas because when I was in the Auckland NPC team a guy like Gary Whetton never said a word to me. And I was in the team for six years!

One of the greatest characters rugby has brought me into contact with is Buck Shelford. I have written about him previously but not so much about him as Harbour's coach.

I thought Buck was a good coach. I'd played with him so I knew that he knew his stuff. But I think he was a bit hard for some of today's breed. He'd tell you the way he wanted things done and there was no arguing. It was Buck's way or the highway. A lot of today's coaches will try to empower the players by letting them make decisions, but Buck wasn't sensitive to things like that. Buck wouldn't hold your hand — he'd expect you to show up and be ready to put your body on the line for the cause. To be honest, that was quite alien to some of the Harbour boys, which, when you think about it, says a lot about some of the new breed of player.

Like any other coach, to be successful you need to have good players. The squad Buck had at Harbour was good but we had nowhere near the depth of Auckland, Canterbury, Wellington, Waikato and Otago. Coaches need to have the playing staff to be successful — look at Graham Henry. He won everything with Auckland and the Blues and then he went to Wales where his record was average. Buck never had the luxury of coaching a 'great team'.

I would classify both Buck and Titch as tough coaches — both liked to run you into the ground and both demanded everything from you when you were training or playing. There were differences, though. Buck would expect you to know your job — he'd march out to training, expecting players to know their roles and jobs on the field. Titch would rarely give you the benefit of the doubt — he'd ride you all the time. He'd always be reminding you of what you had to do. No one can argue with Titch's record, though.

Buck Shelford was a good coach, but maybe his style was just a bit tough for some of today's players.

Buck was a little misunderstood by the media and public. Contrary to popular belief Buck wasn't one of those 'rah-rah' ranting types of coaches in the shed. He was normally pretty calm — he coached like he led. Sure there would be the odd swear word thrown in but he was capable of making a point without raising his voice. He'd just say matter-of-factly, 'Stand up for yourselves forwards. Don't f . . .ing lie down to these f . . .ing arseholes.' But he'd do it calmly.

Today's players aren't soft — as in any weaker or less tough — but today's game is a lot cleaner than it used to be. A lot of players these days haven't had the chance to prove their hardness. Like it or not, rugby fans want to see their heroes standing up for their team-mates. They want to see a bit of biff. They remember guys like Colin Meads, Kevin Skinner, Mark Shaw, Buck Shelford, Richard Loe and Sean Fitzpatrick throwing punches if they had to and laying down the law. They want to see today's players doing the same thing, but rugby — now that it is professional — isn't the same game. If a modern-day player tries to imitate Skinner or Shelford, the media call them thugs.

Look at Troy Flavell. He plays his rugby on the edge of the law. People called him a thug back in 1997 when he was pictured eye-gouging Wellington's Steve Skinnon in an NPC game. But when television images were produced in front of the judiciary it was clear that he wasn't eye-gouging and he had his 12-month ban reduced to three weeks. Flavs probably thought he'd dodged a bullet, but the price he paid for the original picture was that many of the public — and a few commentators — were convinced he was guilty and he never lost the 'thug' tag.

I'm not saying Flavs was an angel on the field. He wasn't. The worst thing he did was stomp on Greg Smith in a Super 12 in 2003. We've all done that sort of thing down the years. The difference was Flavs stomped on him without checking that Smith's head was out of range. It was predictable that Flavs was dragged through the mud by the media after that.

The good thing about the pro game now is that the New Zealand Rugby Union is finally doing a good job getting the boys ready for life after footie. Most of the provincial teams have their academies up and running, and I know that the Auckland and Canterbury ones in particular have been a great success. Young players are beginning to realise that life as a professional rugby player is fickle. You can be in the headlines one day and forgotten the next. Or, worse than that, you can be in the headlines for all the wrong reasons.

One of the costs of being a modern-day rugby professional is the loss of privacy and the higher standards that the media and public force on you.

There have been plenty of mornings where I have been sitting at the table to have a nice breakfast when I grab the paper and see headlines like *Blues stars get into post-match punch-up*, *Two-week ban for player's bar blunder*, *Flavell in bar brawl* or *All Black in no Rush to go home after night out*. My heart automatically goes out to the players. Heck, I

Troy Flavell was no angel on the field, but neither was he the thug that the media made him out to be.

know what it's like to have that media scrutiny focused on you. And it's unfortunate that every time a player gets into trouble my name gets brought up for the accident that I had in 1998 — but I have learnt to live with that.

You can't blame the media. Some would say it's gutter journalism, but the media — when they discover a story — are just doing their job.

The way I look at it is like this: if you put any section of the community under the spotlight that rugby players live in, the shit is going to rise to the surface. Just look at what is happening with the investigations going on into the police and all the allegations. Those cops think they have had it bad, but if they had been rugby players, the fact is, the outcry probably would have been worse.

When I think about how many rugby players I know that have been done for drink driving, and then I think about how many lawyers I know that have been caught driving drunk, it's about 50 to 1 in favour of the lawyers. You never hear about that, though, because as far as the media are concerned lawyers aren't important but rugby players are.

Rugby players getting into trouble isn't going to stop. They are young men making their way in life and they are going to make mistakes. All I say to the people out there is that before you judge them, look in your own closet first and if you have no sin, well, like it says in the big book, you throw the first stone. There are plenty of people throwing them that haven't looked in their own mirror to remind themselves of the trouble they've been in over the years.

I try to stand by the guys. When Mils Muliaina got into trouble for being in a fight at an Auckland bar in 2003, I rang him up and told him I knew how he was feeling. I waited three or four days before giving him the lecture. I didn't want to lecture him straight away because he would have been hearing that every time he turned on the radio. But I eventually told him: 'You know what to do, boy — cut out the piss. You obviously don't handle it very well. Stop drinking and get on with playing good footie.' The fact is Millsy is no different to any other young fella growing up in this country. He's made mistakes now and again and so have we all. The difference is he's a name people know so he's public property.

And when you have a profile you are a target. People like to have a crack at you when you are in public. It happened to me in 1999. I had just played a game for Harbour against Waikato and after the game Dad thought it would be a good idea to support my marae, which was having a fundraising social in Mangere. It was about 11.45 p.m. when I got there and said hello to all my cuzzies. I was making my way across the room to pay for my ticket to the social when one of my cousins came up to me and told me that there was someone there who really wanted to meet me. So I went over to him and he introduced himself by saying: 'So, you are that f . . . ing murderer . . .'

It just happened that that week was the first anniversary of the accident so it had been on my mind — so much so that Buck Shelford had given me the week off training because I was really struggling with it. I looked at the guy, and thought about saying something, but I held my tongue and started to walk away. 'Oh, so you are a f . . . ing coward and a murderer.' I said to him, 'You want to fight mate? Let's go!' Eventually we were pulled apart and he still wanted to fight. He then invited to me to step outside so we could finish it. I hit him twice and he was on the deck and that was that. Or so I thought.

A week later I got a letter from his lawyer and he was suing me for $150,000. He'd set the thing up. He had been asking to meet me all night and when he did he picked the fight. In the end his case was thrown out before it got to court because of all his ridiculous claims, but it still cost me about $10,000 in lawyers' fees.

The incident never made it to the newspapers, even though this character threatened to tell them about it, but I told all the players about it to warn them about what can happen. There are people out there that want to take you down. I'm not saying that all the rugby players that end up in trouble are angels — they're not. But having said that, it doesn't take much to upset you if someone decides to make a target out of you.

No one has had to deal with the media spotlight more than Jonah Lomu.

We all know how the women's magazines and, in particular, the *Sunday News* follow his every move. **He lives in a goldfish bowl. The guy can't go for a walk through Ponsonby without his picture ending up in the tabloids around the world.**

He knows — whether he likes it or not — he's a star in this country. Nothing is off limits. We know that now because you would have thought that if a donor and the recipient of a kidney wanted to keep the identity of the donor secret, the media would play along. Wrong! The interest from the media was so intense that Grant Kereama was forced to put out a statement and identify himself.

One plus to come out of his battle with kidney disease has been the way the public have responded to him. When he got up at the last Halberg Awards this year people could, for the first time, see how sick he was. He could hardly walk. He got a standing ovation from his peers and the reality hit home that he had never used this debilitating disease as an excuse throughout his career.

Everyone has an opinion about whether Jonah can make a comeback and play rugby again. Some people think he is delusional to think he will ever pull on a pair of rugby boots again while others wish he would stop even thinking about a comeback and just concentrate on getting his health right.

For Jonah, the thought of playing just one more game of rugby is the light at the end of the tunnel. And I think he will play again. He never said he would come back and play for the All Blacks. He just wants to play a game of rugby. And he knows there will always be a place for him on the wing at East Tamaki. When he plays that one last game it will mean that he is finishing his career on his terms — not on the terms of a disease.

I had a glimpse into what it's like to have your every move watched by the media when I was involved in my car accident

The big fella stands tall at the 2004 Halberg Awards. Back then, though, Jonah Lomu was struggling big-time.

in 1998. I was being stalked by a *Sunday News* photographer and my phone didn't stop ringing with what seemed like every journalist in the country chasing an 'exclusive' interview.

But nothing I went through compared to the life and times of Jonah Lomu. One incident that I witnessed during the 2001 Wellington Sevens sums up the pressure on the guy more than any other.

Jonah had played for us the previous year but he wasn't in the side for the tournament. He rang me up to see if I wanted to catch up and, of course, I was keen to. He said we couldn't 'go out because it would be too much hassle' but he would come and get me and we'd get a kebab.

His girlfriend at the time, Teina Stace, was in the front seat of the car and I was in the back with one of Jonah's cousins. We stopped at a set of traffic lights on Courtenay Place. The streets were packed — as they normally are during the sevens — and all of a sudden a girl who had recognised the big guy opened up the passenger door, reached across in front of Teina, and started talking to Jonah.

I'd never seen anything like it. Jonah was being civil but after a few seconds he told her that the lights would soon change to green so she'd better go.

'There's no need to be like that,' she said.

'We have to go . . . the lights are going to change.'

'Well, give me a kiss then!'

Remember, Teina is sitting right there.

'I'm not going to kiss you. That's my girlfriend there in case you hadn't noticed.'

'Don't be a snob. I heard you were a snob.'

Teina had had enough of this carry-on by this stage and she said, 'Excuse me, but can you please get out of the car?'

With that, the girl got out of the car and then punched Teina in the face.

Me, the cousin and the big fella were out of the car in a flash. Half of me wanted him to slap her but we knew he couldn't do anything. And she knew it. She was standing in a crowd of people taunting Jonah. 'What are you going to do? What are you going to do . . .'

The whole time the crowd was looking at Jonah wondering why he was picking on this little lady. Meanwhile, Teina is sitting in the car with a blood nose and a split lip.

I couldn't believe what I had just seen. When we got back in the car, Jonah started to drive off and he looked at me through the rear-view mirror. 'Bro, now you know why I don't go out.'

It's extraordinary what Jonah has to put up with. I have been with him a number of times in Hong Kong when we have been walking down the street when someone will come out of nowhere and tackle him. **One time a drunken Pom ran across the street and tackled Jonah from behind. Jonah got up and pummelled the guy. I let him get in a few good ones and then I pulled him off the guy. Jonah could have killed him.** He was still angry so I went across and talked to the guy's mates and told them: 'You fellas did that to your mate, not Jonah. You guys shouldn't have encouraged him.'

I get frustrated when things like that happen to Jonah because he doesn't deserve any of it. If he was the type of person who threw his fame in your face, well, then I could almost understand why people would target him. But Jonah has never been like that. That's not his style.

This is the guy who never used his kidney problem as an excuse. When Laurie Mains and John Hart dropped him, when the press got stuck into him and when the fans booed him, it would have been easy for him to let us all in on his illness. But he didn't.

We're good mates. We have been for a long time. I have seen a few 'friends' of his come and go. Too many people have their hands out wanting things from him. Maybe we are still tight because I have never asked for anything from him — and he nothing from me — except for friendship.

And, to be honest, sometimes I feel like I have been a pretty shit-house mate in the last year or so. When he was going through his dialysis treatment I only went down to Middlemore Hospital to sit with him a couple of times. I would have liked to go more often but I found it too difficult. It hurt me to see this fella who dominated rugby on the world scene reduced to a guy who needed dialysis treatment for eight hours a day.

I felt so sorry for him. It was hard to be there. But his spirits were always up. He'd look around the room and say, 'See that fella, he's way worse off than me. I'll be all right, Rushie. I've got it good. You wait and see.'

He was the star of the ward, too. When Jonah Lomu gets dialysis treatment he takes his DVD player, his X-Box and his PlayStation with him. I wonder if he ever thought about reading a book . . .

Same band, new players

THIS IS THE CHAPTER where I tell a few tales about some of the boys I have come into contact with throughout my rugby career. This is the chapter where we all have a bit of a laugh at their expense. This is the chapter where I usually get into trouble. After the first book Christian Cullen never lived down the fact that I called him Beer Bottle — because he is empty from the neck up. (I want to make a public apology for that because I made it up.) This is the chapter that bruises egos and sees my number deleted from a few mobile phones belonging to high-profile players. I suppose I ought to live by that rugby mantra 'What goes on tour, stays on tour', but, nah . . .

Orene Ai'i

I first played against him at the Commonwealth Games in 1998 — he was playing for Samoa. He was lucky he was only a teenager because his ability to pull on the black jersey wasn't affected by the IRB regulations. We played against him in the semi-finals, where he played really well. He hasn't come on as well in 15s as he would have hoped. The guy is so talented but he hasn't really dominated at NPC or Super 12 level yet. His time will come, though, and he knows it. A few of the boys call

Charlie Baxter — cops a head high against Harbour. Knowing Charlie, though, he probably deserved it.

him Pony — because he's a bit of a show pony. But I call him Wheke — Maori for octopus — because whenever the free stuff is being handed out it's like he has eight arms on him.

Charlie Baxter

He's a good young boy, although he couldn't lay claim to being the sharpest tool in the shed. Baxter's best asset is his speed. I beat him once in a speed test over 40 metres and he got a bit cheeky. I challenged him to another race over 40 and he said:

Alan Bunting tries to split the Wellington defence . . . watch out, AB, there might be a stray fist in front of these defenders.

'That's not fair because you are almost there.' One time at training things got a bit physical and he stomped on my chest. I let it pass and he sent me a text message after I fought in the 2003 Fight for Life saying, 'Bro, that fella never even touched you — you smashed him.' I sent a message back saying, 'Bro, now you know what will happen if you ever stomp on me again.'

Alan Bunting

AB takes a pretty good punch because he was on the end of a prominent Auckland Warrior's fist in a bar-room brawl which hit the headlines for a while there. He is a good player for the Bay and these days is also focusing on his teaching at Tauranga Boys College. It's funny because both Alan and Nathaniel Walker teach at the school that gave the sevens team our schoolboy sensation Tanirau Latimer in 2004 — the youngest person ever to play for the New Zealand sevens team.

Roy Kinikinilau

He's a real homeboy but I don't know if he still has street cred with the fellas he grew up with because he has turned to surfing in a big way. Justin Wilson, Tafia Ioasa and Kini have become quite good surfers. Whenever we have camps in Mt Maunganui the boys — following an hour's rest after Titch has had his way with us on the training field — either go fishing or surfing. I usually go swimming — I go for a surf but end up swimming. Liam Messam and I are probably the worst when it comes to surfing but we ain't the worst when it comes to water sports. That dubious honour has to go to Amasio Valance. He hired one of those plastic kayaks that are unsinkable . . . yes, he sunk it. Talking about water sports, it must be said that Kinikinilau has the weakest bladder of any team-mate I have ever had. He is always going to the toilet — one time he didn't quite make it there. I probably shouldn't say any more . . .

Tanirau Latimer

The youngest player to start for the sevens team. I met my match in the beep tests when this 17-year-old arrived at the camp at the beginning of the 2003/2004 season. Normally, I do pretty well in the fitness tests, but I was no match for this kid. It was like he had four lungs. In true sevens tradition, if you can't beat them on the field, you jerk 'em . . . so I did. We were in a taxi in Hong Kong on our way to a media interview. As we headed into the Hong Kong tunnel I got my passport out.

'Got your passport, bro?'

'What for?'

'Because we are going to Hong Kong Island.'

'Oh shit! You need a passport? Oh shit! No one told me!'

'Come on man. We're going across Hong Kong Harbour. Of course you need your passport! Tell you what, when we get to the other end I'll see if I can sneak you in.'

We got to the toll booth and the taxi driver wound down the window, said hello in Chinese to the operator and paid his money.

Roy Kinikinilau heads for the toilets during a NZ sevens match in Wellington. My best advice to Roy is 'go before the game'.

'What happened?'
'The guy recognised me so he let you through.'
'Sorry Rushie. I never knew I needed a passport.'

Grant McQuoid
He became our token white fella after Craig de Goldie signed to play his rugby in Japan. Matua Parkinson was the captain of the team when Grant was in the side in 2004 and as the skipper he is in charge of the different team committees. Muts put Grant in charge of the REO committee and it was his job to come up with a Maori word every day and explain it to the team. Grant loved it.

'Okay, boys, the word for today is "kaupapa" — it means we all have to sing from the same sheet.'

Good boy, honky! Grant is a real religious fella and by the end of the World Series he had all the boys in prayer sessions. He is one of the nicest guys involved in rugby and deserved all the accolades that came his way during Bay of Plenty's brief Ranfurly Shield reign in 2004.

Liam Messam
He made his debut for the team in 2002 but really came of age in the last couple of seasons. At his first camp I asked him what he wanted to achieve and he gave me the typical answer about how he just wanted to play well. When I got to know him a bit better I asked him again. He told me his goal was to beat me in the beep test.

'I'm 39, man! You should be kicking my ass.'

He vowed to beat me at the next camp and I laughed at him, but as soon as I got back to Auckland I trained like never before. I was determined to see off his challenge. When we met up again and were in the middle of the test I looked at him and said, 'I feel good, bro. How 'bout you?' That broke him and I held on until level 15. He's a good boy, though. He's very aggressive, which is good, but he often gets in trouble with the refs. We call him the Chinaman because he is always seeing yellow — yellow cards.

Mils Muliaina was gutted he never got a mention in *Rushie*. Make the most of it this time, Milsy, it won't happen again.

Mils Muliaina

The first time I came into contact with Mils was when I grabbed his privates at a sevens tournament. He'd stepped inside me and I reached out in desperation and grabbed his package. To be honest, I had to hold on real tight because there wasn't much there. Samoa dropped him after that tournament and Titch swooped. Now, time for an apology. Mils was there in Manchester when we won the Commonwealth Games gold medal in 2002, but for some reason I didn't devote much ink to him in my book *Rushie* — in fact, I don't think I mentioned him at all! He was gutted, and he told me so. So Mils, this time, it's all about you, bro. We could talk about what you brought to the team, the way you played touch growing up and became a great sevens player and a great All Black, which all the sevens boys are proud of. Or the time when you had a scrap with one of the Fijians and you complained to the boys afterwards that we didn't come and help you. We had to tell you the reason we didn't help was that you never threw a punch at the guy — you have to throw a few back so we can jump in. Remember how we called you Buba after that — petit wasn't exactly the way to describe your lips at the time after a Fijian right hand to your face. In fact, they took up half your face. I don't want to say too much about your other problem.

Ma'a Nonu

Ma'a first appeared at a sevens camp in 2004 after missing out on the All Blacks. He wore the jersey in 2003 but for whatever reason wasn't able to recapture that form for the Hurricanes. I take my hat off to the guy because after missing out on the ABs he could have easily just thrown his hands up and felt

Ma'a Nonu only had one word after training with the New Zealand sevens team . . . and I couldn't possibly repeat it here.

sorry for himself. I know how tough it is at that stage of a career because I have been there. But instead he fronted for the sevens and the training sessions and went back to work. He loved it, too. Sure, he was close to death at the end of every day but he never gave in. There have been plenty of guys that have come to camp and given up. At the end of his first day in camp I asked him if he was okay. 'F . . ., f . . .,' was all he could say.

Norm Berryman

Another centre who took up Titch's challenge after losing his All Blacks spot was Norm Berryman. He hated the diet stuff — no fries, no meat, ice cream or fizzy drinks. He didn't care much for the fitness stuff either — no wonder when so many of the new boys spew up. Titch said to him once: 'Normie, look on the bright side — you didn't throw up today.' Norm looked at him and said: 'I didn't spew because you wouldn't let us eat anything!'

Because Titch's trainings have been built up so much a lot of players are reluctant to come to his camps. But the reality is that once you survive the first day, it's not too bad. I've watched the Warriors train a fair bit and they train just as hard every day for eight months. And the hockey guys — they are running the whole time. The sevens boys wouldn't be able to handle the league and we certainly wouldn't be able to handle the hockey. However, if we worked at it every day we'd be able to keep up with even the league and hockey guys — hitting the ball with a stick would be another thing. We'd be able to hit the other team with it, though . . .

Glen Osborne

I thought I'd update the regular readers of my books on the life and times of Oz. You'll remember Oz. He was always getting into trouble for being a bit, well, you know . . . he's not exactly a rocket scientist. Every rugby team has a dress call and one day when we were flying out to Australia with the Harbour team the call was made that we would travel in our No. 1s with our purple shirt. So Oz, who lived with his Harbour team-mate Peter Woods, arrived at the airport in his suit but with his green shirt on. A minute later Woodsy walked in with his purple shirt on. Brad Meurant — the coach — was dumbfounded. 'Oz, you live with him. He's wearing a purple shirt. Did you talk to each other before you left your flat? How the hell did you end up wearing the green one? One of you had to be wrong!'

Oz looked at him a bit confused and said, 'I just put it on.'

To be fair to Oz, Woodsy was hardly a scholar either.

Oz is playing up in Japan now and is as tactful as ever. When he heard I was retiring he rang me and before I could even say hello I heard this voice screaming, 'About f . . .ing time someone got on to you. You have been past it for the last 10 years!' Oz spends all his time in Japan teaching his new team-mates how to speak English — quite a stretch for a guy who can't actually speak English himself. His team toured New Zealand in the summer and he introduced a few of his mates to me. 'This is my mate Jackie . . . Jackie Chan. And this is my bro Bruce . . . Bruce Lee.' But the worst thing was what they said when they met you. All these Japanese rugby boys were walking around introducing themselves as Bruce and Jackie and saying 'primo'. He is cloning a whole team of Ozs — what a scary thought.

Oz is a mate but he didn't make it easy for me when I started missing out on All Black teams. I played my last game for the All Blacks in 1996 but Oz racked up another eight games for the team — seven of them in 1997 and one test at the 1999 World Cup. Before every test he'd ring me and say, 'Rushie! Rushie! There's a team meeting in five minutes downstairs. Oh, that's right, you're not in the team any more.' His other favourite was to ring from the All Blacks camp at the beginning of the domestic season. 'Rushie, how 'bout the new gears, eh? Choice, eh? Oh, that's right, you didn't get any . . .' And he wonders why I like to tell tales about him!

SAME BAND, NEW PLAYERS

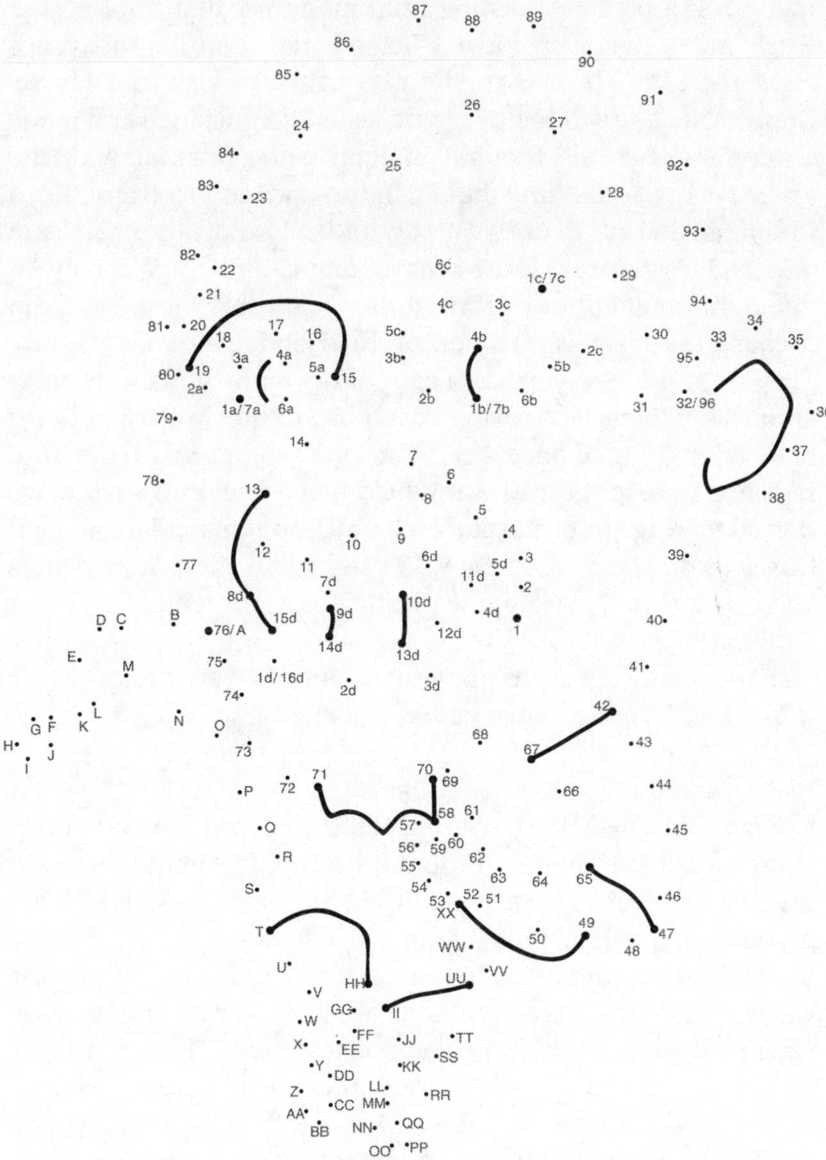

This is for those rugby players who can't read — people like Glen Osborne,Tafai Ioasa, Chris Masoe and tight forwards in general. Enjoy. **(Solution on page 72)**

Lindsay Raki

Raki took a bit of a roasting from me in my first book, *Gold Rush*, so to make up for it I helped train him for this year's Fight for Life. He was in the ring against Mark 'the Horse' Bourneville and while he lost, he lasted the distance and made a few fans. But the thought of Raki being popular with the masses is not something that I can live with so I feel compelled to tell this story. Every year my under-11 East Tamaki team play the Ardmore Marist team from Counties. We play in different competitions during the year but we play them because the team is coached by Raki and Lance Goldsmith. They beat us every year. These little white kids run rings around my team. The losing coach has to buy McDonald's for both teams and I have been the one paying up. I ran into Lance at the Fight for Life and he'd had a few drinks when we started talking about the game. 'It's all about man management Rushie. You just haven't got it.' Then he had a few more drinks and he let slip: 'Next time we won't stack our team.'

'What?'

'Raki stacks our team up with 12- and 13-year-olds.'

Yes, that's right. Lindsay Raki is a cheat.

Joe Rokocoko

I called him The Mike — because like a microphone he's long, black and slender with a little tuft on top. It would be easy to say that as soon as he arrived at his first sevens camp in 2002 he reminded me of Jonah Lomu or Christian Cullen. But he didn't. Those guys were naturals right from the get-go. Joe wasn't. He was fast — both he and Tony Koonwaiyou registered some of the fastest speed-test times Titch and I had ever seen. Joe did all right in the fitness test as well, but once we got into the training games he couldn't go. He'd have one run and that'd be it. He was on my team and Titch was yelling at me to get the ball to Joe with some space ahead of him. We did, but he was stuffed.

Chris Latham — the Queensland and Australian fullback —

Long, black and slender with a little tuft on top — Joe Rokocoko, the microphone man.

played in the Brisbane Sevens tournament one year and he told me that he'd always loved the idea of playing sevens because of the space on the field. He couldn't wait to exploit it. But he admitted having heaps of space to move in and having the legs and lungs to do something about it are two different things. He had a newfound respect for the game. Mat Rodgers and Wendell Sailor said the same thing.

So, Joe found that out, too. The first 50-man camp was set to be cut to 15 guys to go on tour to Argentina and Chile. Joe didn't make the cut. He was really disillusioned. Titch told him to go away and work on his fitness and because we lacked a bit of speed in the team we pulled him in a few weeks later and worked and worked on him. By the end of the year he was our best player. He wasn't just doing one good run a game — he was doing 10 or 12 of them. He scored 28 tries in six tournaments for us before he broke his leg playing for the Colts. He had to sit out the Commonwealth Games. But he bounced back pretty quickly. He was in the Blues' Super 12 squad in 2003 — the same year he became an All Black. And 24 test tries later he keeps getting better. You have to put him in the same class as Jonah and Cully and, to be honest, I don't think we have seen the best from him yet. I just hope he gets the chance to play for a gold medal at the 2006 Commonwealth Games.

The fact that Joe never lost faith in his ability after missing out on those first sevens teams he trialled for says a lot about his character. I remember telling him in those early days not to get down because plenty of good players have been through Titch's camps and not made it but have gone on to play for the All Blacks. I always use Marty Holah as an example. He came to a couple of sevens camps and never made it. I tell the young fellas, 'Just because you miss out doesn't mean you are no good — it might just mean you are not suited to sevens. Look at Marty Holah. He came two, three years in a row. He never had the top-end pace and was exposed a bit in the practice games — that was the only thing that let him down, but look at him in 15s.

Looking back, he is probably pleased he missed out on sevens because he's a regular in the All Blacks 22 now.'

Rodney So'oialo

Rodders was another guy like Joe. He came to his first camp and bombed out. He came back better, but Titch still didn't put him in the team. Then he came back better again and he made it. He won a gold medal at the Commonwealth Games and was absolutely awesome when we won the World Cup in 2001. With Jonah, Craig Newby and Rodders in the forwards, we were unstoppable. Off the field he's a pretty quiet and serious type of guy. I call him Sushi because he likes eating fish and seaweed and stuff like that — and, if you look closely you can see it growing on his head. He doesn't have the worst haircut in the team, though. Matua Parkinson used to look pretty

Rodney So'oialo — loves fish and seaweed.

good when he had his dreadlocks. But then he cut it and he just had this fuzz. I introduced him once by saying, 'He used to have dreadlocks, now it's just dreadful.'

Scott Waldrom

Scooter used to push Titch to the absolute limit all the time. He's so laid-back and that isn't necessarily the best quality to have when you are dealing with someone as intense as Titch. Scooter would sit in team meetings and he'd be texting someone on his phone. He'd even do it just before games. The rest of us would all be getting ready and trying to get in the right head space and you'd hear this faint 'beep, beep'. The first time I ever met him I didn't realise that he had already been on TV. He entered *Sports Café*'s Nude Day competition — he was the guy on the scooter who rode through Parliament grounds naked on his scooter. That was him! He would be one of the fittest guys that has been in the sevens squad. His background as a 400-metre runner made sure of that. Some of the guys call him Wild Bill because he looks exactly like that psycho guy in the *The Green Mile* — the movie that starred Tom Hanks. He acts like him, too, especially when he's in the Red zone at the Wellington Sevens.

Nathaniel Walker

Nathaniel is a bit of a character. He's about five-foot nothing and he has hairy feet. After the *Lord of the Rings* films came out everyone started calling him Frodo. But my inspiration for his nickname came one day when I was introducing the team after meeting a couple of executives from Cadbury at a team function. I introduced the team and when I got to Nathaniel I called him 'Fredo' . . . because he's the chocolate version of Frodo.' The next day Cadbury sent me a box of Fredos for the boys. He has relatives from my home town of Kaeo. Nice.

Rudi Wulf

Ruds is probably the fittest Island kid I've come across. We trained together at North Harbour and often I'd try him out in the fitness tests and he always stayed right with me. He's very quiet and a bit shy but he'll grow out of that. He's got a lot of ticker and I expect that he will be one of the stars of the sevens team in the next couple of seasons.

Scooter Waldrom — this was the best picture I could find. Nice, eh.

ADRENALIN RUSH

Join the dots solution (reproduced especially for Oz).

Fight for Life

IT HAS ALMOST BECOME A RITE OF PASSAGE to retirement for rugby players. The Fight for Life has given a number of former All Blacks the chance for one last moment in the spotlight. It has given us the chance to raise money for charity while asking ourselves one last time: 'Can you handle the heat and pressure of competition?'

My chance came in 2003. Fight for Life organiser Dean Lonergan had asked me a few times to step up and be counted. But I couldn't do it in 2001 because I was still recovering from the broken leg I'd got at the Sevens World Cup and then in 2002 I wasn't available because I broke my hand at the Hong Kong Sevens.

I wasn't sure if I wanted to do it when the call from Deano came. Raina, my wife, wasn't that keen for me to do it so I said no. But Deano kept ringing. And, being Deano, he got a few others to put a bit of pressure on me. **Sure enough, I heard from Frank Bunce, and he basically said I would be a pussy if I didn't do it.**

I didn't decide to do it because of the call from Buncey, but I did feel a bit of peer pressure from some of the boys. And, to be honest, I wanted to test myself. I had boxed a fair bit at school and I guess I wanted to ask myself the question again — could I step back in the ring and box? It's not like getting on a bike. To step inside those ropes takes a bit of courage and

Mr Fight for Life Dean Lonergan battles with former All Black giant Mark Cooksley. The big rig got the money this time.

a whole lot of hard work. I guess I wanted to know if I was strong enough — physically and mentally — to do it.

Deano knew that I had done a bit of boxing so he pitted me against someone called Michael Long. The name meant nothing to me. Someone told me he was a former Australian Rules player. Then I saw him on television being interviewed.

It turned out Michael was some athlete. He'd retired in 2001 after a stellar career for Essendon in Melbourne. He'd played on two championship teams in 1993 and 2000, winning the coveted Norm Smith medal for being the best player in the first of his finals appearances. He told the interviewer: 'My goal is to box for Australia at the Athens Olympics . . .'

What the f . . .!

This was going to be tough. Buncey and I headed off to Lance Revill's gym to begin our five weeks of training. He killed us at every training but he made it fun as well. We had three sessions each week for the first three weeks and then we trained every day for the last two weeks.

I enjoyed the training but it was hard for me to fit it in because of my work commitments. I had a few speeches to do in Australia so I tried to organise training sessions while I was there. I was talking at a conference on the Gold Coast and I met up with an old pro, Johnny Rule. It was great because I was able to get into a ring and spar with him.

Lance — a former New Zealand heavyweight champion — wouldn't let Buncey and me spar. All the other fighters — guys like Inga Tuigamala, Mark 'Horse' Bourneville and Stephen McIvor — were all sparring but we weren't allowed to. Basically he thought we weren't good enough. 'If I let you in there, you are going to do the bad things you are doing now even worse. We'll get rid of the bad habits and then chuck you in.'

He probably had a point. At the first training session he put us on the pads. Lance stands there with these two pads on his hands and we have to hit them on cue. He had us on one-minute rounds but we could only get through one. 'You are going to have to be able to do four three-minute rounds by the end of this! When you can do that, then you can spar.'

It was tough. It's not like I wasn't fit. At the time I was still playing sevens, but a different type of fitness was required. It's all upper-body stuff and Frank and I knew we had a long road ahead of us.

Getting to the fitness level to be able to last four three-minute rounds was going to take a while so to get the chance to spar in the Gold Coast was exciting. **I hadn't boxed since I was at school so to be inside the ropes again — even though it was just sparring — was good.**

One of the guys attending the conference caught on to the fact that I was going to have a session with Rule and he volunteered to come along and spar with me. We only had one pair of gloves and one pair of mitts. He told me to use the mitts because he knew that I couldn't afford to get cut just weeks out from the fight.

I don't know if it was Lance's training or what but the first two punches I threw cut him. He came at me straight away with this big right hand so I thought, 'It's on.' This poor guy — having a bit of a holiday on the Gold Coast — walked out of the gym with blood pouring from his forehead and cheek.

A few days later I was giving a speech in Sydney and I was given the chance to train at Anthony Mundine's gym. **I've always admired Mundine. He has to be one of the best athletes of this generation. To fight for the world title after being a league star at St George and Brisbane takes some doing.** His mouth does get him into trouble a fair bit, though.

I was excited about the prospect of working out at his HQ and after I'd found his gym I could understand the anger that sometimes pours out of him. He's one of the few Aboriginal athletes that is outspoken. I'm guessing that it would take a bit of courage to stand up and be counted in Australia because normally Aboriginals — through no fault of their own — are usually only seen and not heard.

But Mundine is a proud man who has built a successful life out of nothing. The gym he trains out of is in the suburb of Redfern. Being a Maori boy in Sydney I had no idea where or what Redfern was like when I caught the train from downtown with my gym bag slung over my back. When the train pulled up to the station, things looked a bit run-down but nothing too bad.

When I got to the street I asked a cop if he could point me to Mundine's gym. He looked at me as if I was crazy. 'It's almost dark — are you sure you want to go down there?' He gave me directions and within a minute I realised why the cop and his partner were standing on the corner of the road. I was in a place referred to as 'The Block'.

The locals — almost all Aboriginals — were burning anything they could get their hands on in the middle of the street. It was their way of staying warm while they played their drinking games on the footpath. The Block is a notorious trouble spot in Sydney and the cops — keen to avoid a riot —

Anthony 'The Man' Mundine unloads against gutsy Sean Sullivan. I was privileged to work out in Mundine's gym.

were just hanging back, making sure things didn't get too badly out of control. **As I walked down the road towards the gym I was happy that I was Maori. If I didn't have a brown face I think it would have been easy to be intimidated.** I was also lucky that I was dressed for the gym — they must have assumed I was a boxer. 'Maaaate. Maaaate. You looking for the gym, maaaate?'

There was no aggro, until I got in the gym. You worked hard in that gym — you didn't have a choice because people desperate to make a success of their life surrounded you. Boxing was their ticket out of Redfern, in much the same way rugby and league have become a way out of South Auckland.

When I was in Australia I asked a few people about Michael Long. I didn't want them to play mind games with me so I didn't tell them I was going to be fighting him in a charity boxing match.

'Oh, maaaate. He's a goer.'

'Can he throw a punch?'

'He can throw 'em. Maaaate, he's not afraid of a blue.'

Talking of Aboriginals . . . earlier that day in downtown Sydney I was on my way to meet the great Wallaby David Campese at his shop at The Rocks. I passed this guy playing the didgeridoo. He was pretty good and he had a bit of a crowd around him so I threw five bucks into his hat.

'Thanks, cuz.'

'Huh?'

'Yeah, bro, I'm from Kaitaia. You're Eric Rush, eh?'

He had the loincloth on and Aboriginal painting on his face. This Maori boy's picture was in the photo albums of thousands of tourists around the world who thought they had a picture of a native Australian.

'I'm not worried, eh. These tourists don't know any different . . .'

When I got back to New Zealand, Frank and I were a bit worried because even though I'd had a bit of ring time, it was nothing like the sparring that all the other boys were doing. Stephen McIvor from Sky TV kept saying to us, 'You fellas

I thought I knew a thing or two about boxing — that's until I jumped into the ring with Sean Sullivan.

have got to spar. You can't step into the ring without sparring.'

Finally, with two weeks to go until fight night, Lance decided to let Buncey and me spar. But not against each other. He got one of his mates to spar with us. A guy called Sean Sullivan. A guy who has won five New Zealand titles in five divisions. A guy who has recorded 51 career wins — 22 by knockout. *Yeah, that guy!*

We jumped into the ring and he just didn't stop coming at me. They reckon he is one of the fittest men in boxing — I can testify to that. I couldn't get a glove on him. It was a bit disheartening because fitness wise I was at the level that Lance had wanted me to be at, but once you start sparring it's a different level again because you have to avoid shots and take shots. After one round I was gone. The next two rounds he just killed me. He hit me with this uppercut . . . my nose bled for about a week.

It was worthwhile, though. I'd watched a few of the other Fight for Life guys sparring and they were getting beat up. They were just trying to survive. And you can't learn much when you are in survival mode. Sean was beating up on me but he was talking to me while he did it. He would tell me that my left hand was dropping. 'Keep it up!' Then we'd box a bit more. 'Feet! Feet!'

By the last round — before he whacked me on the nose — my left hand had dropped again.

'Get your left hand up.'

'Yep. Yep.'

WHACK!

'Get it up, Rushie.'

'Yep. Yep.'

WHACK!

'I'll hit you again, Rushie. Get it up!'

(Silence)

WHACK!

I was so tired and my hands were that heavy it was easier to take a punch in the face than it was to lift my hands two inches to protect myself.

Even though he gave me a lesson in the ring, Sean obviously had held back. He took it relatively easy on me but when he had the chance to pop me, he did. 'You have to get used to taking shots,' he'd say. His trainer, Alex Sua, was there watching and after the session he grabbed me and in his best Samoan broken English offered me some pearls of wisdom.

'When you in the ring you have to watch out for the dog. Like when the dog, it chases you when you go for run. If the dog, he chases you, if you turn and run, he chase you faster. So, no run, eh? Turn and look at the dog. Pick up the stone and throw at the dog. Never run from the dog!'

That was his way of reminding me that I had to keep sparring to train my eyes so I could see the punches coming. It's one of the most important things a boxer needs to do. And, there was one other thing the Suaman wanted me to do.

'Always smiling. Always smiling to the other guys. Cause then he don't know what you thinking. He don't know if you tired or just crazy. Always smiling to the other man.'

I also sparred with Kahu Benson. I'd met him at the Commonwealth Games in Manchester in 2002. He was — along with Soulan Pownceby and Danny Codling — one of the best amateurs in New Zealand at the time. He offered a different challenge to Sean, who played the role of the old pro; he'd work you around a little bit before peeling you back. If Sean got you once, he'd get you twice.

Kahu on the other hand was like a machine gun. If he got you once, he got you four times. The first time I saw his jab . . . I didn't. Boof! What the f . . . was that? *Boof!* What the . . . *Boof!* Holy shit. *Boof!* After a couple of sessions with Kahu I started seeing his punches. Just like Alex Sua had said I would. That gave me a bit of confidence, as the fight got closer.

I still needed to drop some weight, though. Michael Long was going to come in at about 87 kg. I was 95 kg when I started and Deano told me I had to drop about 7 kg to make it a fair fight. I'm not a big guy as it is and I knew that it would be a real struggle for me to drop my weight. Deano was worried because Long was losing weight while he was training and was down to about 84 kg. I'd been training for three weeks and was still 95 kg!

TV3's cameras were due at a training session and they had requested a shot of me weighing myself. Before they arrived Lance got me to jump on the scales and I was 94 kg. We knew we were in trouble and I didn't know what to do. **I knew Deano would be a bit annoyed if he switched on his TV and saw that I hadn't dropped any weight.** And Lance was feeling a bit of pressure because one of the jobs given to him by Deano was to make sure I dropped the weight.

When the cameras arrived, the first shot they wanted was me on the scales. I looked at Lance and he winked at me. I didn't know why he was relaxed all of a sudden because I sure as heck wasn't.

'Sweet as, Rushie. Jump on the scales.'

I got on and Lance for some reason came right up beside me. Then, quick as a flash, I felt his thumb up my arse and he lifted me slightly off the scales.

'Eighty-nine kilos. Rushie! Good boy! Okay, get off.'

Get off? I couldn't get off quick enough. I didn't want to say anything at the time but I have to tell you that Lance left his finger there probably a little longer than he needed to.

Because the weight wasn't coming off Lance decided to put me on a diet. For breakfast I was only allowed to eat cereal and one piece of toast. The only other carbohydrate I was allowed for the rest of the day was one potato at lunch. I could eat as much protein as I wanted but I wasn't allowed the things I loved, like rice, bread and pasta. It wasn't easy to literally go 'cold turkey'. I have a sweet tooth and on one particular day I couldn't help myself. I was on my way to deliver a speech in Taupo and I rang Lance after I'd bought a packet of marshmallows.

'What about marshmallows? Can I have some of them?'

'What! We are trying to lose weight.'

'Come on, mate. It's only sugar and air.'

'You have already had some, haven't you, Rushie?'

'Yep.'

'How many have you had?'

'A packet!'

'You f . . . ing Maori bastard! Wait until I get you back in the gym!'

At the end of each training Lance would get us to lie on the ground and he would stand above you with a big medicine ball and throw it at your stomach. Buncey and I would always try to go first because whoever went second would be in Lance's ear, saying things like, **'He told me last night that he thinks you're fat!' On this day, though, Buncey went first and I knew I was in for it. I lay on the ground and Lance grabbed the medicine ball.**

'Ah, Mr Rush. Mr Marshmallow Man, eh?'

Lance Revill — he fingered me good and proper during the Fight for Life weigh-in.

BOOM!
'One marshmallow!'
BOOM!
'Two marshmallows! Buncey, how many marshmallows in a packet?'
'About 50, I think.'
BOOM!

We normally did 10 on the middle and each side but he went through to 15 before letting me off.

By the time the fight came round I was down to 86 kg. Long weighed in at 82 kg.

Lance wasn't allowed to be in our corner on fight night because he was refereeing some of the bouts. I'd been up north a couple of times during the build-up to the fight and did some training at the Kaeo boxing club where I'd learnt to box under the tutelage of Bill Woods. His son Nuku — who fought for New Zealand at the Commonwealth Games — and one of my relatives, Rusty Poata, worked with me and agreed to be in my corner on fight night. When I told Rusty that I was a little nervous because I'd heard that my opponent wanted to fight for Australia at the Olympics he pulled me aside: 'Yeah. You'd want to fight for New Zealand at the next Olympics as well. That doesn't mean it's going to happen, bro!'

I was happy with my preparation for the fight because I knew that there was no way Long could be as good as the best pro in New Zealand and the best amateur in New Zealand. And even if he is, I thought, at least I'll know what I am in for.

As the day got closer I was getting more and more nervous. I was having nightmares about this bogeyman Michael Long. I didn't know much about him and I kept imagining that he was this great big Neanderthal. I would lie in bed and wonder, 'What the hell were you thinking!' The chance to see him would come the day before the fight at the weigh-in.

Originally, I was booked to do a speech the night of the Fight for Life. Deano was really keen to get me into the ring. While the whole night was about charity — raising money for the prevention of youth suicide — everyone knew that Deano was making some money out of it — and good on him, I reckon. I told him that I couldn't fight because I was getting a lot of money for the speech. In fact, it was the most money I had earned for a speech at that stage, and I couldn't afford to turn it down.

He rang me back and said, 'If I can get you the same money, will you fight then?' It turned out all of the Australian boxers had been paid so I certainly didn't feel bad about taking a payment.

Deano did a deal that meant I would have to give a little speech at the weigh-in to earn my dollars. It wasn't something that I really wanted to do. All the fighters were there and I was nervous about my fight. I just wanted to sight Long and get out of there.

Eventually someone pointed him out to me so I went across

to shake his hand and introduce myself. He wasn't an intimidating bloke but you knew he was fit. This was a hard man and I knew I was in for a battle. I didn't have time to think about things too much because I had to weigh in and then give the speech.

I didn't do the whole routine but I broke the ice with Long.

'I'm glad I have met Michael because I have been imagining this big bogeyman for some weeks. It's good to meet him and see that he is just another nervous fella like me looking forward to the fight. I take my hat off to the Aussies — it's hard enough for us to do this in our own backyard, but to come overseas and do it must be twice as hard.'

Long came up to me afterwards and thanked me for saying what I said and we got talking. He told me he had been locked up in his hotel room and he was desperate to get out and see some of New Zealand.

'You are the first Maori I've met. I really want to meet some Maori. I want to experience a little bit of the culture of this place.'

Before leaving Australia he had been told that if he wanted to meet some Maori, the best place to go was to a pub in Otara.

I pointed out that that wasn't the best advice he could have been given and I invited him to come out to my kids' school, Te Kura Maori O Nga Tapuwae — a place where they speak Maori exclusively.

The next day — the day of the fight — he was at the school with a few of the other Aboriginal guys in the Australian team, including league's Ken Nagus. The kids put on a powhiri for them. It blew them away. During the singing and the haka I looked at them and some of them had tears rolling down their faces. During one of the songs I explained that the kids were singing about 'my language is my strength'. It really struck a chord with him. Maori think they have it tough with this ongoing debate about the foreshore and seabed but compared with the status of the Aboriginals in Australia, we have absolutely nothing to complain about.

To lighten the atmosphere I told the guys that they had to

sing a song. 'Mate, it's Maori culture. If you don't reply with a song, you'll be cursed.' They all looked at each other as nervous as they could be. In the end Michael grabbed a guitar and sang a song in his native language. The kids loved it. It was a great day . . . but there was still the small matter of a fight — against the bogeyman who had turned out to be my new mate, Michael Long.

When I dropped him off at his hotel he looked at me and said, 'We are both sportsmen, bro. We'll shake hands before the fight, do what we have to do, and then we'll have a beer afterwards.'

Perfect.

Later that night I was sitting in the changing shed with Frank Bunce. We'd been through a lot in the past few weeks and soon we'd be in the ring. He was due up before me and we knew that if we won our fights, New Zealand couldn't lose this trans-Tasman battle. We started to get changed and he pulled out two pairs of All Blacks socks.

'Put these on, eh. Remember what you're wearing when you get tired.'

There was no way I was going to lose now. It gave me a real lift.

On the way out to the ring I saw Michael while we waited for the TV people to introduce us. He gave me a hongi.

'Maaaate, I loved it today. It was one of the great days of my life.'

Once I walked out it was time to switch on. It was time to bring out that killer instinct. Michael had become a mate but this was no time for friendship. As a rugby player — or any sportsman for that matter — you have to have a bit of dog in you and I do. I've never had a problem with going head to head against mates. Nuku told me not to look at anyone during the introduction in the ring. 'Just look at the judges. Give them a wink. Let them know you know who the important people are.'

And then it was on. 'See what he's got first, Rushie.' I threw a jab. He threw one back. It was slow. I'd been used to sparring with Sean and Kahu. This was nothing like them. I saw his

Above: I've got my eyes closed, but I've still managed to connect with Michael Long's chin. Below: Relief!

punch the whole way. I knew I'd be okay. I hit him early with a right hand and it stung him. I knew he didn't really want to be in there after that. By the middle of the second round it was over. I'd won. It was better than losing but there was no real joy or even relief. This guy had become a mate and I had a lot of respect for him. The overriding emotion was to make sure that he was okay.

Not all the fights ended that way. The guy Frank fought, former league player Mark Warren, was a bit of an idiot. Warren eyeballed Frank before the fight and gave him a bit of a nudge when the referee was giving his instructions. It fired up Frank like never before. He went after him and at one stage he had Warren down on the canvas on one knee. Instead of stepping back and allowing him to get back on his feet, he planted him again.

'Well, the ref said at the start of the fight to protect yourself

Buncey's got his eyes closed here (what is it about us footie players?) but still managed to deal to Aussie Mark Warren.

at all times until he said stop. He never said stop!'

Frank told me later that he hit him because he knew that if he let up he would have had to fight for at least another minute. 'I was buggered, bro.'

Ironically, the guy that got the headlines the next day was Sky TV's Stephen McIvor. He'd lost his fight to George Kulcsar really easily and was being treated as a bit of a laughing stock. Before the fight he was quite confident. He was building himself up — something all boxers have to do because if you don't believe you are going to win you should never get in the ring. **There's no hiding place in there — no teammates to rely on. I had a feeling he was going to struggle because I'd watched him spar and he just didn't have it.**

As soon as I saw Kulcsar throw the first punch I just turned around and headed back into the changing room. The next

Stephen McIvor took a lot of crap after his two Fight for Life bouts. Not from me, though. He showed a lot of guts.

time I saw him he was being helped into the room with a broken nose and blood all over him. He was shattered. But he is no laughing stock. I headed for him straight away.

'Bro, I'm proud of you. It takes some balls to get in there. You don't see too many other people doing it. Good on ya. Keep your head up, you did alright.'

His big disadvantage is that he hasn't been in the heat of battle. He's not a sportsman. Kulcsar had the physical toughness and the mental edge. **He was the Vinnie Jones of Australian soccer — he'd been sent off 11 times in his career. He was a tough bastard, and he was always going to beat McIvor.**

My next experience with Fight for Life was as a part-time trainer for Lindsay Raki in 2004. His mates had volunteered him for the fight. They'd all been drinking at the Ardmore Rugby Club when the subject of the Fight for Life surfaced. Lindsay — being his usual big mouth — was talking big about how he would front up if he were ever asked. It was well known that Deano couldn't find an opponent for Mark 'Horse' Bourneville and when his mates asked him if he would do it, Lindsay put his beer down on the table and said, 'Bloody oath, I would!'

When he left the group his mate Lance Goldsmith rang Deano and said that Raki — a former Maori All Black and Counties star — would not only fight Horse but he'd knock him out as well. 'And by the way, Lonergan, he'll knock you out as well!'

Deano reckons he had a bit of a laugh and said he'd call back the next day when everyone was sober. When the call came, Lance, Raki and a few mates were just about to get on a plane for a holiday on the Gold Coast. Lance — who still hadn't mentioned anything to Raki — agreed to enter Raki in a fight-off to win the right to fight Horse.

In the meantime Raki was sinking piss like it was going out of fashion. He was in holiday mode, drinking and eating his days through his Gold Coast jaunt. There were only three weeks to go until the fight — the only trouble was he didn't know he was fighting. Lance didn't tell him until they were on

Let's get it on . . . and they sure did. Lindsay Raki and Mark Bourneville banged away at each other all night.

the plane flying back to New Zealand.

'Oh, mate. I forgot to tell you. On Tuesday night you have a fight.'

'What do you mean I have a fight?'

'You're in a fight-off to see who fights Horse at Fight for Life.'

'Oh yeah, no worries. I'll take him on.'

'No, I'm serious. I have entered you. You are fighting on Tuesday.'

'What!'

By the time I saw him he'd convinced Deano that he should fight because of his profile and he'd asked me to help him get fit. We went for a run. The first hill we came to we had to stop to walk.

'Well, mate, there are two ways we can approach this fight. There is only going to be so much gas in the tank. You can either bluff your way through the first two rounds and come hard in the third, or just turn it into a scrap.'

He knew there wasn't enough time to get him fit. But he worked hard. We sparred every day. He dropped about 10 kg before the fight and once he was in the ring he held his own. He had a go, and he tried to take it to him. He hit the canvas a couple of times but that was due more to how tired he was than how hard Horse hit him.

Another fella to fight in 2004 was my mate Tawera Nikau. I have gotten to know T really well over the last few years. We — along with former All Blacks and Kiwi star Frano Botica — are directors of a motivational speaking company, Team One.

One of the programmes Team One has is called the Power Train. Throughout my career I have been to countless goal-setting seminars but, while they tell you that you have to set goals, they don't tell you how to get there once you've set them.

The Power Train was life-changing for me and I know that it has been for T as well. He's had dozens of different motivational experts around him throughout his league career in New Zealand, England and Australia but nothing has made as much sense as this little train.

There is a statement that Team One always focuses on:

Tawera Nikau, on just one leg, showed everyone at Fight for Life that any handicap can be overcome. T was inspiring.

The quality of life you ultimately enjoy is not decided by what happens to you but by what view you have of it and what you then decide to do about it. T needed something to grab on to when he lost his wife to suicide and that statement was one of the things he focused on.

And then he lost his leg in a motorcycle accident. He had a choice — he could stay in hospital for another year and let the doctors save his leg with countless operations or he could be out in six weeks and be a family man.

'Chop the bastard off,' he told the surgeons. When we saw him after the operation he told us: 'Boys, you know that statement? I've got to live that now.'

Instead of feeling down about things, T was filling out forms for the Paralympics. 'My kids are stoked. They get a car park at the front of every movie theatre in the country now!'

Then he fought in Fight for Life. Some people criticised the lack of aggression in his bout against Tea Ropati. But they missed the point. For T, stepping into that ring was saying to every person going through the tough stuff, 'Don't worry about it. Just do it.'

It's easy to look at that statement and say that you live by it. The key, though, comes when you are tested. Can you live that statement through the hard stuff? What about when you lose someone close to you? Or you get bad news from a doctor? Or, as in my case, when I was involved in a fatal car accident? What about when that stuff happens — can you live it then? That's the question we also ask at the seminars.

We get a foot in the door of a lot of companies because of our names. A lot of the people we talk to are those on the factory floor or on the roads — the blue-collar people. We can relate to them because we are the same sort of people. They listen because of who we are, but unless you have any substance to what you are saying they'll see right through you.

T has a powerful story to tell them. So does Frano. He left the All Blacks in 1989 after spending four years in the giant shadow of Grant Fox to play league for Wigan. When he arrived in England the first thing he discovered was that while the club's chairman Maurice Lindsay was a big fan, the person picking the team wasn't.

The first newspaper billboard he saw on the way to his first training said, *Coach doesn't want Botica*. He got to training and went into the gym — he'd never been into a gym before; 'I thought it was a fella's name' — and his new team-mates killed him on the weights. After he bombed out, he had a shower and when he grabbed his underwear he found some of his team-mates had cut the crotch out of them. They all cracked up laughing. He went home and wondered why he'd left the security of a place on the All Blacks' reserve bench.

But he didn't give up. The team had 12 Great Britain internationals. He figured that because they didn't have a decent goalkicker and the only spot not taken up by a test player was one of the wing spots, he would reinvent himself as a goal-kicking winger. By the time he left the club he had turned the situation around and left as Wigan's record points scorer.

I can't imagine that I will ever step into the ring again. My wife didn't enjoy watching it and she has made more than enough sacrifices for me over the years, so the least I can do is say no if I am asked again. I don't have anything to prove to anyone — it's very much a case of been there, done that.

There was an opportunity to fight at another charity event in Invercargill in September this year. But instead of saying no I asked Frano Botica if he wanted to attend a function on my behalf.

As a former All Black and Kiwi he is just getting into the after-dinner speech thing and I told him it would be a great opportunity to 'grow his brand'. He had no idea that he would be required to box until the sponsor rang and thanked him for putting his name forward.

(My mobile rings . . .)

'Hello?'

'Rushie!'

'Hey Bots.'

'What the f . . . is this about a fight in Invercargill?'

(Click.)

He lost the fight but he went okay, according to all reports. I'd just like to point out that he is the only person from Team One who has lost one of those fights.

The day after the fight he was interviewed on the local radio station and was asked if he had learnt anything.

'Yes, as a matter of a fact I have — never trust Eric Rush!'

Retirement

I PLAYED MY LAST GAME OF SEVENS for New Zealand at the Hong Kong tournament in 2004, but I didn't actually finish playing rugby until the end of the Auckland club rugby season in August.

I coach two of my boys at East Tamaki. It would be one of the poorest clubs in Auckland. The majority of players are Samoan, then Tongan, Rarotongan, followed by Maori. I love coaching the team — the under 11s — because they all have so much enthusiasm. **I tell them, 'Don't come when it's raining,' but they come anyway . . . in case it stops raining. Pacific Corn Beef sponsors the club — the player of the day gets a choice between a big tin, a little tin and a bag of lollipops. The Island kids always take the corn beef.**

Rugby for them is something they love doing and something they can excel at. Their families aren't rich — far from it. Half of my team don't even have telephones. But rugby is a great leveller and when they are on the field they are equal to any of the players in the fancy teams. It reminds me of why I loved the game so much when I was a kid.

After training one night I played a game of touch with the reserves and then the next week they told me they were short of players that weekend. Their coach Lui asked if I wanted to play for them. I said I was too old but he convinced me that they were short of numbers that weekend. So I turned up *after* halftime on purpose but as soon as I got there I was thrown into the game. I was useless. I got hit in the first tackle and I was hurt. 'What the f . . . am I doing here?' Then, just when I thought it couldn't get any worse the coach of the top team — Francis Leilua — asked me to stand by for his team. Sure enough, I was called onto the field and the next week he had me down to start for the team.

This is rugby at it purest and I must admit I loved it. Here I was, playing in the Auckland club rugby competition — the same comp I was playing in 20 years earlier. Making it fun was the fact that I was back at flanker instead of being stuck on the wing and making it even more fun was the Pacific Islands flavour at the club.

Before the game they have a prayer. I struggle to understand what the boys are saying, though, because their English isn't the best. One player started his prayer by saying, 'Okay, boys, heads off . . .' I think he meant 'hats off' (but by the way he tackles maybe he knew what he was saying!). It's tough in the games because when they are fresh they all speak English, but when they get tired they can't be bothered and start issuing instructions in Samoan or Tongan! I guess it's a good thing that you don't have to play your club rugby in Japan or France to come up against a language barrier.

Before a game for the reserves I asked the first-five what the call for the ball coming back to the forwards was.

'Okay, okay. That's any of the colour — like the red or the blue or the yellow.'

Then I asked him what the call was for the ball that goes out wide to the wingers.

'That's any of the fruit — you know that one? The banana, the apple . . .'

So we got into the game and at the first scrum I looked at him and asked him what the call was. 'Orange . . .' I looked at him and waited for him to start laughing but he was serious. I figured the best thing to do was hang around and see what happened! At halftime I asked our prop Sammy — a Cook

Islander who speaks good English — what does 'orange' mean because it's a fruit and a colour?

'Oh, bro, you're the first one to pick that up . . . we've been using that call all year.'

Lui's team talks were tough to grasp as well.

'Too much talking, eh. You fellas too much talking, eh. You got no mouth guard now, eh. What? Because coming in the game, nobody doing any talking, ah. You all gotta mouth guard in. Come to training take mouth guard out, too much talking bullshit.'

The success of the East Tamaki side in 2004 surprised a lot of people. I was talking to the Auckland B coach, Jeff Mooney, who selected our hooker Tai.

Jeff said he asked Tai what the secret to ET's success was, because there were no stars in the team. Tai replied: 'We have no game plan, eh. We play with the ball. When you have the ball run fast. When you got no ball, then the three Ds.'

Mooney figured Tai was talking about words like discipline, desire and dedication.

'No,' Tai said. 'Dackle, dackle, dackle.'

I'm glad that I played out the season because it's important for fellas like me to put something back into the game. So many of our top players end their careers overseas and never repay the game for what it has given them. I have been hearing for years about how bad our club rugby is these days but I hoped that when I ran out with the East Tamaki team it lifted our team and the opposition. That's why it's great to see former All Blacks like Shane Howarth playing for Suburbs, Ofisa Tonu'u playing for Ponsonby and Charles Riechelmann turning out for Grammar. Stu Forster came back and played in Hawke's Bay and Jamie Joseph did it in Wellington. It's a great trend. Club rugby is crying out for leadership and all those guys are doing their bit. It's a shame others choose not to.

I would have been coaching at East Tamaki regardless of whether I was playing sevens or not. I started coaching my boys' team three years ago. But as for playing for the club — I never thought that would happen again.

But when the chance to play came along I had to take it because people say the reason the club game is struggling is because people like me aren't playing and passing on all the things we've learnt to the young fellas. This was my chance to change that at East Tamaki.

Getting back into club rugby reminded me of how important volunteers are to the grassroots game. People who give up their time to run a club, coach teams or make meals — those people are the real heroes of New Zealand rugby. We should never forget that.

As for my rugby career, I was feeling okay until halfway through 2004 when my body just packed in. I was struggling with my neck and my shoulder, but then everything else starting blowing up. I was getting through the games okay but it was the build-up to the games that was the problem. I just couldn't get through Titch's trainings.

I really knew it was time to hang up the boots when I went up to the letterbox, slipped on the concrete and pulled a muscle in my groin. That was a bit of a sign. Then I asked myself, 'What if I don't play again next year?' When I realised that I wasn't fussed either way it was obvious that it was time to walk away from the sevens field.

It wasn't a tough decision. In the past I had asked myself that question every now and again and I always wanted to keep going. But this time I knew that my body had had it. I could still deal with the rigours of international sevens mentally but not physically. I remember talking to Dad about it. **He said, 'Boy, don't worry about it because there is going to come a time when you can't do mentally what you used to do physically . . .'**

Titch did his best to prolong my career. In the last couple of years he didn't make me play all the trial games and then during a tournament he'd give me one or two games off. But that can only go on for so long. I didn't want the team to carry me. I figure that I have set a standard for myself on the field and if I can't maintain it, then it's time to go. The time was right.

In sevens I always wanted to be in the starting seven. I stayed there for 17 years, which isn't a bad achievement when you look at the list of players that have come through the team in that time.

Towards the end of my career I'd always wonder if I'd be good enough to still make the seven when guys like Jonah Lomu were available for selection. And Titch would always remind me of that, too.

A lot of players want to play every minute of every game — I used to be like that myself. But in the last couple of years I've had the odd game off to give my body a bit of a break. Normally I wouldn't have to play in the second game on the first day of a tournament. It was good because I was able to save myself for the business end of the tournament and it would also allow one of the young guys to get a run. **Even starting on the bench didn't bother me. A black jersey is a black jersey.**

A few people have asked me if I ever feel like I don't want to help the young guys when they come into the squad because eventually those are the guys that would take my place in the team from me. But, no, I have never felt like that. I think that's one area where sport is a little bit different from business. If you are involved in sport and you are one of the senior guys the whole point is to try and get the young guys to outperform you. If you can get that guy to be a much better player then you have done your job. If a young guy came along and was putting pressure on me I always thought that was great because it made me work harder. **A big thing for me has always been to try to leave sevens in a better position than it was when I first made the team in 1988. In business, though, it's not like that.** If you are a senior executive you want people below you to excel, but not too much because the last thing you want is to lose your job.

One of the first things Titch said to us when he took over the team in 1994 was that one of his goals was to make sure that he coached us to be far better players than he was when he played for New Zealand.

Both Titch and I take great delight in seeing these young fellas come into the team and then leave us to go on to bigger and greater things. The most recent to rise up to the highest level was Rico Gear, who made his All Blacks debut against the Pacific Islanders in 2004. He was in the 1998 team that won the gold medal at the Kuala Lumpur Commonwealth Games. At the beginning of 1998 only Jonah, Christian Cullen, Dallas Seymour and I had played for the All Blacks. Since then Caleb Ralph, Roger Randle, Joeli Vidiri, Bruce Reihana and Rico have all discovered what it's like to play for the All Blacks. Even the team that played in Manchester in 2002 has produced its share of All Blacks. Mils Muliaina, Craig Newby and Rodney So'oialo all played for the ABs after they won their gold medals.

Back to 2004 and my retirement . . . Titch knew the writing was on the wall for me. He called me into a meeting at the start of the year and asked me if I was going to play and I told him

Rico Gear is the latest in a long line of sevens stars to take the step up to the All Blacks.

I'd give it a go. He told me he would never drop me. 'We've been through too much,' he said. 'But I know if you don't think you are up to it, you'll come and tell me.' And that's what I did. I finally rang him — after a week trying to get up the courage to make the call:

'Hey, Titch. You said to ring you when I don't think I want to do it any more. Well, I'm ringing you to tell you . . .'

'Oh no, mate! Matua Parkinson has just signed to play in Japan.'

'Yep.'

'Craig de Goldie has gone to Japan.'

'Ah, yep. I know Titch . . .'

'Karl Te Nana has just gone to Japan.'

'Yes, Titch. I know.'

'Well, you'd better keep running just in case . . .'

He wouldn't even let me retire gracefully! So I went to the camp at Mt Maunganui before the French and English legs of the World Series in May, but Titch was able to pick a team without selecting me.

I never made a big announcement or anything like that — that's not my style. If the big romantic retirement was something I wanted, I would have walked away after we won the Wellington leg of the World Series for the first time in 2003. But I was only 38 then . . .

When Titch came to terms with me retiring he was keen for me to make the big announcement, but I told him that I wanted to be like my grandfather's pig dog Nigga. It was on its last legs and we were all going on about putting it down but Granddad wouldn't let us. 'Nigga will know when it's time.' Sure enough, one day he walked into the bush, lay down and went to sleep. He knew when his time was up — no fanfare, just walked away. I could relate to that.

It has always been my thing to play until I knew my time was up. After winning Wellington, I wanted to play for at least another year. I felt the same at the beginning of 2004 but once I injured my neck, it put the rest of my body out and it was just too tough to get back to the level of fitness you need to play sevens at the highest level.

Will I miss it? No. Not the playing side of things anyway. When the boys were in England and France the only thing I missed was the inside oil on the team. When I heard a result on the radio I'd be a bit frustrated because I didn't know who had played, who was injured, what the build-up to the game was like or what sort of mood Titch was in.

The feeling I will miss the most is the feeling you get when you win. Whether it's winning a gold medal or a World Cup or any of the World Series events, the one thing I have learnt is that nothing can recapture that feeling. I don't care how rich you are and what sort of car or anything else you can afford, nothing can give you the feeling of euphoria that comes with winning something that you have spilt blood to earn.

My greatest memories from rugby aren't based around individual things I've done. Being the Player of the Tournament in Hong Kong was nice, but the memory that sticks with me from that day is celebrating the team's win. It's the same thing when I think about the All Blacks test against France in 1995. **I scored a try — probably the most satisfactory try of my life — when I scored an early try in a 37-12 win. That victory came a week after we were stuffed 15-22. It's the turnaround in the score and the fact that we were able to win Laurie Mains' last test for him that sticks with me — not the try.**

Another highlight was in 1996 when John Hart's Incomparables won a series in South Africa for the first time. Unlike the end of 1995, I wasn't in the test team but it didn't matter. I get frustrated when I read some books by All Blacks who bitch about not being in the test side and having to play in the midweek team. I have always thought that if you are good enough you'll be in the test side. If you're not, get over it. Work hard and see if you can change the minds of the selectors. If I was playing a midweek role — great, because for that midweek game, when we ran onto the field we were the All Blacks! If we lost it would be reported as the All Blacks losing — not the midweek team losing.

The personal highlight for me on that 1996 tour was leading

On the way to a try against France in Paris in 1995. It was probably the most satisfying score of my All Blacks career.

a haka for the team after we'd beaten the Springboks at Loftus Versfeld Stadium in Pretoria to secure the series win. I didn't play in the test but there was no one prouder of the boys on the field than the midweekers on the sideline. I was sitting next to Jonah Lomu and Carlos Spencer in the stand and I told them we should do the haka.

I told the boys: 'We haven't been able to do much on the field today but we can contribute in some way. Let's do the haka for the boys when they come back towards the stands.'

The All Blacks were on the other side of the field paying tribute to our supporters and when they headed back to the sheds and towards us, we started one of the best hakas I have ever been involved in. The boys on the field appreciated it — it was a great feeling to pay tribute to the 22 players that had made history. It was also about acknowledging all the All Blacks that had been trying to register a series win against the Boks in the Republic since 1921.

There's no doubt that Harty's team was helped by the fact that — for the first time — an All Blacks team had the opportunity to compete with South Africa on a level playing field because neutral referees were controlling the tests. Every All Black who had toured the Republic since 1921 had a story to tell about how the All Blacks had been robbed of victory by a dubious decision. **Anyone who played in the midweek team in 1996 could relate because, unlike the test players, we had to put up with South African refs.**

Every game — with the exception of an easy win against Western Transvaal — was a struggle. We beat a Boland Invitational XV 32–21 and Eastern Province 31–23. Calls were going against us throughout both games, but nothing compared to what we had to put up with in our last game against Griqualand West, which was controlled by Tappe Henning.

It looked like we were going to lose until the last minute of the game when Glen Osborne scored a try in the corner. That made the score 18–18 with time up on the clock. Up stepped John Preston to take the kick but he couldn't find his kicking tee. We asked the ref where the kicking tee was and he just shrugged his shoulders. After a short while of JP frantically looking for it, Henning told him to 'dig a hole'. So JP started to dig a little mound for the ball when I spotted the tee in one of the touch judges' hands behind his back.

I told JP and he pointed it out to the ref. 'No, no,' the ref said. 'You have placed the ball so you must now take the kick.' It was like a dark comedy but the South Africans seemed happy because JP missed the kick and the game was drawn.

Despite the odd refereeing, the tour was one of the highlights of my career. South Africa isn't the easiest place in the world to tour but it was made bearable by the boys winning the series.

Tackled against Western Transvaal in '96. This was the midweek All Blacks' only easy win on tour in the Republic.

And of course touring is all about having a good time with your mates, so if you are surrounded by good people it doesn't matter how bad everything else is because you can always have a laugh.

Marc Ellis was a great tourist. In South Africa a year earlier during the World Cup he got into the habit of stealing buses. The bus driver would park the bus at the training venue and wander off for a smoke. Macca — with an All Blacks sock tied around his head — would jump in the driver's seat and park around the corner. By the time the driver got back his bus would be missing and he'd start panicking. On cue Macca would come speeding around the corner, honking the horn and waving. Priceless.

It's important to have one or two characters in the team when you are touring. At the end of the day we all play the game because we love it. Yes, the boys get paid these days, but if they didn't enjoy rugby and their mates, they wouldn't be pulling on their boots every week.

Every rugby player has screeds of yarns to tell. Heck, I make a living from talking about my life and times in rugby.

Every tour has a story. When New Zealand Maori toured Europe in 1988 we were travelling through the south of France to Spain. It is, apparently, some of the most beautiful countryside in the world. But I missed seeing it because all the curtains on the bus were pulled while the boys were watching a porno film on the video screen. I tried to look outside, but when I pulled the curtain back all the light came into the bus and about 20 guys turned around and told me to 'f . . .ing close it!'

At a sevens tournament in the Middle East a few years ago Scott Pierce was sent away to get the game tape of the final. He stopped at a bar and never made it back to the team room. Simon Tremain — who had played a good game in the final — was a bit dark so he hunted out Scottie's bag and put three big plates of food underneath all the clothes Scottie had packed for the flight the next morning.

When we arrived back in Auckland the Customs people asked Scottie if he had any food in his bags.

'No.'

'Are you sure sir?'

'Yes.'

'You are telling me you have no food in your bags?'

'That's right. I have no food in my bags.'

'Did you pack your bags yourself, sir?'

'Of course.'

They opened up his bags and he saw the food and you could see his heart sink. It was beautiful.

Another great tourist to the Republic was Craig de Goldie. When we arrived at the airport there were two mini buses waiting to take us to the hotel. 'Because we are in South Africa,' he said, 'we should have one van for the whites and one for the blacks.' One of the drivers seemed a little offended and explained: 'We are trying to get away from that sort of thing — we prefer to think that everyone here these days is

Marc Ellis — bus driver, practical joker and, to my knowledge, the only All Black ever to invite Princess Di on a date.

Springbok green.' Goldie, not missing a beat said: 'Okay, then. All the dark green boys over there and all the light green boys over here!' It is those types of yarns that help provide material for my new lease of life on the after-dinner talk circuit and appearing on TVNZ's *Sports Café*.

The star of the TV show is definitely Marc Ellis. I knew he was a character ever since we toured together for the first time in 1993 when the All Blacks were invited to Buckingham Palace to meet the Queen, Prince Edward and Princess Diana.

The invite said, 'You are invited to tea at the Palace' — we all thought we were going to have a big feed but it turned out to be only a cup of tea.

'What's up with this?' Arran Pene was heard to say. 'It's not like she is short of a few dollars.'

Boys being boys we had a bit of a sweepstake to see who could get a memento from the palace. Richard Loe had two bucks on every darkie in the team! One of the boys got an ashtray from one of the toilets. I won't name him because he's a bit of a royalist and he'd never forgive me. Let's just say he is playing his club rugby in Wellington now and his last name features prominently in the Bible. As for his first name — I always thought it was a girl's name . . . He got on the team bus at the end of the night and shouted, 'That's for all the land you pinched from us, you honkies!' **(Political comment: It's no wonder we lost our land if we were happy that we had levelled the score after nicking an ashtray. We actually found out later that they leave these things for people to take home).**

Before meeting the Queen, Jamie Joseph and the rest of the team were all told about the rules that applied at the Palace. Obviously, you weren't allowed to swear. Not allowed to say anything controversial. You had to stand in groups of three or four so the royal party could circulate around all the groups. And when you shake hands with the Queen you aren't allowed to squeeze your hand in case you hurt her.

We were all waiting around when all of a sudden trumpets started playing and a big glass mirror opened up and out strolled the Queen. It was an awesome experience — we'd all grown up with her on our stamps and on the TV and now, there she was, standing in front of us.

She walked past our group and I remember seeing her yellow handbag and thinking, 'Why is she carrying her handbag when she's at home!' I guess she is watching her money after all.

Edward was the next into the room and five metres behind him was Diana. We'd all been staring at the Queen but as soon as Diana walked in all the boys forgot about the old bird in a hurry. Diana had a shiny dress on and she looked stunning. She'd only recently broken up with Prince Charles and Arran Pene looked at me and said, 'What the f . . . was he thinking?'

Much to our delight, Diana walked straight over to our group. Arran, Marc Ellis, Liam Barry and I were the happiest boys in the Palace. The conversation was a bit one-way at the beginning — none of us could talk and we were all struggling to get the words out. We were just staring. Then she started talking rugby to us. She seemed to know heaps about us so I asked her if she was a rugby fan. She looked around the room to see where the Queen was and then leaned across towards me and said, 'To be perfectly honest, gentlemen, we've been upstairs for the last five hours swotting up on you guys. I know absolutely nothing about you fellows.'

(Within a year she would be involved in a relationship with the former England captain Will Carling. I suspect she would have picked up a few tips about rugby from him.)

She was a cool chick. At the time of our meeting she had been on the front page of the papers in England after revealing photos of her had been secretly taken as she worked out in a London gym. **Bearing in mind that we were under instructions not to mention anything controversial, Arran said, 'So, there's no gym in Buckingham Palace then?'**

Diana wasn't offended. Instead she said, 'In fact, the person who took those pictures was a New Zealander.' Arran offered to give him a hiding if he ever caught up with him.

We then had one of those uncomfortable moments of silence when no one knew what to say, so Macca pipes up and asks her what she was doing later. 'If I'm not mistaken,' she said, 'you have just asked me out!'

Macca said, 'Well, you're free, aren't you?'

Liam was quick to apologise for Macca 'on behalf of all New Zealand', and as she walked away, Diana turned to us and said, 'Don't worry. I was thinking about it!' Macca's hands were up in the air in a heartbeat. 'You heard her! I'm the man! I'm the man!' — and he has lived off it ever since.

There's always a bit of tension on *Sports Café* between Lana Coc-Kroft and Macca but it's all make-believe. They get along really well, although sometimes Macca genuinely annoys her — like the time he was making 'skinny' jokes a couple of months after she got out of the hospital following her near-death encounter with streptococcal toxic shock syndrome. She flat-lined twice — so it was serious — but that didn't stop Macca.

The first time Lana belted him (the show was live on air) was the day Macca asked her what her name spelt backwards would be.

I ended up on the show after Zinzan Brooke and John Kirwan left. I don't know what I am doing there. Macca, Ric, Lana and Graeme Hill talk so much I can never get a word in. It's a pretty easy job for me — I just sit on the sofa and say nothing. Ric reckons I must have the best per-word pay rate in the world of entertainment. One day I said to Ric that I am only on the show because I am the token darkie.

'Yes, Eric. That's right,' he said.

Every now and again he'll tell me who's going to be on the show but most of the time I have no idea. I usually get to the studio five minutes before the show starts and Macca has never beaten me there. Never. He has arrived after the show has started at least a dozen times. I can't criticise, though, as there have been times when I have been sitting next to a guest and I have absolutely no idea who they are. Ric reckons it doesn't matter. 'Don't worry,' he says, 'no one is watching.'

Of course he's joking because whenever I travel round the country people love to talk about the show. It's big with schoolboys — they can't get enough of Eva the Bulgarian. Lana was originally offered a spot on the show because she was supposed to be the dumb blonde. **But she was too clever so Ric hired Eva. Eva is clever but she's only clever in Bulgarian so that makes it okay to typecast her in New Zealand as the blonde babe with the big . . . eyes.**

Since I wrote my first book, *Gold Rush*, in 1999 I have been doing a lot of speeches. There's a big demand for it. But the only rugby players who do it in New Zealand regularly are Colin Meads, Sean Fitzpatrick, Stu Wilson and occasionally Grant Fox.

I got into it by mistake. I was in Hong Kong with the sevens team and Telecom invited us out on the harbour on a chartered boat. We thought it would just be for the team but when we stepped on board there were about 150 supporters already there. The Telecom people asked us to stay on the boat for an hour and mingle with the fans. No worries there — it's always good to rub shoulders with people who have paid good money to travel halfway round the world to support you. But then they asked me to give a speech . . . so I did what I normally did, I roasted the team by introducing them one by one.

'This is Glen Osborne — we call him Laser Breath; you'll find out why when you talk to him later on . . . just don't get too close.

'This is our esteemed coach Gordon Tietjens. We call him Titch. He's the only man in New Zealand rugby who parts his hair in a circle . . .

'This is our manger Tony Ward — he has 99 parts in his hair.

'This is our physio Kevin McQuoid — we call him Oxygen: you know he's there somewhere but you just can't see him . . .'

I got a lot of practice doing it because when we have our sevens camps in Mt Maunganui — Titch's territory — we go to every school in the area every time we're there. First, we visit the schools that Titch's kids attend and then every other school. At one stage we were doing three or four schools a day so I got comfortable talking in front of a crowd pretty quickly. **'This is Nathaniel Walker — he used to go to this school. And, as you can see, he hasn't grown up much . . .'**

These days it's not uncommon for me to do two or three talks — either at corporate events or at rugby clubs — a week. And it doesn't matter how many I do or how well they go, I am always nervous before I step up to the mike because you never know what the audience will be like.

I showed up at a Bledisloe Cup lunch in Sydney once ready to take the piss out of everything Australian. When I walked into the joint it turned out that it was an all-women's lunch. I couldn't stop sweating — first the gig was in Australia so they wouldn't know who I was and, second, they're women. What am I going to talk to them about? In the end it was okay because I took all the swearing out and talked about meeting Lady Di and the Queen, but it was a good lesson never to relax because you just don't know who will be in the crowd.

Some audiences are better than others. I have been lucky that I haven't bombed too badly (yet!). There have been one or two speeches that I have given that I know could have been better, but I have never been booed off the stage. The biggest problem is when there is someone in the audience who's drunk — normally they keep talking through the whole speech. When that happens I usually just cut my speech short and finish up. There's no point trying to compete with them because if they are drunk, they just don't care. I tried competing once — at East Tamaki where a woman kept talking. **She was getting married the next weekend so I told her: 'Lady, let me give you a piece of advice for your wedding reception — don't drink because you are not a pretty drunk.' It only made her louder and more obnoxious.**

Sometimes, even the veteran after-dinner speakers misjudge the audience. There are some audiences you can swear in front of and others you can't. I've seen people look really offended when a speaker has started to swear. Some people will just walk

Speech-making has become part of my life in recent years. Here I do my bit for Jonah at his book launch in Auckland.

Mike King — part-time racing driver, but full-time comic. No one swears as eloquently as Mike.

out. Mike King is a bit like that in that he doesn't care. And, anyway, if swearing offends you then you should know better than to go and listen to Mike King. He really is the king, though.

He is one of my favourites. He normally offends everyone. One classic speech Mike gave was at Eden Park before an All Blacks test. He started it like this: 'Good evening, ladies and gentlemen. What a great night. Here we all are looking forward to a great game. All the men are dressed up and all the women are dressed up . . . my God, guys, aren't there some beautiful women here?'

The crowd all cheer.

'Don't get me wrong; there are some f . . .ing pigs here, too. That's probably a good thing, though — all us fellas from West Auckland need to get a root, too!'

I haven't had the balls to use that opening yet.

The former Wallaby Peter FitzSimons is another favourite on the guest-speaking circuit.

Former Wallaby Peter FitzSimons is one of the cleverest speakers on the rugby circuit.

There's an MC in Australia, Vince Sorrenti, who is outstanding. He's Greek and loves to take the piss out of his people.

'Greek men wear gold chains so they know where to stop shaving.'

He has a great line about American intelligence in the war against terrorism:

'American intelligence — that's a contradiction in terms. **They couldn't find Saddam for a long time. How tough could it have been to find a guy with a five o'clock shadow and a moustache in Iraq? What's going to happen when they invade North Korea — there are 14 million Kim Il Jongs there!'**

One of the toughest crowds I had to talk to was the one I ran into after the All Blacks had lost the semi-final of the 2003 World Cup to the Aussies.

It's never easy watching the All Blacks lose but I wasn't too gutted after the Sydney defeat. If it had been a close game it would have been hard to accept defeat, but the fact is once Stirling Mortlock intercepted that pass from Carlos Spencer, the All Blacks were never in the game.

As I went up to the podium later at an after-match function I was greeted by a chorus of 'Baa, baa, baa'. When you are surrounded by a bunch of Aussies having a go at you, you have to fight back, so I did.

'Let's face it, anyone can shag a sheep. Kangaroos, they fight back. You have to build a relationship with them. It's the only animal I know that's learnt how to box . . . there has got to be a reason for it!'

I ended the speech by telling the crowd that the All Blacks would be back next year to try and win the Bledisloe Cup back. There was a murmur in the audience and one fella said that the All Blacks still held the Bledisloe. And I said 'Pardon?' He explained it again. 'THAT'S RIGHT!' I left the stage with a smile . . .

It took a while to be able to enjoy watching the All Blacks because you always think you are still good enough to be out there. You know you're not — but when someone makes a mistake you always feel you wouldn't have made the mistake. It's a pretty easy game from the stands!

These days, because I have been doing a lot of speeches, I get to watch most of the tests. And I enjoy watching them now, although when they lose I always hurt for them. When they win, I guess I am like every other Kiwi. But when they lose — because I have worn the jersey and I know what it's like to lose in that team — I probably hurt for them a little bit more than most.

And in the era that we are in now, the All Blacks are losing more tests against the top countries than ever before. That's not a criticism of the current players, it's just a fact. Professionalism has been great for the game in a whole lot of ways but it has hurt the All Blacks because all the other teams have been able to catch up to us. Back in those days the All Blacks — even though they had full-time jobs — trained like professionals. Teams like England and Australia used to train hard but not to the same level as the All Blacks sides. Nowadays everyone is professional and the advantage we used to have is gone.

People say the fear factor of the black jersey is gone. I'm not sure about that. If you ask players from France, England, Ireland, Australia and South Africa who they'd like to beat the most, most of them would say the All Blacks. If you asked them which would be the toughest test to play, they'd all say the All Blacks. Maybe that's just arrogance on my part or maybe the players I talk to are just telling me what they think I want to hear. But I am sure there is some truth to it. So, the aura is still there, but because we play so many tests these days the opposition get to work you out a bit better.

A good example of the gap being closed can be found in sevens. When the only two tournaments that were going were in Sydney and Hong Kong, it was almost always New Zealand and Fiji playing in the final. Occasionally Australia and Samoa might sneak in but that was a rare occurrence.

Now that the World Series has finished its fifth year, not only are teams like Australia and Samoa making finals, they are winning tournaments, along with the likes of England, Argentina, France and South Africa.

It's the same in fifteens. Everyone is able to analyse everyone else and work out ways to counter their strengths. One of the English boys who played against us at the Manchester Commonwealth Games went out with the New Zealand boys in Hong Kong and got a little drunk and confessed that they'd videotaped our trainings. We'd had practice games against Wales and the Cook Islands and they'd taped them!

It turned out the England team had videos of each of the New Zealand players. They knew which foot we stepped off, which was our strong side in the tackle, which side we passed off was the weaker. We had no idea we were being watched. We'd actually gone out of our way to get out of the village to train in private.

Maybe one way for New Zealand rugby to fight back is to allow our overseas-based players to play for the All Blacks.

Would we have lost the tests against Australia and South Africa this year if Bruce Reihana, Mark Robinson or Andrew Blowers had been available? Who knows if they would have been good enough to wear the black jersey but they are certainly playing well for Northampton.

At the end of the day they are New Zealanders and if we are going to compete with the best we need to be able to pick our best team. At the moment it seems we are cutting our noses off to spite our face. I appreciate it's a difficult one for the NZRU because they want our best players playing in New Zealand. But they need to remember that the All Blacks have to be the priority. You can talk about grassroots but if you have a winning All Blacks team the grass roots side of things takes care of itself.

John Mitchell predictably came in for a lot of criticism after the 2003 World Cup. I thought that was a little unfair. After all, he'd brought the Bledisloe Cup and Tri Nations championship trophy back to the trophy cabinet at the NZRU offices in Wellington.

It is easy to say Mitch was passionate about the All Blacks but he has proved it. He came back from England to coach the team. He could have made more money assisting Clive Woodward's England team and he would have had less pressure on him. But he was determined to coach the ABs and he ought to be admired for wanting to take on that role.

I've always had a lot of admiration for Mitch. He was the All Blacks' midweek captain on the tour to Britain in 1993. Before our first game against Midlands he scared the shit of me. I don't think I have ever seen anyone as passionate as him about his rugby.

During the warm-ups he was ferocious. His eyes were popping out of his head. Walter Little and I figured the best thing to do was head outside and do our own warm-up. With 10 minutes to go we went back to the shed and he was still fired up. It was his first game as an All Black and he was the captain. It was good to see that passion. It's something he has never lost. He's a bit calmer and more collected as a coach but he's still passionate about his jersey — whether it's the black one or the red, yellow and black one.

John Mitchell — Tri Nations championship and Bledisloe Cup-winning coach. It wasn't enough to save his job.

One thing he tried to get the All Blacks to do when he coached them was to enjoy their victories. All Blacks are often so relieved not to lose they forget to enjoy the moment. Mitch wanted to change that because he knew the value of balance. When we were playing in the All Blacks 'balance' was something we all talked about. You prepared, played hard and then celebrated. Guys like Mike Brewer, Zinzan Brooke, Walter Little and Frank Bunce enjoyed a night out with one or 10 beers. But the next day, when it came time to train, they were ready to go.

It's an attitude I will hope to encourage if I ever get the chance to coach the New Zealand Sevens team. That's my goal. That's the reason I have stayed loyal to New Zealand rugby and not cashed up and headed overseas.

I have had a few chances to head offshore. In 1998 **I was offered a deal worth $400,000 to play in France. But that wasn't the first offer that came my way. In the late '80s Graham Lowe offered me the chance to join Matthew Ridge at Manly in the Winfield Cup.** My sevens team-mate Scott Pierce was also offered a deal. I'd already turned down an offer to play league for Bradford Northern but the Manly deal was a bit more attractive. I thought seriously about it. Lowey was good — he told me not to sign for the money because if I did, I'd never be a success in the game. 'Sign if you want to be a good league player and because you want to enjoy it. Don't do it for the money.'

I was enjoying rugby so much at the time, though. I was travelling the world and I wasn't even an All Black. I couldn't see the logic in leaving that behind to join a professional game that was only played in Australia and Great Britain.

In the last few years I have been offered the chance to play in Japan with the opportunity to earn big dollars. But the most enticing offer came from the bosses of another country's union who wanted me to coach their sevens team.

They were offering a massive amount of money for three years but I couldn't do it. I thought about it and even came close to agreeing on terms. But, when it came to the crunch,

Graham Lowe (centre) offered me big money to switch to league. The offer, though, came with some great advice.

there was no way I could coach against New Zealand — not yet anyway.

I almost went after the way I was treated before this year's Wellington Sevens.

Ever since the first Wellington Sevens in 2000 I have bought tickets to distribute to my family and friends. This year I was injured and unable to play, but a couple of days before the tournament I rang up to pay for my tickets, which I had ordered six months before. I was told that because I wasn't playing I couldn't get them! They told me that there were no tickets available because the demand for tickets was so great after the team won in 2003. **Um, hello! Do you know who captained the winning team?** After 17 years of service I was pretty peeved to say the least.

Tony Ward put in a gold medal performance to sort out the problem and my family and friends were, thankfully, able to attend the tournament.

All that was going on as I had this offer to coach overseas on the table. In the end I spoke to Titch about it. He didn't want me to do it, so I turned it down.

I was happy to walk away from it because my dream is to coach the New Zealand team. Titch is trying to work on an arrangement where I can observe things for a year. It's a great way to do it because I need to have a year or two away from the players so I can make the transition from player to coach if it ever happens.

It's not always an easy thing to do. Someone told me that when Mitch took over the coaching reins at the Chiefs there were one or two guys in the team he had played with. At the first team meeting he said: 'I owe you guys a hell of a lot. As team-mates we went through a lot and I will never forget that. But as coach, I owe you absolutely nothing. Everyone starts from square one with me.' It's a tough attitude but one you have to take when you make that transition.

I presume Titch will hang on until the 2006 Commonwealth Games before handing the torch to someone else. I'll know by then if I have the passion to think about applying for the job.

If I am lucky enough to get the job I'll certainly take on a lot of things I have seen Titch do over the years. If I can take on his organisational skills and work ethic then that will go a long way to making sure I am a successful coach. He is also a meticulous planner. He is always planning — something that has ensured we have stayed at the top of the World Series tree.

Laurie Mains was the same. Wayne Smith — I loved playing for him when he coached the sevens team. He and Peter Thorburn had the ability to say the right things at the right time. Another coach worth attempting to emulate is John Hart.

He was a master motivator. His team talks were inspiring. Before my first game for Auckland he addressed the team. Frank Bunce and Brett Craies were also making their debuts. He challenged us and the older guys in the team at the same time. 'You see those three young fellas there — they are going to run till they drop today. It's their first game for Auckland and it's up to you guys to show them how it's done.'

He'd motivated the debutants by saying we were going to run until we dropped and he'd put the onus on the older guys to show us the way — all in one statement. Before I went out he pulled me aside: 'Just enjoy yourself, fella.'

Laurie was the same when I first played for the All Blacks. He had picked me as a winger, even though I had played all my representative rugby in the forwards. He rang me in Hong Kong and I heard this voice saying: 'Hello, Rushie. It's Laurie Mains here . . .'

I hung up because I was convinced it was one of the boys pulling my leg. I'd taken plenty of calls from what I thought was the media but had turned out to be Glen Osborne or Stu Forster. Oz had me on the phone for half an hour one day before he asked me his last question. 'Is it true that you have the smallest penis in the New Zealand Sevens team?'

Stu had got me a few times as well but before Harbour played Otago once I got my own back. I wrote a letter to him with my left hand (so it looked like the writing of a child).

Dear Stu. You are an inspiration to every child in New Zealand like myself because you are so small against all those really big men. Do you enjoy reading books? I ask this because it seems like the other team seems to read you easily.

When we got down there for the game Buncey asked him whether or not he got the letter.

'How do you know about the letter?'

After Frank told him I sent it, Stu was furious. I spoke to him after the game and he said he'd been dark all week. **Normally, if you get a letter from a kid it inspires you. But Stu walked around with a cloud over him for the whole week.**

Anyway, back to the hotel room in Hong Kong . . . Laurie rang again and this time I heard him out. 'Look, mate, I am not going to give you an All Blacks trial.' I thought, 'Well, why are you ringing me?' I figured he was the first All Blacks coach to call everyone he doesn't pick before naming the team! Then he continued: 'But if you want a game on the wing then we will give you a try out there. You are a good rugby player but you are too small to play in the forwards.' I said yes straight away and three days later I was playing in an All Blacks trial.

Paul Cooke, the Otago winger, was a reserve for the game and he gave me some advice. **'Rushie, you know the film *Top Gun?* Yes. You know what he says to his mate — "You never leave your wingman." That's all you've got to remember. If the wing you are marking is there, never leave him. And, if you get the ball, run! Run fast!'**

I scored a couple of tries and was given another go in the New Zealand B side that played against England B. And the third game was for the All Blacks. Before the game Laurie came up to me and said, 'This is your third game as a winger now. You just get out there and enjoy yourself. Do what we picked you to do — turn up wherever and have fun. This is your first day as an All Black — you'll never forget this day, so go and enjoy it.' Well, I was on top of the world. There was no pressure on me and I just went out there and played hard and enjoyed it. I even managed to get a try.

Before the next game he came over to me and said, 'You have had three games as a winger now. We have allowed you to make a few mistakes. But you are a winger now. No more mistakes!'

I wish Amasio Valance would listen to that advice . . .

Dad

HE NEVER TOLD THE FAMILY HE HAD LEUKEMIA. But he knew he had it before Christmas in 2003. But my old man made a point of telling us it wasn't leukemia. 'I don't know what it is, but I know it's not leukemia.' That's what he told us.

So, we all had a good Christmas and a few days later he told us the truth. Turns out he stayed quiet about it because he didn't want to ruin Christmas Day for everyone. That was typical of my dad. He didn't even want to tell us after Christmas but my mother got it out of him. Then in the first few months of 2004 he was told he probably wouldn't last through to Christmas — he didn't want us to know that either but Mum told us. She wanted us to know. At the time of writing this book, having him around at Christmas 2004 is something we are all hoping for . . .

He's been crook for about five years. It started when he first began to get a lot of pain in his feet. Sometimes they would turn black because of a lack of circulation. We knew he was sick because he came down from Northland to paint my aunt's house and he couldn't finish the job. He could only work for an hour at a time.

His mantra was always, 'If you are going to do a job, do it properly', so it was obvious that something was wrong. The doctors up north struggled to identify the problem so I took him to see the All Blacks doctor, Doc Mayhew. As usual, I was running a bit late and when he finally arrived Doc looked at me and said, 'Ah, finally . . . the late Mr Rush.' The old man calmly said, 'I'm not that sick, Doc!'

He was in hospital in Auckland for three weeks. He underwent a load of tests but all the tests for leukemia came back negative. In the end they just gave him aspirin and told him to try to keep his blood thin.

Complicating things for him was the news that because of all the work he'd done in old houses and buildings over the years, he had breathed in a phenomenal amount of asbestos. It turns out he had a calcified ring of it right throughout his lungs and heart. The doctors originally thought it was another cancer, but when they X-rayed him to have a look they discovered it was the asbestos. The doctors told him then that it was lucky he had stopped smoking 20 years ago — if he hadn't he would have already been dead.

I learnt a few things from my dad but the most important one that I have tried to pass on to my kids is his work ethic. My kids have it pretty easy compared to the way I grew up — there was no running water or electricity in our house. There was no septic tank either — it was all long-drop.

I remember the first time Raina (then my girlfriend, now my wife) went up to the old house. She was there for four days and never went to the toilet. 'Look at all the flies, I'm not going in there!' I told her to go at night — when the flies are asleep.

Dad built a new house across the creek where he and Mum live now. He's worked hard and paid it all off. He'd still be working now if he weren't crook — that's the way his generation is. The greatest generation. He was a boy who was born in a small village in Ireland called Cavan before he was adopted by the Rush family in Belfast. He made his way to New Zealand and raised a family of brown Irish kids.

He was always a funny fella.

Dad always had a way of embarrassing us and the embarrassment usually involved the school bus or his cars.

One time me, my brothers and sister were on the bus on our way to school and all the kids on the bus saw these feet poking out of the entranceway to the Post Office. As we got closer I realised it was the old man. Everyone on the bus was laughing at us. We got home and we were really dark with him. It turned out he was sleeping off a hangover. *It's better than drinking and driving!* He's right, of course, but it would have been good if he had chosen a place a little more private.

My brother Robert (Bru) was embarrassed again when he made the North Auckland secondary schools team. We had two Triumphs — a red one and a white one. The white one was broken down so Dad put the bigger motor from the red one in the boot of the white car. It wasn't the best idea as the motor was too heavy for the white car, which travelled along with the back scraping the ground and Dad looking straight into the sky. Sure enough, Bru's team bus pulled up alongside it and all the boys were laughing. *Look at that fella!* Bru didn't want to get off the bus.

Dad also had a habit of crashing his Valiant on the same stretch of road. It was on the school bus route. We were on board when we spotted the car in the ditch. We got out to see if he was all right. We could see him lying on the front seat.

'You alright, Dad?'

'Of course I am! You go off to school and let me have my nap.'

I didn't have the heart to tell him that it was the afternoon and I was on my way home.

After each of these episodes, he would stop drinking for a whole year as a sort of self-imposed punishment. Then, one year later to the day, he would have a beer again. I think Mum secretly wished he'd crash more often.

He was also in the habit of hand-painting the cars. One afternoon one of Mum's friends, Mere Muka, came to the house and they went off fishing. By the time she came back her white car was green. Dad said he'd painted it because he didn't like the colour.

As well as being a real character, he was emotional, too — once he cried when we were watching *Lassie*. 'It's an Irish trait,' he'd say. 'There's nothing to be ashamed of. Cry as much as you want. Nothing wrong with showing your emotions.' Which is an ironic thing for him to say because when it came to rugby he very rarely showed those emotions to me. He never praised me. When I made a rep team as a kid he said, 'I'm pretty proud of you.' But that was as good as it got.

When I made the All Blacks I rang him — all excited — and he came back with, 'Choice. Ah well, make sure you go all right, eh.' Mum told me later he and my grandfather were pissed for a week.

As a father now it's tough because everyone expects my kids — especially the two older boys — to be really good rugby players. I would love them to be good but I don't want to put too much pressure on them. They'll train hard anyway — they have no choice about that! I want them to be able to handle anything, on the field or off it. Life can be tough so you have to be tough.

Any toughness I have I would have got from the old man. As a little fella my brother and I always used to fight. He bought us a pair of boxing gloves and if he caught us fighting he used to make us box until we both cried. If one of us started bleeding, the other used to have to start bleeding before he let us stop. One day, he caught us fighting and he went to get the boxing gloves but my brother and I had cut them up into little pieces so that we wouldn't have to use them. I can't remember it but the old man reckons that when he found them in the cupboard he started laughing his head off before coming out and looking at us and saying at the top of his voice: 'What happened to these gloves?' My brother and I — with innocent looks on our faces — said, 'We dunno . . .'

More than anything he is just a great dad. He may not have said too many positive things about my career, but whenever I needed support he was there for me. In 1998 when I was involved in a fatal car accident he was a pillar of strength.

Me and Dad at the Kaeo Rugby Club after he was made a life member. He kept his acceptance speech short and sweet: 'Thanks for all the entertainment over the years.'

It was the same early in my career when I missed out on teams. I'd be disappointed and he'd just say, 'Why do you play rugby?'

'Because I like it.'

'Well, don't let them destroy that. Just keep playing because you like it. If you get in teams, good. If you don't, at least you are having a good time. Never let them take your ability to enjoy the game from you. It's up to you if you want to enjoy it.'

So I went out there, didn't care what the selectors thought, had some fun and enjoyed my rugby. And because I was enjoying it, I was playing well and, sure enough, the selectors picked me.

It was a great piece of advice. I was able to pass it on to Glen Osborne in 1996. He had been one of the stars of the All Blacks the year before but when John Hart took over the coaching reins he told Oz that he needed to get a bit bigger. So

Oz started swallowing Creatine and spent every waking hour in the gym. He was transfixed on getting big. But while he got bigger, he lost all of his speed.

He had an ordinary Super 12 and was dropped from the All Blacks. He went to play club rugby and he had no confidence. So I pulled him aside and told him, 'Never mind being big — you are never going to be Jonah. I'd rather be a yard faster than a kilo heavier. There's no point being a kilo heavier if the other fella is already a yard in front of you. Get out there and have a good time. Just be yourself.'

Oz used to yell out 'Woo hooo' or make sounds more common on a karate floor like 'Aaaaawwwww' as he stepped you. He started doing that again — having a bit of fun — and, just as my dad would have foreseen, Harty came calling and he was back in the team for the trip to South Africa.

As a professional footballer you are surrounded by hangers-on who are forever telling you how good you are. That's why it is important to have a support network around you of people that you trust. For me that's my family. We're tight. We always have been. It's funny because Dad doesn't have too much time for the Maori way of life. He's used to a different culture. If a European wants to borrow your lawnmower, they'll ring up a week before, then ring up the day before, they'll announce themselves when they arrive and then have a cup of tea. When they're finished with it they'll return it clean and full of petrol and leave a packet of biscuits.

With my family I have to ring around to see who has my mower. I rang up my brother one day and he said: 'Yeah, I've got it, bro, but it's broken. Can you come round and fix it because I haven't finished the lawns yet.' That's the Maori culture — *what's mine is yours and what's yours is mine.*

As well as the laughter in the house, there was plenty of swearing as well. One time my cousin and I were helping Dad paint Mrs Atwell's house. We were painting away and my cousin Darryl saw a spider and lost his balance and yelled out 'F . . .!' Dad came around the corner and went into one of those shouting whispering rants: 'What was that? I told you not to swear in front of the old lady. Don't swear!'

Later in the day the old man was on his ladder painting the highest point of the gable when the wind blew and he nearly fell off. At the top of his voice, all we heard was, 'You f . . .ing bastard of a f . . .ing thing, for f . . .'s sake keep still . . .' My cousin and I were rolling around with laughter but the old man had had enough. 'Let's go and get a f . . .ing beer.' On the way to the pub I looked at him and said, 'Lucky we didn't swear in front of that lady, eh?' Luckily for me, Dad saw the funny side of it.

He may have sworn a lot but one thing I am proud of is the fact that he never hit Mum. Most people will take it for granted that their parents don't fight but up north — in the area where I grew up — it was commonplace for fathers to hit mothers. It's just the way it was.

I knew it went on because I had seen Dad get a few hidings after sticking up for women while they were getting beaten. I remember one of my uncles in particular getting stuck into him. When I was 16, I was talking to that uncle and he mentioned that he'd had a go at Dad. I told him I could remember it and I said, 'Just make sure it never happens again.' As soon as the words came out I thought, 'I'm in trouble now.' This uncle was right out of the script of *Once Were Warriors*. He had a temper on him like Jake the Muss. Everything was dead quiet and then he looked at me over his beer and said: 'Good on yuh, boy. You look after your old man.' After I got my breath back — 'cause I was panicking there for a minute — I knew that he'd leave Dad alone. Dad didn't need protecting by me, but it was good to know that he wouldn't be targeted for doing the right thing.

If anyone was going to protect Dad it would be my mum. They have a great relationship — although if you didn't know them, you might be left wondering. They always have a bit of fun at each other's expense. When we were talking about where Dad wanted to be buried she said she didn't care as long as they put him in deep so that there was room for her to eventually be buried on top of him. 'You're not going on top of me!' yelled Dad. 'I've been carrying you for 40 years, now you are telling me I am going to carry you through the afterlife!'

I remember a mate of mine was talking about his wife and he mentioned to the old man that 'My wife's an angel.' Quick as a flash Dad shot back with 'Lucky bastard — mine is still alive.'

In a way I guess it has been a blessing that we have had time to say goodbye to Dad — a kind of long goodbye. But I never took the chance to really tell him how I felt about him. We weren't brought up to say things like 'I love you'. We never said that in our house. I'd go to other houses as a young fella and hear people say it all the time — but we never did. I've said it to him plenty of times in the last few months, though, just to make sure he knows. I guess this chapter is another way of saying those three words.

Rushie: the stats

ERIC RUSH
FIRST CLASS CAREER

TEAM	GAMES	TRIES	POINTS
New Zealand	29	18	90
Chiefs	18	10	50
North Harbour	92	37	182
Auckland	13	7	28
New Zealand XV	4	2	10
New Zealand Trials	4	3	13
North Island	1	1	5
UK Barbarians	4	4	17
New Zealand Maori	30	13	56
Maori Trials	8	8	37
Invitation XV	1	1	5
	204	104	493

INTERNATIONAL SEVENS TOURNAMENTS ATTENDED

YEAR	VENUE	PLACE
1988	Hong Kong	2
	Australia	1
1989	Australia	1
	Hong Kong	1
1990	Hong Kong	2
1991	Hong Kong	2
1992	Hong Kong	2
1993	Hong Kong	*
	Scotland	* (World Cup)
1994	Fiji	*
	Hong Kong	1
1995	Argentina	1
	Uruguay	1
	Hong Kong	1
1996	Hong Kong	1
1997	Hong Kong	* (World Cup)
	Dubai	1
1998	Argentina	1
	Uruguay	1
	Chile	1
	Australia	2
	Hong Kong	*
	Malaysia	1 (Commonwealth Games)
	Japan	1
	Jerusalem	*
	France	2
1999	Argentina	1
	Uruguay	1
	Chile	1
	Australia	1
	Hong Kong	*
	France	1
	Dubai	1
	South Africa	2

YEAR	VENUE	PLACE
2000	Argentina	2
	Uruguay	1
	Australia	*
	Wellington	2
	Fiji	1
	Hong Kong	1
	Israel	2
	France	1
	Dubai	1
	South Africa	1
2001	Argentina	1 (World Cup)
	Dubai	1
	South Africa	1
2002	Chile	1
	Argentina	*
	New Zealand	*
	China	1
	Hong Kong	*
	England	1
	Wales	1
	England	1 (Commonwealth Games)
2003	Australia	*
	New Zealand	1
	Hong Kong	2
	Wales	*
	England	*
2004	Hong Kong	*
	Singapore	*

* Indicates New Zealand did not feature in the final

SEVENS SUMMARY

Tournaments attended	62
Tournament finalists	46
Tournaments won	35

EAST TAMAKI UNDER 11s

I loved my time coaching (and playing) for East Tamaki this year. But the best thing about being at the club was taking a big group of the players to Taupo in the winter. Last year I took them all up north to Kaeo (most of them thought 'up north' meant Takapuna), but as most of them had never seen snow before, this time around we headed south. The trip was a blast and — like most things at rugby clubs — couldn't have happened without the support of volunteers and great sponsors like Stevensons, Manukau Pak 'N Save, Exotic Timber and Ideal Garages. Thanks fellas.

Back row: Chayce Tito, Teina Wahanui, Blair Rush, William Maea, Tere Miriau. Third row: Eric Rush (coach), Martyn Rush, David Silata, Jordon Tua, Samuel Beech, Junior Pouono, Johnny Tuivasa (coach). Second row: Ulufia Fetu, Jay Wahanui, Maea Laga, Amalale Tafa, Jay Masina, Safale Ofoia, Bryton Kaumoana. Front row: Leonard Brown, Nathan Pamatatau, Roger Tuivasa, Daniel Stowers, Paul Aoina, Johnathan Aoina. Absent: Andrew Aupaau, Aloalii Tapu.

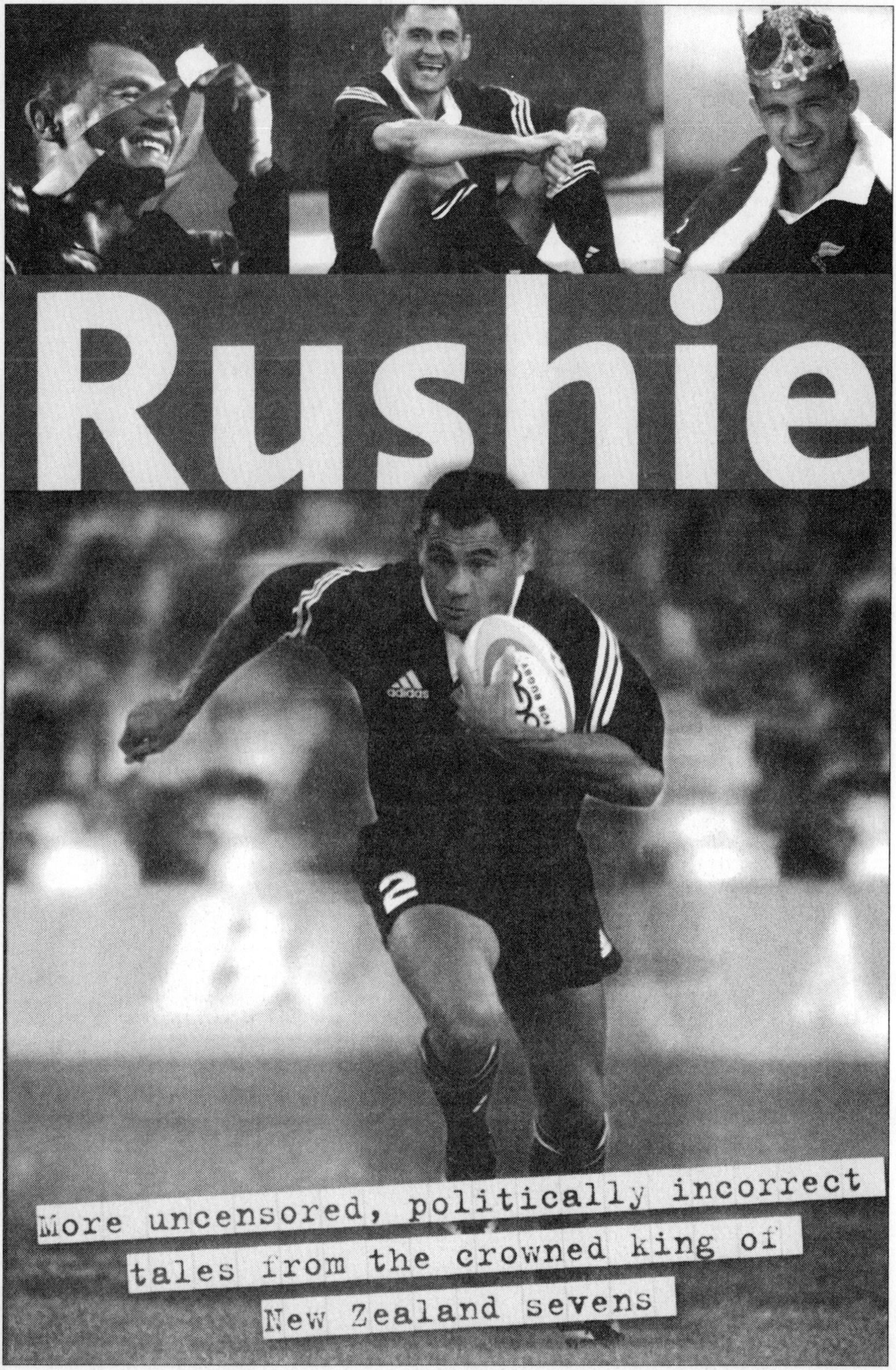
Rushie
More uncensored, politically incorrect
tales from the crowned king of
New Zealand sevens

Foreword

CHARACTER. IT'S THE THING that separates the champions from the also-rans. And it is something that Eric Rush has in abundance.

It was interesting to me that when I selected Rushie for the 2002 Commonwealth Games, some commentators suggested that I had picked him for Manchester with my heart rather than my head. It's true that Rushie and I have had a close relationship since I took charge of the sevens side in 1994, but to suggest that he didn't deserve his spot on merit is doing a disservice to one of New Zealand rugby's greats.

Six weeks before our final trial at Mt Maunganui I pulled Rushie aside and told him that he needed to up his work rate. For years he had dominated the sevens game because of his aerobic capabilities. But sevens has changed. Defence is a big part of the game now and at the camp Rushie had been falling off a few tackles. He needed to get into the gym and do some strength work. I looked him in the eye and I told him I didn't want to be back in the same room in six weeks to tell him that he wasn't going to the Games.

Rushie responded. He got into the gym, worked harder than ever and made my decision at the final camp to select him very simple. He was the best hooker on the park. *Character.*

At the Games, Rushie played some of his best rugby in a black jersey. Against Wales and Samoa he was outstanding.

Titch and Rushie . . . 'if there is anyone who epitomises the pride and passion in the black jersey, it is Eric Rush.'

But he was injured in the semi-final against the Samoans and I was faced with the prospect of going into the final of a Commonwealth Games without my captain.

I left the decision on whether he would play or not up to him. Rushie — who had worked harder than he ever had to be in his second Commonwealth Games final — did a fitness test. After some time on his own he looked around at his team-mates and decided that he had confidence in them. He decided to pull himself from the final. Can you imagine that? This was his last Commonwealth Games. His last chance to play on such a huge stage. But he didn't want to be the one who cost his team-mates the chance to do what we had done four years earlier — win a gold medal. *Character*.

After his team-mates had beaten Fiji and we had won the gold medal, Rushie did something that will live with me forever. As we were walking away from the dais after the medal presentation he told me that he was going to give me his gold medal. He had tried to do the same thing four years ago in

Kuala Lumpur. This time he insisted. All the work he put in, the personal disappointment of the 2001 World Cup when he broke his leg in a pool game, and the unimaginable emotions of having to watch the final from the sidelines . . . the medal was mine. *Character*.

There are so many things to admire about Eric Rush. He has proven that at 37, age means nothing. If he wants it bad enough, he will continue to wear the black jersey for many tournaments to come.

And like his play, his humour — the basis of this book — is legendary. His way of welcoming newcomers to the squad is to make fun of them as often and as publicly as possible. He is responsible for New Zealand's famous sevens humour continuing to separate the side from other sports teams. He is also responsible for embarrassing a number of people in front of international dignitaries . . . including the coach.

But I wouldn't want it any other way. If there is anyone who epitomises the pride and passion in the black jersey — any black jersey — it is Eric Rush. Whether playing for New Zealand Maori, the All Blacks or the sevens side, he always brought one thing to the jersey that anyone who has ever managed, coached or played with him admires in him. *Character* . . . and that cheeky grin.

Gordon Tietjens
September, 2002

Gold Rush II

THIS WAS IT. A new beginning. The venue for the beginning of the sequel to New Zealand's sevens success at Kuala Lumpur in 1998 began in an unlikely place back in July . . . Mt Maunganui.

Coach Gordon Tietjens had selected 22 players for the Commonwealth Games team trials. Any training camp with Titch is hard work, but with a team to be selected for such an important tournament we all knew that this was going to be something out of the ordinary. Twenty-two players competing for 12 spots. Six games of 10-minute halves. It was as tough as it has ever been.

After the trials everyone left for home. We all knew Titch would be notifying us by telephone that night, so there were a few nerves among us as the Auckland boys headed back together. **Some of the boys suggested we stop at a hotel so they could have a few beers and try to relax a bit. (No doubt we'll pay for that when Titch reads this book and finds out we broke the alcohol ban.)** But the occasion called for a break from all the tension. Players had been dreaming of going to the Manchester Commonwealth Games from the day after we'd won gold in Kuala Lumpur. Once you have a taste of what it is to stand on that podium and hear the New Zealand national anthem with a gold medal hanging around your neck, you can't wait to get back there.

Once I was home I got a call from Titch saying I was in. The perception might be that I always knew I was going to be in the side, but that couldn't be further from the truth. There was no real elation when I was told the good news . . . it was more a feeling of relief.

Titch had put the acid on me a month out from the team trials by telling me he wouldn't be talking to me at the camps. Normally I am involved in most management meetings and Titch always asks my advice on how we should train and which players we need to work closely with. During the camp before the previous Commonwealth Games I had been involved in every meeting, and in the selection of the side. **There had been no question that I was included in the side. And I had had a broken hand at the time! All I had needed to do was get through the camp and I knew I was there. But this time, I knew something was up.**

Before we went away on our last World Series trip Titch hauled me in and told me that people were starting to ask him why he was still picking me. He basically told me to go out and prove myself because, he said, I hadn't played well. I was informed that I had to do weights to get stronger. I'd never done weights in my life, so it was a bit of a shock. I didn't like the way it was handled. I would have preferred to have had my situation explained a little better. It would have been nice if they'd asked me to start doing weight work, rather than delivering an ultimatum. That meeting showed me that there was no doubt that I was either on the outer or very close to it.

At the tournaments we played before the Manchester Commonwealth Games Titch started leaving Craig De Goldi and me out of teams. We played the important games, but it was a new thing to have to spend time on the bench when we were fit to play. **I was convinced he was starting to lay the groundwork for dropping us later on. I guess it was his way of saying, 'You aren't at the Commonwealth Games yet.'**

At the camp Titch went so far as to purposely not talk to me. He would come into a room, talk to everyone else and ignore me.

Here we go again! Back in one of Titch's legendary training sessions for the 2002 Commonwealth Games.

I was angry about that. I never showed it, but inside I was fuming. I'm very competitive and so I was thinking, 'Bugger you. I'm gonna show you I am good enough.'

So when the phone rang I didn't really know what to expect. I knew I had done well enough at the trial to make his team. I know how Titch selects his teams and I knew I had done my job. The other hookers — Damian Karauna and Johnny Leo'o — had trialled well, but I thought I still had the edge. **The big concern for me was that maybe Titch was trying to retire me gracefully. Perhaps he thought my time was up. That's what I couldn't read . . . so when I was told I was in it was a massive relief.**

I guess in hindsight I have to give Titch the credit for motivating me like that. But if I wasn't such a stubborn character his plan could have backfired. Other guys might have reacted by saying, 'Stuff ya. Stick your team.' Luckily I hadn't done that. I had something I wanted to prove.

Titch asked for my views on some of the close decisions that needed to be made. Josh Blackie had played out of his skin at the trial. It was a really tough call to leave him behind. The other close calls were Dallas Seymour, Justin Wilson and Hayden Reid.

Obviously the hardest thing about the night was learning that Dallas wouldn't be making the trip. We'd been playing for New Zealand together since 1988 and the thought of him not being there was difficult to get used to. When we were in South America or South Africa and there would be thousands of people screaming for your blood, it was comforting to look across at Seymour and realise that nothing fazed him. He'd say, 'We're all right.' And we would be.

So I gave Titch my opinion about Seymour and the others. But the thing you learn about Titch is that when he's asking you something, well, he's not really asking. **Titch will ask you what you think, but until you come round to his way of thinking, he won't hang up the bloody phone.**

Eventually I got to sleep, although I was a bit nervous about what lay ahead and how tough the Commonwealth Games tournament was going to be.

Monday, 15 July 2002

HERE WE GO AGAIN. Training camp at the Mount. Training started at 7 am. Back to the motel for a shower, some food, and then training again at 11 am. **Titch doesn't muck around. There are no 'bonding' sessions. Just straight into the hard yakka.** We played a game against the Tauranga Boys High School First XV. They scored two tries against us, which we weren't happy about. The one-and-a-half hour warmup might have been a factor. It was an interesting day actually. It was obvious that a few of the boys that had been selected were carrying injuries. Titch had picked them on past performances rather than anything they had done recently. But we all had faith that they would come right in time. If we were going to win in Manchester they had to!

Tuesday, 16 July

WENT TO TAURANGA INTERMEDIATE School's assembly. Got up on stage with Tai Mitchell Shield team before training for a couple of hours. It's funny, people have asked me if these school visits are a necessary evil — they reckon we must hate them. Some of the guys think it's a bit of a nuisance and, to be honest, I used to feel like that sometimes. But now that I have my own kids, I always tell the boys to talk to the kids.

It's good for us to spend time at schools because it grounds us. It wasn't that long ago (well, a bit longer ago for me) when we were kids in the same position. I remember North Auckland's All Black Hamish MacDonald came to our school and, man, he was a giant — at least, at the time I thought he was. I have never forgotten that, although I'm sure he has. But for me, it was the best thing. And then Sid Going came to a boxing prize giving once. He had always been my hero and all of a sudden there he was, shaking my hand. It's strange that now I play with Sid's son Jared in the sevens side. I remember saying to Jared once: 'Your dad used to be my hero. He was awesome, eh?' And he said, 'Well, I've never seen him play!' Good old Jared . . . always knows how to make me feel old.

Wednesday, 17 July

OUR LAST DAY AT the Mount. The boys wanted to head back to Auckland early so we could see our families. We were due to fly out to Manchester in a couple of days so any time you get to see your partner or your kids is pretty precious. We trained at 7 am again so we could start the bus trip earlier than first planned but we need not have bothered. **Titch held us up for an hour. When he eventually made it to the bus it was classic Titch. We were all watching him and sure enough he dropped his bags on the footpath, hopped on the bus and made the driver get out of his seat and put his bags in the luggage compartment.** There is never any doubt that Titch is the boss. The players knew it and now so did the bus driver. In Auckland that night the NZRFU and adidas put on a farewell function for the team. It was a nice gesture. It was also a reminder of the expectations that were being placed on us. This wasn't going to be a holiday.

Thursday, 18 July

WE TRAINED AT THE Southern Cross Campus in Mangere, which is the site of the former Nga Tapuwae College. Nowadays it has a mainstream school, a Samoan school and a Maori school. My kids go to the Te Kura Maori O Nga Tapuwae — a full immersion Maori school. We were supposed to train somewhere else in the city, but I convinced Titch to let us train in South Auckland. **I rang the principal to ask if we could train there. She said we could and she even allowed us to speak English when we addressed the kids. Thank goodness too because I don't speak Maori.** I wish I did . . . that's why my kids go there. The songs raised the hair on the back of my neck. Even the five-year-olds were into it. There was just so much pride. The whole team were amazed by the singing and the haka. It was great to leave New Zealand shores with that sort of pride ringing in our ears.

Friday, 19 July

WE TRAINED AT LES Mills gym in Auckland. Saw the Team New Zealand guys there. They wished us all the best for the Games. In fact a lot of people at the gym did. There was a good vibe. Not sure if Karl Te Nana would have heard any of the well-wishers, though. When he's in the gym he goes into his own little world. **Karl is a beach muscle fella — he only works on the beach muscles, the ones that look good on the sand.** If you arrive at the gym and want to know where Nana is don't bother looking in the changing rooms, the sauna or the steam room. Just head to the mirrors . . . that's where he'll be.

Someone that isn't a huge fan of the gym is Amasio Valence. He struggles to bench-press 80 kg. The top guys are at the 120

Amasio Valence (centre) . . . can run, but struggles with the weight training. With 'Moji' are Rodney So'oialo and Brad Fleming.

and 130+ kg level and then there is a group at about 100–130 kg. Then there is me and Moji. We just sit there disillusioned. I just tell him, 'Don't you worry boy. You do your thing when you have the ball in your hands.'

We were given the rest of the day off. As we didn't need to be at the airport until 6 pm, I spent some time with my family and did a bit more painting at a house I am doing up. **A TV news crew had come by earlier in the week when I was working at the house for a few hours and when I did the interview I was caught on film eating some fish and chips. Titch wouldn't have been too happy about that.** I expected him to ring me up and give me some stick. He's good like that. He's aloof enough to be able to make the hard calls and give you the hard word when you need it, but when he is with the team he is capable of having a laugh.

Our best way to have a crack back at him is in one of the warmup drills we do called two-ball. We all form up in a circle and have two balls going. Basically we fire passes at each other, trying to get the other guys to drop the ball. We always try to get Titch out first. But once he won . . . it was the darkest day in the history of New Zealand Sevens. He has never let us forget it. He used to be a bit of a character in his young days. **One time, there was a horse by the hotel his team was staying at so he led it into the coach's room and tied it up to his bed and the horse wrecked everything in the room.** Titch ended up getting dropped. So God help him if we ever find a horse somewhere . . . it will be straight into his room!

Once on the plane, we found ourselves sitting among the Silver Ferns. It was good to catch up and talk to a few of them that had been with us in Malaysia four years earlier. They got the best seats — I guess they needed room for those long legs. One of the great things about going to a Commonwealth Games is that you are a part of a big team. You have the chance to talk to a whole range of athletes, all with different ideas about training and being in camp.

We had a stopover in the USA for a few hours and while most of us spent the time looking around the shops, Chris

Masoe couldn't because he didn't have the right visa. When we saw him on the plane a few hours later I asked, 'Where have you been mate?'

'Bro, I've been in nicotine.'

'You been having a smoke?'

'No, no, no. I don't smoke. I have been in the nicotine.'

'It's quarantine bro. Quarantine!'

Saturday, 20 July

THE TEAM WERE PRETTY excited when we arrived at the Games Village. **We all had a look around. Well, everyone except our manager Tony Ward, who was crook. We didn't see him for a couple of days. Things went real smooth . . . I actually thought about putting some more stuff in his food!**

Got our gear issued and went on the orientation around the Village. In the Village you must wear your identification tag everywhere. Titch stuffed up the Village security when he forgot his tag. He walked right through to the dining-room hall without a pass. When the security people finally asked him for it, he'd been through three security checks. The next day all the chefs de missions found out about it because there had been an inquiry as to why security had failed. It was just another sign that nothing is Titch-proof.

After Titch had caused a few red faces within the Games' security ranks the boys had a pool session. The New Zealand team had hired the use of a school next door to the village, which had astroturf courts and a swimming pool. It was great to have somewhere the New Zealanders could escape the Village and have somewhere to hang out with other Kiwis. It was a good set-up.

On the way back to the Village we saw the boxing boys in the gym. It was pretty impressive seeing them work out. Kahukura Bentson, Shane Cameron, Daniel Codling and Daniel Headifen all looked sharp. Couldn't help but think how handy they would be on the footie field when things got a bit rough.

Sunday, 21 July

WOKE UP FOR THE first time in the Commonwealth Games Village. No time to get excited though as the day started with a cardio and weight session followed by some lineout work. Titch wanted us to get out of the Village, so we got in the van and headed on a tour to look at all the sites. **We drove by Manchester United's ground Old Trafford. Titch missed it as he slept all the way. He only woke up when we passed the 'Coronation Street' set.** As it disappeared from view, he settled down for another kip.

While we were in Manchester the rugby team was given the use of three vans with three drivers. One of them was a fella called Rupert. A croquet player who had never had any contact with rugby. Can't begin to think what he thought of some of our boys, especially the ones with dreadlocks. They'd hand him their gangsta music to play. It was all *Mother . . . this and mother . . . that.* You could see him cringe. But I think he learnt to enjoy it by the end of the Games.

That night we all had dinner at the dining hall. The New Zealand team had grown during the day with the arrival of all the athletics, table tennis and bowls teams. I was pretty tired by the end of the night but my sleep wasn't the best I've ever had. My room was right by the footpath on the first floor. **I woke up when I heard some commotion outside my window. I looked out and saw two girls streaking through the Village. Turned out they had lost a game of cards against two table tennis guys.** Rumour has it the boys cheated. It's like they always say . . . if you can't beat 'em, cheat!

Monday, 22 July

THE DAY STARTED WITH a fitness session at the school next door. Titch ran us real hard. The session only went for 40 minutes, but he really pushed us. Later in the day we trained at the Manchester club. They had the bar open and there were about 100 people watching. It was another intense training

The boys outside the New Zealand Commonwealth Games compound in Manchester.

session. Before we left, we picked up our rubbish and threw it in the bins. The people watching got a real shock. They said that had never happened before. It was good to see the rubbish committee doing their job. Wardie was as proud as punch.

Went to the Village for lunch. The dining hall was packed. Titch let us have an ice cream as a bit of a treat. I know, I know. It's pretty sad when you are 37 and have to be told when you can have an ice cream.

In the afternoon TVNZ's Bernadine Oliver-Kerby arrived and wanted to get a tour of the village so Craig De Goldi and I obliged. During the interview Goldi mentioned how he hadn't received very many good luck faxes or emails. Well, in the next few days he got heaps. He'd never seen anything like it. Like a real rookie he sat down to try and answer every single one of them, but there were too many. In the end the team sent a few back to some schools and kids that had written to us. It was a real eye-opener for the team, and reminded us how many people back home were supporting us and the rest of the New Zealand team.

Before checking in for the day, the rugby boys were given

With the Manchester school group who put on a performance for the New Zealand team at our flag-raising ceremony.

their allowance for the week. As usual Roger Randle was the first in the queue.

Tuesday, 23 July

EARLY BREAKFAST. HAD A speed session across the road at Manchester School For Girls. **Went to the gym to do some weights. I bumped into an Aussie woman triple jumper there and she put me to shame on the bench.** A bit of a worry . . . I am 37, though. I could have bench-pressed more if I wanted to, but I figured that I ought to save my strength . . .

Back to the Village for lunch and the flag-raising ceremony. The local school had adopted us and got on stage and performed a song they'd written before doing the haka. They asked us to respond, so we did. I didn't want just the rugby guys to do it. I wanted others in the team to do it as well so I told them not to be shy. The walker Craig Barrett and the hockey and boxing guys joined us on stage. **We knew we'd had a pretty good haka when we realised that we'd scared some of the kids.**

Back at the Village all the netball girls came back from training battered, bleeding and bruised after playing the Australian Institute team. They were really gearing up for a big tournament. Had a late dinner. Got dressed up in mufti and headed out to get some different food outside of the Village. Ended up at the Hard Rock Café. Everyone had crashed by the time we got back.

Wednesday, 24 July

ANOTHER EARLY TRAINING. WE were starting to get our pattern. Amasio had never trained so hard. Titch broke him for cutting his face out of the team programme and pasting it on a girl's body and hanging it up in the team room. Titch's revenge meant that every time we did a drill Amasio was involved. Usually in a session you get a bit of a rest because five guys normally have a spell on defence while the other seven are going through the drills. But Amasio never got a break for two hours. Titch broke him with 30 minutes to go when he went over on an ankle. Poor bugger.

Back to the Village for a quick lunch before getting into our No. 1s for the big New Zealand team photo at Old Trafford Cricket Ground. After the photo it was into the bus and off to the official function for the flag-bearing ceremony. **Sarah Ulmer got the job. She was a good choice because she seemed to get along with everyone. I won't name names but one of the boys in the team reckoned that we had the spunkiest flag bearer at the Games.** This player — a young fella that plays for North Harbour — reckoned we'd won the first gold already with Sarah's selection. The ceremony was the first time the whole team had been together. I had the chance to mix with a few of the New Zealand team. At one point netball's Irene van Dyk was asking about our training regime and she came out with: 'I hear you

Little and large . . . up close (but not too personal) with the easily embarrassed New Zealand netball goal shooter Irene van Dyk.

are a machine, Rushie?' **I replied: 'I don't like to talk about my sex life in public.' She went bright pink.**

Later in the evening I was approached by swimmer Jon Winter, the unofficial leader of the swim team, and asked if the sevens guys wanted to do a haka at the opening ceremony. The swimmers really wanted to do it, as they had never really had the chance to perform one as a part of such a big team. They wanted to make an impact. I said we would think about it.

Thursday, 25 July

AFTER TRAINING IT WAS time for haka practice. Not too many of the boys turned up, but I was quite rapt with our Pakeha friends who were determined to learn how to do it properly. At 6 pm we were off to the opening ceremony. We had to wait in a stadium next door to the main stadium for about an hour. Jon Winter and the hockey boys had convinced our Chef de Mission Dave Currie to let them do the haka, but he said he wanted it done properly. He told them that if they were going to do it, the rugby boys would have to do it. We weren't too keen. A few of the boys feel that if we do it too often it can lose its importance. To me the haka is a respect thing. You only perform it when you want to pay respect to the people who are witnessing it. Normally we don't do a haka until we have won a tournament. We certainly won't do it if we lose.

When we saw the look on the faces of guys like Winter and Craig Barrett we thought it would be a good idea to do a haka because it would bring us together as a team. **We walked into the stadium and we'd organised that we'd jump out of the line and the rest of the team would keep marching behind us.** We didn't want to stop people from marching! I asked Bruce Reihana to lead the haka and everyone — the wrestlers, the hockey players, the swimmers, the boxing boys and a few others — took part. One of the New Zealand wrestlers, Ricardo, is originally from Iran. When we asked him to join in, he thought we were taking the piss. When I asked him again, he said he thought I was joking and that he didn't know the actions, anyway. I said he didn't need to know the actions, he just needed to give it everything he had. Afterwards, the look on his face was priceless. When he said he really felt like a Kiwi now, I knew the exercise had

Stealing the show at the opening ceremony . . . Bruce Reihana leads our impromptu haka.

been worthwhile. The whole crowd roared their approval. The thing is, if we hadn't done the haka the Queen wouldn't have had any idea what team was marching in front of her. **The Queen and Duke were smiling and applauding. They reckon it was the only time she smiled during the entire Opening Ceremony. We made sure we bowed afterwards as a mark of respect.**

The cheer for us wasn't anywhere near as big, though, as the one the crowd saved for Manchester United star David Beckham when he entered the stadium with the baton. I didn't know it then but the next day I was going to get the chance to see him up close and personal.

Friday, 26 July

TITCH GAVE US THE day off so Wardie organised a trip to Manchester United's training ground at Carrington. We were told the team was training and we could watch as long as we didn't attempt to disturb them. We got our photo taken at the front of the training ground and I remember noticing that there were no flash cars around. We were a bit surprised that these guys would be driving Ford Lasers . . . but then we headed around the back and there they were: Mercedes, Ferraris, Porsches, the works. And then there they were . . . the players. We waited like little kids to see them. As they walked past us our driver gave us a running commentary: '£50,000 per week, £100,000 per week, £100,000 per week . . .' The club had spent £23 million on the training facility, apparently not enough to buy a decent defender these days. **The United boys were having a laugh among themselves about Ruud Van Nistelrooy's BMW parked beside the pitch having a smashed window after someone tried to break into it. (It wasn't us!)**

As they were warming up, the side's coach Sir Alex Ferguson walked up to us and asked, 'Who's in charge here?' Titch introduced himself and they talked about training concepts and ideas. Sir Alex invited us over to watch the training up close. They worked quite hard and the skill level

Two of the biggest names in world soccer — Sir Alex Ferguson (above, centre) and David Beckham (below) — took time out to meet the sevens boys in Manchester. I think Becks liked my hair.

Two of Man U's big money men with one of New Zealand's little money men . . . Rio Ferdinand (above) and Ruud Van Nistelrooy (below).

was amazing. When training was about to wind up, the players that had played at the football World Cup were told to do extra work because they had rejoined the club later than the rest of the team. Titch would have loved seeing that!

The first player to come across and talk to us was United's striker Van Nistelrooy. He started chatting with Karl Te Nana and Brad Fleming. I walked across and introduced myself — there is no point in being shy. **Then Beckham came over and posed for pictures. I reckon he must have just come from the hair salon. He looked immaculate.** He made us all feel pretty stink. We like to think of ourselves as reasonably good-looking men, but we felt positively ugly standing next to that fella. He asked us about rugby and I had to ask the obligatory question: 'How's the missus?'

Rio Ferdinand asked how much beer we had. He couldn't believe we couldn't drink alcohol. He asked about Jonah too. He had met him at a function, and wanted to know how fast the big fella really was. We talked about Ferdinand's switch from Leeds United to Manchester United. I think he sensed we needed a bit of a release, so he offered up the names of a few clubs to hang out at. Rio was surprised, and pleased, that none of us asked for autographs. I said: 'We're quite happy for you to put one on a cheque for us mate.'

We also chatted to Diego Forlan — the Uruguayan international. He knew a few of our mates from Montevideo. Apparently he used to watch the sevens there each year. He told us he loves rugby — he has an All Black autographed rugby ball on display at his house.

We were then shown around the Carrington training complex. The physio room was like a hospital — Paul Scholes and Nicky Butt were getting treatment. In their gym they had a high altitude chamber, all the latest gear and some boxing gloves. Their personal training guy asked if any of us were good scrappers. The boys volunteered me to go one-on-one with him. He tried to nail me and he almost succeeded, but I managed to get out of there with some mana. Masoe was next and he was hammering the trainer before he called things off pretty quickly and went off to continue doing whatever it was he did all day.

It was a great way to spend a morning. When we got back to the Village the soccer ball came out and all the boys were playing with it on the lawn out the front. We started calling Anthony Tuitavake David Blackam.

At lunch we sat at our normal table. When we looked up we saw security guys standing around. The Queen was sitting two tables away. A great day had turned into an even better day.

Later we learnt that the netball girls had a mascot called Wiki. Each day it was the responsibility of a different player to look after it. On this particular day it was Anna Veronese's turn. She had left him in the team room and a couple of the guys kidnapped him and left a ransom note for the girls.

With that out of the way I went to watch Shane Cameron box. He won his first fight. I caught the bus back to the Village with him. He was wondering how I managed to get into the venue, as there were no tickets available for team members. I just told him that I'd given it the old boxer walk when I walked past security. He said: 'They must have looked at you and looked at that nose and figured you'd taken a few.'

Saturday, 27 July

AFTER BREAKFAST WE WATCHED the Wallaby-Springboks Tri-Nations game on TV. **The two guys that kidnapped Wiki took some ransom photos to send with the notes to keep the netballers guessing.** The girls were really worried about it. They asked us if we had him. They said they knew it was us, but they couldn't prove it. It was under those dubious circumstances that we caught a bus to Preston to get out of the Village for a few days. Bruce Reihana held up the bus for an hour because he'd lost his bag. So we had to ring security, which caused a big fuss. It turned out he had grabbed the wrong bag. What is it about this team and buses?

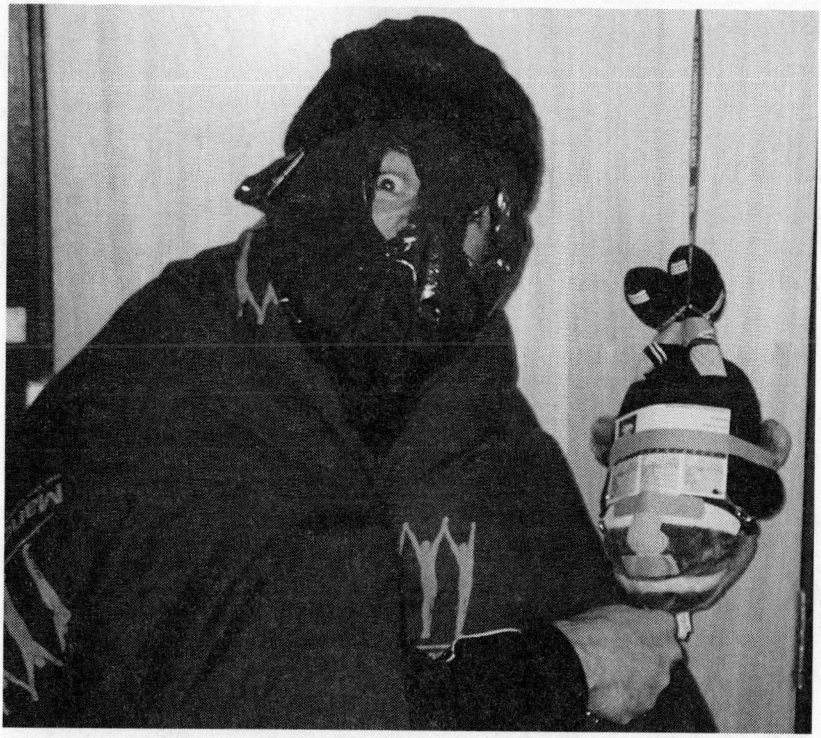

A well disguised kidnapper (Craig De Goldi, actually) with the netballers' mascot, Wiki.

We stayed at an old English manor. When we arrived there were two weddings taking place on the front lawn. We rolled up in our big bus and spoilt the wedding photographs. Went to training at the Preston Grasshoppers Club. They were hosting a pagan festival in the clubrooms. **One of the ladies said she read palms so she read one of the boys' and said that we were going to win the gold medal.** A few of the Christian boys were unimpressed. 'We'll rely on the other fella.'

In the evening we had a birthday cake at dinner for Craig Newby. Newbs was also under instructions to ring the Village in Manchester and speak to another of the Kiwi athletes to leave more notes for the netballers. We didn't want everything to come to a halt just because we weren't around. That would have looked a little too suspicious!

Sunday, 28 July

AFTER A TOUGH, THREE-HOUR training session in the morning we all headed to Blackpool to the theme park, and a trip on the world's highest roller coaster. Titch doesn't normally enjoy things like that but we made him front up. During the ride I remember looking back and, sure enough, he had his eyes closed. After that was over we headed for the water log ride. Titch paid for a raincoat but as the ride was

This is the world's highest roller coaster. As predicted, Titch kept his eyes closed the whole way round.

starting we ripped it to pieces and he had to trudge back to the van soaking wet. Next it was back to the hotel, where it was like a little piece of paradise. The beds were big and that was a luxury we didn't have at the Village, where there were only bunk beds in very small rooms. It was also good to get away from the distractions of the Village. Everything had a rugby focus, which is what we needed with the tournament starting in a few days. It turned out to be a good move.

Monday, 29 July

WE PLAYED THE COOK Islands in training. John McKittrick — who coaches North Harbour and the USA when not on Commonwealth Games duty with the Cooks — made sure his boys were up for the game. It was good because they exposed us in a couple of positions early on. **They got three tries, which showed there were things we needed to work on, but all up it was a good run for us.** John was pretty happy with the way his boys played. It was good to catch up with Dazz Robson and find out that Takapuna, our club back home, had won the North Harbour club final. Oh, yeah, Anthony Tuitavake, if you are reading this book, you still owe me £10. And so do you Craig Newby.

In the afternoon we went and had a look around Liverpool. We checked out Anfield, the home of the Liverpool Football Club, and had some dinner. Titch got pissed off after we had stopped to do some shopping. I was a bit tired so I stayed on the bus and read my book. I could have gone with the boys but a good part of a book is better entertainment than watching the boys blow out their credit cards. The boys went one way and the management went the other and apparently it wasn't long before they bumped into each other. **Titch was furious because they were all eating ice creams. He hit the roof. He got back on the bus and asked me to call a team meeting.** He wasn't upset because they were eating ice creams . . . it was because they had gone against the rules. It was a discipline thing. If they were eating ice cream behind his back, what else were they doing? It was a quiet trip back to the hotel.

Tuesday, 30 July

WOKE UP FOR AN early morning weight session. Had a bit of time to kill before a late session in the afternoon so I decided to play a joke on my old mate Stu Forster. Karen Paewai, Stu's girlfriend, was in Manchester with the New Zealand hockey team. In all the time I have known Stu he has never paid for anything. So I rang him up and pretended to be a Telecom operator: 'Hello Mr Forster. Will you accept a collect call from a Miss Paewai in Manchester?' Lo and behold — and I thought it must have been a cold day in hell — he accepted the charges. I said: 'Hello darling.' He went off! **He was going to hang up on me until I told him that it wasn't a collect call. After a while he asked where Karen was. I said I'd go to my room to wake her up. He hung up!**

We began to hear from home that the team had been criticised for staying outside of the Village and even for visiting Manchester United. The situation arose because a reporter from the *New Zealand Herald* had had an argument with our manager Tony Ward. He had been to a couple of trainings and had rung Wardie to see who was in the team. Wardie was a bit surprised because he thought the reporter would be able to figure it out. After all, the New Zealand sqaud had been named three weeks before! After having watched the team training, Wardie had told him to do his homework and offered to write the story for the *Herald* himself. **The reporter hung up. I presume he then went off and wrote the scathing story about the team.** The thing is, we had thought about what was best for us to try to win a gold medal and getting away from the Village distractions seemed the right thing to do, which it proved to be. The same reporter talked about us not being popular with the rest of the New Zealand team for leaving the Village for three days and also made comments about us riding on the coat-tails of the All Blacks after we got our invitation to visit Manchester United. I thought, hang on a minute, I am a bloody All Black! Frankly, I didn't care about what the bloke wrote. Our focus was winning this tournament and we would do whatever was needed to achieve that.

Back to the footie. Nana hurt his back at the afternoon session. Hayden Reid got a call back in New Zealand and was put on standby.

Wednesday, 31 July

PLAYED AGAINST THE WELSH in a practice game at Preston. Titch made Nana play, but it worked out because he played well and he gained a lot of confidence from it. We all played well. The Welsh had no answer and we were all over them. They didn't score a try in 30 minutes of rugby and we scored a hell of a lot. Titch finished off with a real hard blow-out. As the Welsh boys headed to the changing rooms, we had to stay out there for another 15 minutes getting thrashed.

We headed back to Manchester and the Games Village and then to the adidas factory. We'd rung Jonah a couple of days before to see if he could organise a visit. He did a bit more than that. He'd made sure we were given a great discount and the boys went crazy.

When we got back to the Village it was surprising to see that the place was nearly empty. The athletics events had finished and most athletes had bolted.

As soon as we got there the netball girls wanted handwriting samples from us. They wanted to match them to the notes. So we all complied and Donna Loffhagen wanted to go through everyone's luggage looking for Wiki. Donna suggested there should be a strip search. I've never seen the boys' hands go up so quickly. The boys that were responsible for taking Wiki sent another note. Part of it read: *Now's the time to use your height. If we are not happy with what's in sight, Wiki will stay another night.* Half an hour later there was a G-string and a bra hanging up on a sign outside the New Zealand HQ.

Obviously the kidnappers were happy enough because the girls got another note with a map and Wiki was found sitting behind a tree.

Thursday, 1 August

WITH THE SEVENS TOURNAMENT only a day away it was time for a tour of the stadium. We were shown the changing area and where to warm up. Six minutes before a game we had to assemble underneath the grandstand. And for the last two minutes before heading out on the field we were told we would have to stand in a little room with the other team right next to us.

The netball girls made us a little poster and signed it for us. Chicks are always better at that kind of stuff, eh. It was a nice thought — a reminder that the New Zealand team were supporting us. Our manager Tony Ward suggested that we do something for them and so we did a poster for them and both the hockey teams as well.

Friday, 2 August

GAME DAY. EARLY BREAKFAST. Chilled out until lunch. Meeting at 2 pm. Bused to the stadium. Warmed up. Played Canada at 6.40 pm. Won 28–7. Played Niue at 9 pm. I didn't play that game but the boys played really well, posting a 66–0 victory. Did our hot-and-colds in the ice, hot shower, ice etc. We went back to the Village and were at the New Zealand compound by 10.30 pm. Had dinner and straight to bed. No time or thoughts for anything else.

Saturday, 3 August

HAD BREAKFAST IN THE common room. **Too far to walk to the main dining room. Watched the start of the All Blacks-Australia Bledisloe Cup test on TV before we had to go and do our warmup.** Heard the All Blacks lost in the last minute, so everyone was

Try time for me in our pool match against Scotland. It wasn't our most convincing performance . . . good try, though, eh.

pretty despondent heading to the stadium, but we had to block it out and concentrate on what we needed to do. We played Scotland and won 26–12.

On the way out to the main stadium to the warmup track I had been walking alongside Roger Randle. **Usually when you walk on the concrete you can hear the clack clack clack of the sprigs. With Roger it was more of a click clap click.** Turns out he was wearing one boot with sprigs and one with a moulded soul. Nana was also a little distracted. He started the game as a reserve and was only on for one minute when he got a yellow card. When he was coming off we noticed he still had his watch on. It was pretty funny but, boy, it was a good thing we were winning otherwise Nana would have been in a bit of trouble. We were up 26–0 when Nana was sin-binned and Chris Masoe got injured, so we had to play the second half with six players. Later in the evening we played our quarter-final against the Welsh. We played well, but again didn't score too many points, winning 24–0. We had played better against them in training three days earlier.

So the focus wasn't great, but sometimes when you are a reserve — like Nana and Roger were — it's a little harder to maintain that focus. Other teams can get upset by incidents like that, but we just laugh at them. That's our team. We're on when we have to be and off when we don't need to be on. It can be a long day at the stadium. **It's not uncommon to be at the venue for 12 hours straight. You can't stay focused all day. So we use Jonah's boom box. He donated it to the team — he doesn't know he has donated it but he has, trust me.** We put the sounds on, play cards and read books. I've got a lot of the boys reading now. It used to be just PlayStation, but I banned that because it is a waste of brainpower (and I'm not good at it). So now they read. I lease books to them for $5 per book. They complain that I am making money off them, but I just explain to them that the more they pay me the easier it is for me to buy another book for them to read.

Once in Japan we were waiting for our final and all the guys were reading or playing cards in the changing shed. Titch came in. He doesn't like seeing us do anything but focus on the game. He puts up with the cards and reading and things, but you just know he'd prefer it if we were studying game film or something like that. Anyway, Titch came in to give his talk to the boys. I knew he was angry because he just stared at me and said nothing. I noticed he was looking in my direction so I told the boys to turn the music off and listen up. Titch gave the team talk and after he was done someone came in and told us our final would be delayed for five minutes. **On cue the boys turned the music on, started playing cards and relaxed again! Titch slapped his head and walked out.** My attitude is just do whatever you need to do to be ready because when that whistle goes you'd better be firing. If you're not, you won't last a day in any team that someone like Titch is in control of.

Sunday, 4 August

GOLD MEDAL DAY. THIS is what the last two years had been all about. We'd won the Commonwealth Games gold four years earlier and then the World Cup in 2001. Now it was time to go out and get another gold medal for New Zealand. **I was a bit nervous because I'd seen Fiji's captain Waisale Serevi before the World Cup and we were talking about how I had never won a world championship. He said he'd never won a gold medal and I told him that we'd swap — let me win the World Cup and you can have the gold medal.** The next year, when we'd won the World Cup, I wondered whether it was written somewhere that he would win the gold medal. So I was a little worried, to be honest.

On this morning, though, my immediate concern was the Samoan team. The other teams in the competition hadn't been playing that well and I knew there was a very good chance that we could win the gold if we could get past Samoa. But Samoa has always been a bit of a bogey team for us. They're a physical side, it's Polynesia v Polynesia, little brother against big brother . . . we knew they would be physical because that's how they had beaten Australia the day before. We knew that we had it over them when it came to the skills in our backlines, so it was up to the forwards to win the physical battle. I had a meeting with the forwards and stressed that point. 'If we let them get an edge on us they will do anything they want in the backs.' We knew our jobs.

We started our warmup at 10 am and left for the ground an hour later. With those words ringing in the ears of the forwards, we blew the Samoans off the track in the first half. We got out to 24–0 before they came back with a couple of late tries. **I got a Samoan head in the chest when I wasn't expecting it and popped a rib. It was bloody painful.**

Before the final I got a pain-killing injection. Titch was keen for me to play and was determined to leave me to make my decision right up to the last minute before the final against Fiji. But I'd played in Wellington with a crook shoulder earlier in the year and I didn't really do myself justice. I didn't play badly, but I knew I didn't play as well as I am capable of. I felt like I had let the team down. This time round, I wanted to play but only if I was 100 per cent right. **I did a fitness test and while I was making tackles all right the pain was getting worse. I knew that I didn't want to be the guy to miss a tackle in the final and cost my mates the chance of winning a gold medal.**

If there had been no one else available, I would have played. But when I looked around and saw Chris Masoe, Craig Newby, Craig De Goldi and Rodney So'oialo, I knew those guys would do the job. Rodney was the one who came into the team and replaced me. That guy at 100 per cent is miles better than me at 75 per cent so in the end it was an easy decision to sit out the final. I knew that it was my last Commonwealth Games and I knew that it could be the last big game of my career, but I have played in the black jersey too many times to be selfish about it. I knew that I'd made the right call.

The final started. Fiji lost their discipline a bit and we came away with a big win in the end. We got a penalty late in the game when they only had five guys left on the track. Amasio was going to kick it out and claim the win but when he looked to the bench and saw everyone was urging him to run it we scored another try to seal the win 33–15. It was good to see that the ruthlessness which New Zealand rugby is famous for was there right to the end.

With the game won, the celebrations began. We did about six hakas around the field for the fans. I remember some of the guys looking at me with a smirk. *Oh yeah. You're not fit enough to play but you can still do the haka, eh?* I got no mercy. But it didn't matter. **We had won the gold. I just remember this massive feeling of relief. There had been a lot of pressure on us to win.** Expectations were high — from the rugby union, the public and the rest of the New Zealand team. We had been determined to play our part for New Zealand rugby and not let anyone down.

The medal ceremony was awesome. For a lot of the guys it

Action from the gold medal game at Manchester. Above, Amasio beats the Fijian defence. Below, Chris Masoe looks for support.

All that glitters . . . Brad Fleming, Mils Muliaina, me and Rodney So'oialo show off our gold medals.

was the first time they experienced it. For myself, Amasio Valence, Bruce Reihana and Roger Randle it was our second gold medal. **We knew what they were about to experience, so after we had got together and said our prayer of thanks, I told the guys that they may never get this opportunity again and told them to make sure they take every moment in and never forget it.**

On the dais we were presented with the medals. Like KL, I started to think about my kids and my family up north and my friends and I knew the tears were on their way. So in the middle of the anthem I started singing to take my mind of the emotional stuff. I thought about all the guys that had helped us get there. All the boys back home who had played in the World Series games for the last three years. Then I looked at Titch, Wardie and our workaholic physio Kev McQuoid. They weren't allowed on the podium but they deserved to be up there with us. I also thought about John Walker — the champion New Zealand miler from the seventies. Throughout the village there were photos of New Zealand athletes with quotes underneath them and Walker's was the one that I really related to: **'Self-belief is what it is all about. Don't watch your opposition. Don't watch them train. Don't watch them warm up. Don't watch them do anything. Self-belief is all you need.'**

The week before I had been saying to myself, 'Hell, Aussie and Fiji have good teams. Man, the English look good.' But when I saw that quotation I knew he was right. It was something I thought of every day throughout that last week.

By the time we got back to the Village it had been a pretty long day, but it was only the beginning of a long night. The beers got cracked open. Bruce Reihana — just as he did in KL four years earlier — refused to take his medal off at any stage of the night. I'm sure he had a shower with it in the morning.

It's hard to compare the feeling in 1998 with this one. With the first gold there was a lot of pressure because it was the first one. This time round, the thing I was scared of was that we might not have the fire and passion to win because we are the reigning World Champions and no one can take that off us for another two years. But when I looked at the team before the day began and realised that only four of us had won the gold medal before, I knew we'd be all right. There was still pressure, though, mostly from the other members of the New Zealand team. It wasn't direct pressure, but every time you'd talk to them it was obvious there was a real expectation that we'd win. **And when we looked at the New Zealand websites there was a poll asking what the best chance of a gold medal for New Zealand was . . . we were streets ahead of anyone else. Those little things added up.** But, hey, a gold medal is a gold medal. And it felt great.

After we got our medals and were walking off the pitch I said to Titch, 'This is your medal too.' He was chuffed. 'Yeah,' he said, 'that's our medal mate.' I said, 'No. This is your medal.' He didn't understand. 'I am going to give it to you. Four years ago you said this is *our* medal. Nothing's changed since then, except this time you keep it at your house. We can have one each.' My only proviso was that I showed my kids the medal first before I gave it to him.

In the months leading up to the Games I had always planned on giving him the medal, but there had been plenty of times when I thought 'Bugger him' — especially when I thought he wasn't treating me and Goldi too well a month out from that last trial! But if anyone deserved it, Titch deserved it.

Monday, 5 August

A QUIET DAY. BREAKFAST was ready at 8 am and none of us had been to bed. **I don't usually drink, but I had quite a few that night. I've been drunk five times in my life and that was number six. I put all the drinkers away, though — Brad Fleming, Karl Te Nana and Craig Newby . . . they couldn't keep up with the old fella.** We spent the day sleeping, cleaning up and drinking lots of water. Had a few quiet drinks — strictly lemonade for me this time — with the rest of the New Zealand team before a relatively early night.

Tuesday, 6 August

HEADED HOME. SAT WITH the squash girls on the plane. They had done well picking up a few gold medals. The hockey boys, who surprised many by getting to the final and claiming the silver, were going off up the back. People thought it would be the rugby boys causing havoc on the plane, but we were pretty well-behaved. Touched down in Auckland at 5.15 am. There was a great turnout of people to meet us.

The media were there and wanted to know my plans. I couldn't really tell them because I knew I had to put something in this book. One job I won't be after is Wardie's. I'd be a terrible manager. Earlier in the year, when we came back from the World Series games in England, all the management crew went up to Manchester to check out the facilities for the Games, so I was put in charge of getting the boys back home. It was a temporary team manager type of role. But before we

One for Titch. I gave my second gold medal to Titch . . . Bruce Reihana shows everyone this was No. 2.

even left the UK one of the boys had decided to stay on in London. Then in Dubai, another two — Josh Blackie and Hayden Reid — jumped off. When we got to Singapore we lost Chris Masoe! I lost a person at every stop . . . and we didn't get Business Class for the flight to Auckland so I almost swapped a trophy for that! So management isn't really my thing.

I'd like to coach the sevens team one day, but not yet. On a day before the Games' tournament started, Titch came up to me and said that I was training well. I told him that we'd get this tournament out of the road before we talked about a decision to retire or not. **When we were on the plane home he said, 'Mate, you'll last another year if you're hungry enough.' I said I was.** He pointed out that he had another year on his contract and, if I was feeling up to it, he'd like me to play for another year too. I have to get a contract, though. Titch might want me to play but the NZRFU board might not!

I spent the next couple of days showing off my gold medal. I took it to my kids' school, Southern Cross Campus, to show them the medal and thank them for their send-off. Then I gave the medal to Titch. Magic.

Gumboots and goalposts

'RUGBY HAS BEEN GOOD TO ME.' It's a phrase a few players have used over the years but I reckon it was written just for me. How could I think anything else . . . I have had a charmed life, a life that has surely been better than anything my parents could have dreamt for me when I made my first appearance in the world way back in 1965.

Ours was a simple life. Kaeo, in Northland, was the typical small New Zealand town. We had a dairy, a butcher, a hardware store, a chemist, a garage and two pubs. My parents, Merv and Unaiki and us six kids — Stephen (Putti), Lawrence, Robert (Bru), Huia (Witch), Brendan (Honky) and me — lived in a two-bedroom house that would have been no bigger than eight metres by four metres. **We didn't have running water. We were allowed to have a bath once a week — on Sundays, so we were clean for school on Monday. During the week, if it wasn't too cold, we would wash in the creek.** Me and my brother Lawrence got tapa a few times. That's when the skin on your feet and knees cracks up because you haven't washed very often. It was really sore. Once it was there, the only way to get it off was to scrub it with sandstone. Mum would scrub us for hours. I still cringe when I think about it. It was pretty rough living, but at the time I thought nothing of it because it was such a great life up there.

We used to make our own fun. Remember, these were the

days before colour television and video games. When we went to school we had to ride a bus for 30 minutes into town. In the afternoons we used to get out a stop earlier at the top of a hill. We all had turns riding the bus down the hill. We used to climb onto the spare tyre until the next stop. When there were floods we'd ride the logs down the river. That was our idea of fun. It was a great life.

If we got hungry, it didn't matter because we all knew where the trees with food on them were. Whenever we found a soft-drink bottle we used to walk for miles to cash it in for lollies at the store. One day we found a whole crate. We knew it was worth about $5. So we walked the 10 km around to Whangaroa to cash it in. On New Year's Eve we would all go 'tin canning'. It was a little like Halloween. We would go door to door with a tin and people used to give us money and food. When we got a bit older we'd stand on the side of the road and wave down the campers that were staying at the nearby beaches. **When they stopped, off came the petrol cap and the hub caps. Then, if they gave us money, we'd put them back on. If they didn't, they went in the creek!**

The family didn't own much, but we did have two cows — a tame one and a wild one. My brothers and I would race home every day after school to try to get to the tame one. After that, we'd go up to the old abandoned Matangirau School where there was a netball court. In the winter we'd play touch on it. Like most country kids our feet were pretty tough. We were used to running along metal roads in bare feet, but when it came to stepping, sprinting and stopping suddenly on concrete it was a little too hard on our feet. We didn't own sandshoes or anything like that so we'd play in gumboots. The trouble was we only had one pair of gumboots between us, so it was first in, first served. **If you could learn to sidestep and take off from the mark with those things on, you were pretty good when it came to the real thing on Saturdays.** We would play until we lost, and then another group of boys would replace us. We'd play until it was dark.

My earliest rugby memory is watching my older brother Putti (Stephen) play at East Tamaki in Auckland. I played my first game at Okaihau. We moved there just after I started school. I used to walk into the hardware shop in the little town there and go to the back and look at all the jerseys in their cubbyholes. I always wanted to start playing rugby so I could get my own one. When I was five I played my first game. I was playing for Mr Collins' Okaihau Primary School team. Mum and Dad didn't come and watch. **Mum was in when I got home, but she didn't believe me when I told her I got two tries because I wasn't dirty.** I tried to tell her that I wasn't dirty because it was wet and the grass was real long. But she just gave me one of those smiles . . . you know the ones. The kind that looks like she feels a bit sorry for me. But I actually did score two tries!

When I was in Standard 3 we had moved to Kaeo. I started playing for the Kaeo Rugby Club, and my new coach was Mr Winiata. My old man had a Valiant ute and every Saturday

On the front lawn in Otara. I'm on the right holding my cousin Ron. Brother Lawrence is holding Bru and in front is 'Mutt'.

Waiting for Mum to come in with the pipis . . . no, I haven't got flippers on.

morning — even in the freezing cold — he'd have a dozen or more kids in the back of it as he dropped us off in Kaeo outside the dairy where all the teams used to assemble. When our Valiant packed up we got an HQ Holden wagon. **It became a bit of a ritual to get nervous every Saturday morning because none of us knew if Dad's car would start.** If it did — and that wasn't always the case — we'd have to put bags over our heads so the dust from the metal roads didn't get in our hair and in our eyes. Even when it was wet and the metal roads weren't dusty, we had the bags on because the car was so full of dust from previous trips. We must have looked like ghosts when we turned up. We used to tell the old man to drop us off down the road, but he always stopped right in front of all our mates, just to embarrass us.

When there was no club footie on we played outside my grandfather's house, which was right next to our place. There, brothers and whatever cousins happened to be around always used to play on the field. The boundaries were pretty clear cut. At one end there was a shed where we used to keep all the wild pigs that we'd caught — that was the tryline. To get a conversion you had to kick it over the shed. On one side of the field was the long grass and on the other side was the fence outside the house. **The other tryline was the blackberry bushes and the ditch. If you scored at the ditch end you had to go to the other end to kick the conversion. If you kicked it too hard it went in the creek.** Sometimes, if it was raining, we'd sneak into our marae's wharenui, put down all the mattresses and play in there. If we had been caught we would have been skinned alive.

I used to pretend to be one of the North Auckland backline. They had guys like Eddie and Ian Dunn, Sid, Brian and Ken Going, Joe Morgan, David Haynes, Chippy Semenoff, Fred and Kawhena Woodman and Mike Gunson. Those guys were my heroes, they really were. I remember listening on the radio when I was 13 years old to the Shield game in 1978 when North Auckland beat Manawatu. Chippy Semenoff kicked the winning penalty goal in the last minute. I went outside immediately and started kicking goals over the shed.

Our Christmases were normally spent playing rugby outside Papa's (my grandfather's) house. The adults would be sitting in the shade on the lawn watching us kids hammer the shit out of each other. **My older brothers would make me cry so I'd make my younger brothers cry. Man, we were all crying at one stage.**

But I loved the confrontational side of rugby. That's probably why I took to boxing when I was 13 years old. Mind you, I had to be a bit careful on the rugby field with my boxing. It's funny, when I used to box I was always real careful not to get into too many rugby fights because I didn't like to fight once I knew how hard it really was. But as soon as I stopped boxing I started getting into more and more fights on the field. Once, there was a bit of a scuffle and a guy squared up to me. I hit him four times before he'd even raised his hands. I had an unfair advantage because I knew how to throw a punch. I had about 20 fights — winning 18 of them and losing twice. Both losses were in the finals of the New Zealand championships in the lightweight and light-heavyweight divisions.

When I was a young fella I was trained by a local, Bill Woods, whose son, Nuka, went on to fight for New Zealand at the 1990 Commonwealth Games in Auckland. **Bill was a real rough bastard but he loved his boxing. So did I. I used to run or bike the 5 km to the rugby club to train.** Because training finished just before dark I used to motor the whole way home. Half of me was scared of not being able to see anything if I took too long and the other half was scared of the dark. But I could put up with it because I loved to box. It was Bill's passion too. He helped so many kids in that little place. The Waitaruke convent — a Catholic school near Kaeo — was a great source of talent for Bill. He used to take his cattle trailer up there and bring all the boys in the back to town with him so they could train. He was a real character. His cars were worse than ours. One of them was a floor shift — he had a big long screwdriver as his gear lever, so he never used to take his keys out of the car. He just took the screwdriver into the pub with him. When he got a column shift, he used a pair of pliers to change the gears.

We never had a gym or anything to train at. We used the rugby club, the church hall, anywhere we could. All that mattered was that Bill was there training us. He loved working with us, so much so that when he lost a leg in a road accident, he used the money he got from ACC to build a gym. He never quite finished it. He was always threatening to get drunk and let us run over his other leg so we could finish the building!

Bill had some strange training techniques. The half-finished gym was on his property and there was about a 100-metre gap between his front door and the gate. **Bill's dogs were pig dogs and every day after training — when we were about 50 metres from the gate — he'd look down at them and say, 'Kill.' We used to run for our lives.** I don't know how high the gate was, but I never touched it on the way out. I just hurdled the thing. Bill reckoned it was good training.

Bill also used to make his own liniment. One time, when we

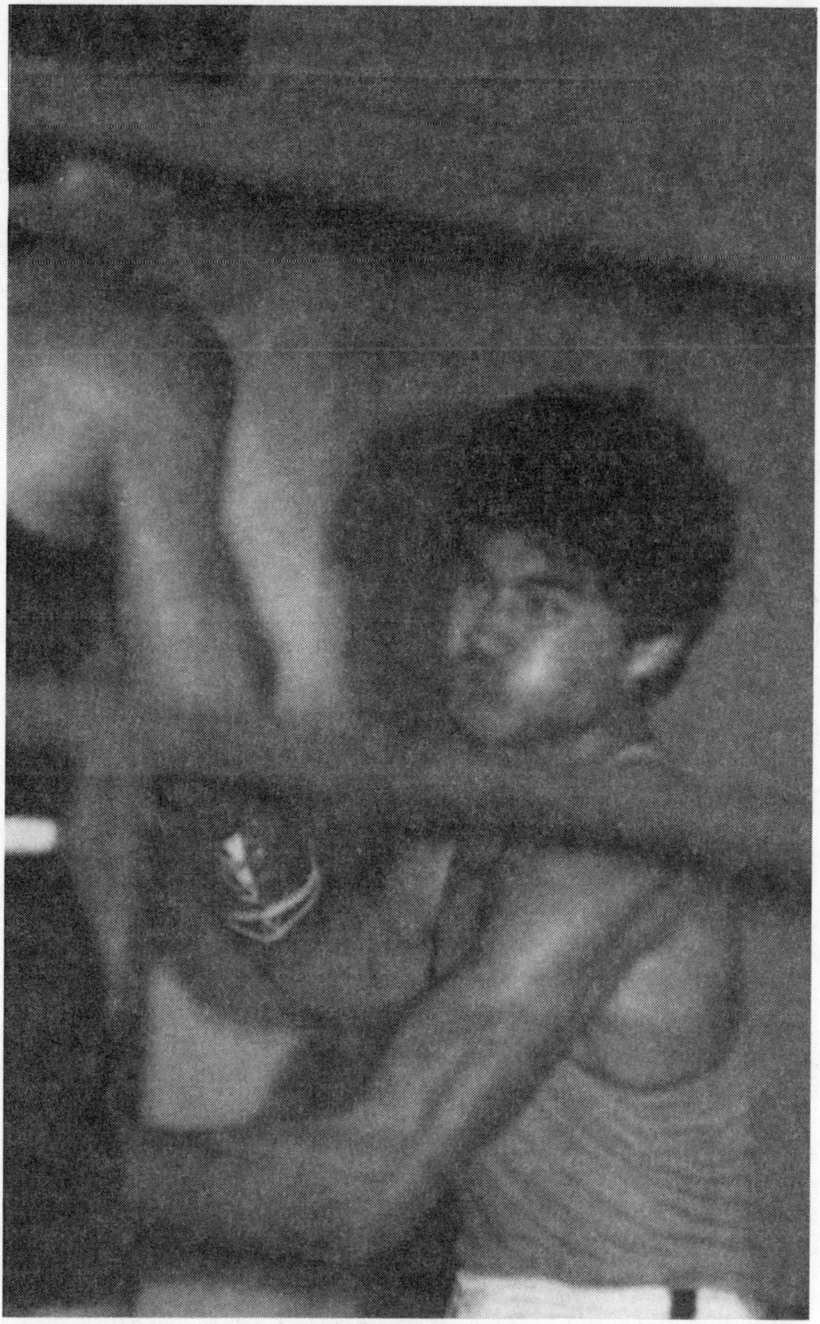

Boxing. To me it is the ultimate sporting contest.

were fighting in Whangarei, we were all putting it on before our fights and it was real hot. Everyone was jumping around. All he could say was, 'Harden up you little bastards!' **While we were jumping around one of the boys knocked the bottle of it over and it spilt on the table. All the paint peeled off. We all panicked and jumped in the showers to get it off us, but it just made it spread and made matters worse!**

I learnt a lot about what hard training was with Bill. He was the first one to teach me that you had to put in the hard yards if you wanted to succeed. He also introduced me to touring, when the Kaeo Boxing Club went to Queensland. To raise money for the trip we used to row across the Whangaroa Harbour in the morning, cut scrub all day, then row back at night. When it came time to pay for the trip we were all quite a few dollars short and we needed help. One of the main cash crops up north is the old marijuana. A couple of the locals decided they would help us out by selling a bit of it down in Auckland. There was a member of our club who also happened to be a cop. I don't think he knew what was going on. If he did, though, no doubt he realised that Bill's boxing club saved more kids from jail than anything else.

I'd never been overseas before, so going to Queensland was pretty exciting. We went to a little town called Beaudesert where we thought we would be fighting the local team, but it turned out our opponents were the Queensland representative side. Typical Aussies. The contest was over 11 fights. One of the first up was my brother Lawrence. Bill loved him because he was a wild character. If someone walked up behind him and tapped him on the shoulder he would swing a punch. He was a really edgy, nervous kind of fella. When Mum wasn't at home I would have to wake him up. **I learnt pretty quickly that the only way you could wake up Lawrence and not get hammered was if you used a broom!** In the ring Lawrence was a brawler, but the kid he was fighting was a classic boxer, so it was a real meeting of opposites. Lawrence hunted him down. He hit him. The Aussie fell through the ropes onto the trophy table and we all thought that that was that. But when we looked up Lawrence had ducked under the ropes and had begun hitting the guy while he was coming back into consciousness on the table.

That fight set the tone for the rest of the night. The fights were hard, and even. By the time my bout came round the score was locked up at five bouts each. The guy I was boxing had been written up in the local paper as a 'fitness freak'. Because our fight was the decider we were instructed that instead of a three-round encounter ours would be a six-round affair. I wasn't thrilled about that, but Bill told me just to box like I always do. I went out and pasted him in the first four rounds, but in the last two he hammered me. The only thing keeping me going was the fact that the boys were doing the haka between rounds. In the sixth round I saw an opening and I thought I'd throw a big right and finish the fight. After I threw it all I could see was a blue light. **After a couple of confused seconds I realised that it was the canvas. Apparently my punch never landed . . . I'd missed and fallen flat on my face. I jumped up and was able to last the final couple of minutes and so snatched the win.**

My hero at the time, of course, was Muhammad Ali. I had no idea that I would one day be lucky enough to meet The Champ. That happened in Scotland when I was on tour with the All Blacks in 1993. We were walking past a bookshop, from which a long queue snaked all the way down the road. We asked what was going on and were told that Ali was signing copies of his book. The publicist was standing by the door and he recognised Michael Jones and Inga Tuigamala. 'You fellows want to come in and meet The Champ?' We couldn't believe it. We were in the shop in seconds. They showed us into a room and we were told that Ali would be in soon. Then, after a few nervous minutes, The Champ walked in.

I was one of the new boys at that time and I looked up to Ice and Inga, who were right at the peak of their careers as All Blacks. They just looked like little kids at Christmas. Ali may have shuffled into that room but the aura around him was just as good as it gets. He shook our hands, talking really quietly. He wanted to meet us because of the All Black connection. I'm not sure if he knew who we were . . . he may have just liked the name All Blacks. He did a couple of tricks. The first one was the hankie disappearing. **And he did a levitation trick that freaked Inga out no end. It actually looked like he was floating on top of the ground.** If you were standing at the side of him you could see what he was doing, but if you were directly in front of him it looked like he was floating. Later Inga was convinced: 'He was! He was! He was floating!' We told him it was a trick but he wouldn't hear anything of it. 'No bro. He was floating. He's The Champ, man. Floats like a butterfly. He was floating. I saw it with my own eyes.'

Apart from Bill, another person to give me a few good lessons was a teacher at Whangaroa College. Rex Jury had taught my mother and he is still teaching there now. One time I didn't bring my PE uniform. He told me if I didn't bring it I wouldn't be able to play rugby on Saturday. I forgot it again and, sure enough, he stopped me playing the game. I never forgave him for it but I didn't forget my PE uniform again either. He was a pretty tough bugger. One day the whole class got the cane because we were making too much noise in the changing room. He marched in, lined us all up and caned us.

It was a good school, though. Volleyball was our best sport. One year we won the senior and junior boys' and girls' Northland titles. It was the sort of school where everyone was encouraged to take part in sport. On athletics and swimming days you had to enter everything. Every year there was a compulsory swim across Whangaroa Harbour and back again. **The whole community helped out by forming a ring around the kids. If you got tired they would whip you out of the water. It was all about having a go.** Even the kids that didn't have a lot of self-esteem when it came to sports loved it. It didn't matter if they only made it halfway across because, for them, it was a huge achievement. That attitude seems to be missing these days. Today, teachers seem more worried about little Johnny getting a cold than they do letting him accomplish something. That's why I send my kids — Natalie, Marty, Blair, Brady and Robert — to Auckland's Southern Cross Campus. It's a strict school and the teachers aren't consumed with political correctness. The other reason why they attend that school is because I want them to learn Maori. I never learnt it because my mother wasn't in the habit of using it. **When she was growing up she used to get strapped and got her mouth literally washed out with soap if she used it at school. It was a Pakeha world back then and it was drummed into her that Maori was no good to her.** My generation missed out on the language, but I'm proud that my kids are fluent speakers.

After playing some reasonable rugby for Whangaroa College and the Kaeo club everything was on course for me to fulfil my dream of playing for North Auckland. But everything changed in my seventh form year. I wanted to play rugby, but I was going to be the only seventh former at the school after all of my friends had finished up after sixth form. I didn't like the idea of that so I headed to Auckland to stay with my Uncle Charlie and Aunt Francis. I'd been going down to Auckland to visit them for years. Their kids, Bett, Sonny and Darryl, were my closest cousins in age. I used to love going to work with my uncle on the meat trucks and out with my aunty in the taxis.

My aunty and uncle decided I should go to Tangaroa College. I thought it was a good idea because I knew they had a good volleyball team and my cousin Sonny was the captain! I'd played volleyball up north and was used to being at a strong volleyball school so Tangaroa was the perfect fit for me. **The coaches there were Trevor Lawrence — who had played hockey for New Zealand — and Reuben Riki, who had been a Stormtrooper, and had played league for Otara.** They were a great coaching team. They coached us to the final four at the nationals. I made the New Zealand under-17 side with their help. It was a tournament team, but never a played a match.

But things weren't always great at Tangaroa. One day up home at Whangaroa College someone stole a box of ice creams

The Rush whanau. Standing, left to right: Honky (Brendan), Lawrence, me, Bru (Robert) and Putti (Stephen). In front: Dad, Witch (Huia) and Mum.

off the back of the ice cream truck. There was an inquest. At Tangaroa, someone stole the truck! It was a real introduction to South Auckland. All these people were talking four or five different languages. Some guys were setting the rubbish bins on fire. It was like a bloody war zone! On my first day there I nearly got into a fight. I beat this guy in a ping-pong game and he wasn't thrilled. His name was Mark Leaver. He went on to play more than 100 games for the New Zealand hockey team. We were good mates from the moment the ping-pong game finished. **We didn't have a First XV because we only played the one game — an annual fixture against Hillary College. I played flanker. The other flanker was a fellow called Tawera Nikau . . . and he was bloody good.**

Because of the lack of rugby at Tangaroa I joined the Otahuhu club. I played in a team that had a reputation for being a bit rough. A bit rough! We were shocking. Pretty much every week there would be a fight in one of our games. The club got sick of us so they banned us. It was the best thing that could have happened to me. I joined East Tamaki and that's where I met my great mate Ron Reti. He took me along to the Auckland Maori trials in 1986. He told me they were the colts' trials. **I walked into the changing room and thought, 'Shit some of these fellas are old-looking colts.' It was the senior trial.** Things took off for me from there. I owe a lot to Ron.

The Auckland coach at the time, John Hart, watched me play a game for East Tamaki as well as a game for Auckland Maori against North Harbour. This wasn't my first taste of rep rugby — that had come in Northland when I was called into the under-16 side. I have never really counted it as a representative team though, because I only made the side after someone else was injured. At the nationals I played against a fella in the Counties team called Kev McQuoid — our physio in KL and Manchester when New Zealand won the gold medals. The nationals were held in Rotorua that year and after the finals we went to watch Bay of Plenty play against the Springboks. Playing for Bay of Plenty that day was a forward by the name of Gordon Tietjens.

Harty must have been happy with what he saw of me playing for the Auckland Maori side because after a whole lot of injuries to his first-choice players — and the fact that no All Blacks were available for the Auckland side to play against Horowhenua — I got the call-up. **During the lead-up to the game, which was a Ranfurly Shield defence, Auckland's captain Andy Haden had been barking at the young fellas in the squad. I was shit scared of him.** I'd grown up watching him play for the All Blacks and thought he was a pretty intimidating kind of character. During the game — and I was a flanker in those days — I took the ball up and the Auckland forwards crashed over the top of me. Haden went to stomp on one of their forwards but missed and got my knee instead. Blood was squirting out of it . . . man, it hurt. Haden came over and stood over the top of me and all I could say was, 'Sorry! Sorry!' He'd stomped on me and I was apologising! He asked if I was all right and we got on with the game. In the second half I sprained my ankle

Warming up with Auckland at the sevens nationals in 1988. We won the final and I was selected for the New Zealand side.

and while I was getting treated he came over, took a look at me and said, 'No one goes off in their first game for Auckland.' My ankle ached but I got up and gutsed it out. I did so much damage to it in those last 15 minutes, though, that I was out of rugby for the next six months!

After I came back from that injury in 1987 I played for the Auckland Colts, and Auckland's sevens coaches Maurice Trapp and Bryan Williams invited me to their trials. I made the team and went to the nationals where I managed to get one game against East Coast and scored three tries. **The next year, Mark Brooke-Cowden went to league and Auckland was looking for a new hooker for the sevens side. Sean Fitzpatrick was supposed to be the guy to step up, but he didn't come to training so I volunteered.**

They chucked me in there and when we went to the nationals at Pukekohe I was getting two or three tries a game. We'd made it through to the final against Canterbury and while we were warming up Maurice came up to me and said, 'They have got to be looking at you.' I didn't know who he was talking about, so I asked him what he meant. 'The bloody New

Zealand selectors mate. They have got to be looking at you.' Well, straight away the nerves set in. I hadn't even thought about playing for New Zealand. I was just thrilled to be playing alongside guys like Terry Wright, Frank Bunce, John Kirwan and Zinzan Brooke. Frankie told me to relax and was really encouraging. By the time the game came round I was reasonably relaxed. I scored three tries (Dallas Seymour was in the other team, but I don't really want to say again that I did him on the outside). We won the nationals and I was named in the New Zealand team.

I ended up playing 13 rep games for Auckland between 1986 and 1991 when I transferred across the bridge to join North Harbour. **I was one game short of my blazer game for Auckland. I had been selected to play my 14th game, but when I was playing for Otahuhu my mate Paddy Masani — who was on my team — tackled a guy I already had a hold of and snapped my arm. So, I never got my blazer. (Thanks Paddy!)** But I had some good times at Auckland, and it was a privilege to be a part of such an awesome team. No one could beat us. Auckland dominated the NPC and the Ranfurly Shield in those days. I had some good mates in the side — blokes like Zinzan Brooke, Michael Jones, John Kirwan, Steve McDowell and Joe Stanley — but a lot of them were real arseholes too. Some of the guys didn't want to know you if you weren't an All Black. They wouldn't acknowledge you at training. I could go through a whole game without some of them saying anything to me.

When I made the decision to join North Harbour I remember having this amazing feeling of relief. And it didn't take me long to realise that the group of guys over the bridge were totally different to the Auckland ones I'd been with for five years. Before my first game against King Country our coach Peter Thorburn came across to have a serious chat with me. He was laying down the law of what it meant to be a Harbour player. Behind him our centre, Scott Pierce, was making faces and pulling down his pants!

Harbour had a reputation — and still do — of being a party

team. We weren't. We knew how to have fun but as soon as that whistle went the boys knew how to switch on. That's why I enjoyed my time at Harbour more so than at Auckland. Even though Auckland won everything that they could, I never felt a part of the Auckland set-up. I was always treated like an outsider. I wasn't the only one either. All the guys that weren't All Blacks at the time were treated pretty poorly. There was nothing like that at Harbour. Our captain was Buck Shelford — one of the greatest All Blacks ever — and he treated everyone the same. There were no cliques in our side.

The most famous NPC game I played in would have been the notorious final in 1994 between Harbour and Auckland. It was a real grudge match. There was a real hatred between the teams. We'd beaten them at Eden Park four weeks earlier. On that day they were missing Sean Fitzpatrick and the Brooke brothers, Zinzan and Robin (Moose). After that game some Auckland players came out saying we would never have beaten them if those three had been playing and some of the Harbour boys had responded through the media saying some pretty dumb things too. In effect, we'd given Auckland their team talk. So both teams were fired up. Some of the Auckland boys — Moose in particular — were saying a few naughty things to us to wind us up . . . and it worked. Richard Turner, our captain, wasn't going to back down. 'Bugger them. If they want it, bring it on, let's go.'

Auckland had targeted Harbour's lock Blair Larsen as a bit of a softie. At the first scrum Moose threw a punch at him, but much to the surprise of the Auckland boys Blair just turned and whacked him back. It was all on after that. While Auckland was having a shot at goal **Moose appeared out of nowhere and smacked me in the jaw. I was out like a light.** When I came to there was a bit of an argument going on. The doc wanted to take me off but Frank Bunce and Walter Little were saying, 'Nah, he's all right.' I spent the next few minutes stumbling around the field. I didn't know it at the time but apparently I was standing in the first five spot and then the second five's spot instead of

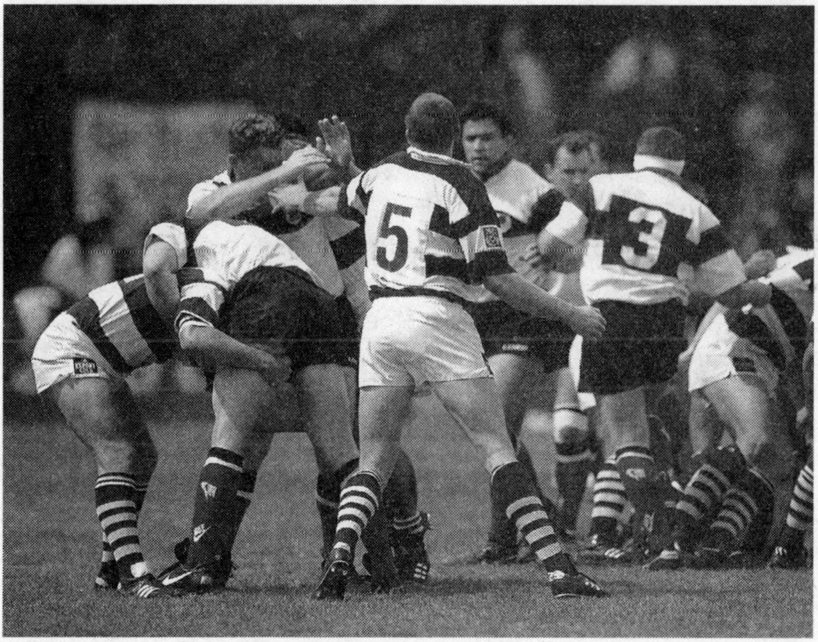

The fur's flying in the 1994 NPC final at Onewa Domain. There was real hatred out there.

on the wing. Then Zinny and I were going for the same ball and he stepped into my line and I hit him with my shoulder. **I have been told by more than one Auckland player that Zin — who was supposed to be injured — was lying on the ground pretending to be knocked out, asking his team-mates if I had been sent off or not. I think they call that a Hollywood!** I was still concussed and the next thing I knew I was sitting on the side of the field after being marched by the referee. History shows that Auckland won that game and Harbour — eight years later — has yet to get that trophy in the cabinet. I love winning as much as anyone but I have never regretted leaving Auckland.

They say winning is everything and I believe that to an extent. However, enjoyment is also a factor and though I was as disappointed as anyone with always being the bridesmaids in that era, I really enjoyed my rugby with Harbour. If someone asked me now which team I preferred to be in — either with that great, winning Auckland team or playing with the less successful North Harbour — I'd pick North Harbour every time. I would love to have won the NPC with North Harbour and the Ranfurly Shield, too. But I also would have loved to have walked on the moon and won Lotto as well. I guess not everything in life is meant to be . . .

I don't get to play much fifteens any more. My sevens commitments make sure of that. Every Labour Weekend, though, I travel back home to Kaeo to play in the local marae tournament. Every marae in the area puts in a rugby team. **Our team, Matangirau, has had a great record in the 22 years the tournament has been going. A lot of the guys that front for the weekend don't play rugby anymore. But they dust off their boots and lace them up for another run every time Labour Weekend comes around.** My eldest brother Putti is 42 now and him and my cousin Rusty Poata haven't missed a single year. That's an amazing record actually because the rugby is *tough.* It's different rugby to anything most people have seen before. It's tribal warfare. You are not just playing a game of rugby; you are playing for your mana. For your marae. For your ancestors buried at your urupa. Sometimes people get a bit carried away — me included — but most of the time it is just good hard rugby. There's some great talent up there — for one little town.

In the games we played outside Papa's house he always used to go on at us that when we could pick up a ball while running at full speed, then we would be good rugby players. I practised that for so many years, just to prove to him that I could do it. The only time I've done it was during a game one Labour Weekend a few years back. I only tried it because I knew he was watching. When I pulled it off all my brothers and cousins knew it would make Papa a happy man.

I remember my first game for Matangirau — it was the first tournament. I was 16 and was playing hooker. We played Wainui in the final. In the opposition front row was my brother's father-in-law, Ace Hona. He was *the* man in the Kaeo seniors. He took all the young guys under his wing and taught them a lot about rugby. So before the final when my dad came up to me and told me Ace would punch me in the first scrum, I didn't believe him. Dad said when (not if) he does, you've got to hit him back. Ace didn't wait long. He hit me in the very first scrum. I was dumbfounded and for the next five minutes I didn't know what to do. I looked across at the old man and I could see him mouthing to me, 'You know what to do.' So I whacked Ace in the next ruck. From the bottom of the ruck I heard this bellow, 'You little dark person' — or words to that effect. **I ran. And he chased me. I ducked in and out of our players. I thought I was going to die. After the game he shook my hand and said, 'Good on you, boy. You're going to be all right.'**

The tournament has grown in status over the last few years. We even had a television crew there last year. One of the reporters asked if there was any drug testing after the games. One of my cousins said, 'Yeah, bro. We'll be testing them all night.'

Corporations, cups and capers

I HAVE NO DOUBT about it, the World Rugby Corporation's failed attempt to take over the running of the international game saved rugby. And not because it failed either. It saved rugby through making sure the NZRFU knew the value of the game and its players. If the WRC hadn't been around to set the benchmark, rugby would have been plundered by rugby league of its players and its dignity.

The first I knew about the WRC was during the 1995 Rugby World Cup in the week leading up to our semi-final against England. I was asked by Fitzy and Mike Brewer to meet with John Hart, who had been contacted by the WRC guys. Harty — who was in South Africa as a part of a TV commentary team — was targeted by the WRC guys because at that stage he wasn't part of the NZRFU set-up and the WRC were keen to not upset the All Blacks' preparation for the semi-final.

After the game I went up to a corporate box with Harty to meet Ross Turnbull. No figures were mentioned, but he said he had already contacted all the teams that had been knocked out of the tournament and had had a positive reaction from all of them. He also said that some teams had already signed up. He said from the beginning that the WRC was set up as a direct result of rugby league's Super League.

I also had the impression that they were keen to get rid of

the IRB — the 'gin-swilling brigade' as they called them. He told a story about officials from various countries that got free business-class trips around the globe, got driven to their five-star hotels and then dined out on the IRB. You can only imagine how much this exercise cost the game. When you consider that the people who are the most important — the players — were getting £20 a day, it was a little tough to accept that a massive amount of money was being spent on flying these guys into South Africa on another free trip. In my opinion, some of the officials deserved it because they were responsible for the running of the game and they got paid very little or nothing for it. But no one can deny that a lot of the officials that travelled were not essential to the running of the World Cup.

The WRC people said they wouldn't talk to us until after the final. Harty was not convinced they could get it up and running, but thought it was a great concept. **I went back to the team's hotel and reported in to Fitzy and Bruiser and told them that the concept sounded like a good one. But I stressed that if it was going to get off the ground it was going to be a huge undertaking by all concerned.** They told me not to talk about it to anyone until after the final.

We trained well that whole week leading up to the final against the Springboks. It was similar to the week before where it was full-on bloodshed at training — the test team against the 'driftwood', as we were so affectionately termed by Laurie Mains. Before the England game he had got us to get in at the rucks and try to kill the ball in order to simulate what England's Dean Richards did in the games. He'd tell us to get in there and he'd come over and make sure we were lying on the ball. At one stage I heard him say to the test team. 'If the driftwood gets in the road, sort the bastards out!' I have never seen so many stitches at a training before. It was out-and-out war. When we were on the team bus, the test team sat at the back. The 'driftwood' piled up at the front. It was like that for three days. Once trainings were over we were one team again,

Laurie Mains did his best to stay out of the WRC wrangle as senior players like Mike Brewer (right) took charge.

but during trainings it was harder than some of the games we played at the World Cup.

I knew at training that the English didn't stand a chance. If the boys were prepared to do that to their mates then the English forwards were in for a bit of a smashing. And then on the day Jonah chipped in as well with his four tries and a 45–29 win was secured relatively simply.

The intensity in the preparation for the final against South Africa was, well, it was intense. We had trained well all week and there was a good vibe in the camp. On the Thursday we all went down to lunch. **The whole team was there. Laurie was a little paranoid about someone nobbling the team, so instead of continuing to eat in the hotel's main restaurant we had our meals served in our team room.** In hindsight it was the worst thing we could have done.

Once in the team room, Glen Osborne, Zinzan Brooke and I bailed. We had been eating pasta and chicken for the past five or six weeks and we'd had enough of it. We decided to get out of the hotel, so we went to the movies, played a few video games and had some pizza. We didn't eat or drink anything at the hotel with the rest of the team. Consequently, we were some of the few players still on our feet at dinnertime. Half the team weren't there. And, at breakfast the next morning, there were only about six or seven of us. All the other guys were sick. **There was a shocking stench coming from the All Blacks' floor of the hotel. As soon as the elevator doors opened you knew it was our floor. There had been a fair amount of diarrhoea and vomiting going on.** It was so bad that all the guys that weren't sick were moved to a different floor.

Looking back, I don't know if we were poisoned or not. I do know that everyone was sick and I know that had the World Cup final been a day earlier we wouldn't have been able to put a team on the field. Some guys never got out of bed until the day of the game — some of them shouldn't have ever got out of bed, but it was the biggest game of their lives. They had to do everything they could to get to Ellis Park and play against the Boks.

As I wasn't one of the sick ones I was put on stand-by for the final. I hadn't expected to play but all of a sudden it was a real possibility. That meant the cancellation of the Dirty Dirties' big night out. **Normally the players not in the test side would be allowed to go out the night before the test. The thinking behind it was twofold. First, it kept us away from the test team and, second, it meant that we could scope out the town and find a place for the team to go to the following night.**

Harty knocked that tradition on the head when he took charge of the side in 1996. By the time he got the All Blacks' job the game was professional and he didn't look fondly on guys having a drink. He was even in the habit of calling 7 am debriefs the morning *after* a test — I guess it was his way of making sure the guys didn't have too late a night. Of course, not all players went along with it.

In 1997 at one of the debriefs, Frank Bunce arrived still wearing his No. 1s from the night before. Harty asked Fitzy his thoughts about the forwards' effort in the test and Fitzy talked for five minutes about the tight five needing to up their work rate, etc. **Harty then asked Frank, 'How about the backs, Frank? How do you think you went?' Frank, with a smile a mile wide, said, 'Sweet as, bro. Sweet as.'** That's all he said. Harty wasn't amused.

It wasn't only the backs that defied the drinking bans. On a Blues trip to South Africa — when Graham Henry was in charge — a certain All Black prop was missing when the side's early morning training session began. While Henry was chatting away to the guys, their concentration was broken by the sound of a taxi screeching to a halt. Out jumped the missing prop. When Henry sent the boys to do a few laps, this player — still in his No. 1s — joined in! The Blues' players then stopped to do some stretches. Again, the missing player joined in, but, this time, he couldn't hold it together and collapsed in a heap on the ground! Props, eh . . . can't take them anywhere.

Back to South Africa . . . On the morning of the final we knew that some of the boys were still struggling, but we wanted to keep it quiet. **Even after we had lost 15-12 after extra time to a Joel Stransky dropped goal, we didn't want anyone to find out about the sickness because it would have sounded like sour grapes.** The players made that call but the management — probably Laurie because he was so passionate about the players — revealed the news that the team had been sick.

Despite the media and public knowing the truth we never used it as an excuse. It was 15 players against 15 players and we didn't win — they did. And it hurt. There were a lot of downcast faces afterwards. A few of the boys shed some tears. We had trained so hard for it, and to lose the way we did was tough. There was dead silence in the shed. Having watched from the stands it is a difficult thing to then wander into the changing rooms after an All Black loss. And this wasn't just a loss — we'd lost in the final of the World Cup. All you can do is walk in, tap the boys on the shoulder, and be there for them.

Of course, sometimes, when you play with a guy like Frank

Bunce, those traditions don't always hold true. After a North Harbour loss in Queensland once, our first five, Warren Burton, was singled out for some Bunce-tude after missing a kick that would have put us in the Super 10 final against Natal. **'Bugger you, you bloody honkie! You know that's the only reason you white guys are in the team.'** Then, at the airport, while we were checking in for our flight back to Auckland, Buncey couldn't resist another dig at Burts when he was handed his airline seat number. 'What do you mean I'm going to Auckland? I'm supposed to be going to Natal!' Lucky Burts had a sense of humour.

After a period of silence in our dressing room, Colin 'Pinetree' Meads — our manager — addressed the team. 'Look boys, you played 120 minutes of rugby. We missed a dropped kick and they got theirs. So don't beat yourself up too much. All things considered, you played bloody well. You are All Blacks. You like taking the wins, now we have to take this loss. **Get out there, hold your heads high and show these bastards that we know how to handle a loss as well.' 'Tree' never wasted words.**

It was a great campaign to be a part of. I got my first test against the Welsh — a test which was my own individual highlight of the World Cup. I was a reserve for the game. Jonah hit his shoulder on the deck pretty hard and I got up from the bench straight way. I knew that this could be my best chance of finally getting on the track. I looked at Jonah and I could see he didn't want to come off. He pushed the doc away and I could see in his face he was determined to carry on. But, when he looked up and saw me jumping up and down on the sidelines, he just walked off. I still owe him for that.

I was on the field in an instant. I was pretty geed up. Frank, Walter Little and Oz came over and congratulated me on getting on the park for my first test. What a moment. Then Walt called a move for me. He wanted me to get the ball in my hands as soon as possible. He called a double miss. The blindside winger came outside the centre — which was where he was meant to be — and Frank missed him, hit Oz and there was a perfect overlap for me on the outside. Oz dummied and took off and never passed me the ball! I could hear Walt shouting, 'Give him the bloody ball!'

Getting that first All Black test was one of the highlights of my career. I had been in and out of the All Black side since 1992 but never got on the field during a test. When you first make the All Blacks, you are so happy that you think just being in the squad is enough. But it's not. Once you are there, you want to play tests. You are desperate to play tests. I'd hear Fitzy after every test talk about what it meant to him to play test rugby and I wanted to know what it felt like. I also knew that once you played a test for the All Blacks you got a test tie. And you only get the one — after your first game. It is presented to you at a court session after the game.

Frank Bunce and Walter Little got up and said a few nice things about me to the rest of the boys and then Fitzy welcomed me to the club before it was my turn to address the boys. It was such a proud moment. Fitzy had made it pretty clear, though, what being an All Black was all about, so it was a pretty sobering moment too. 'Congratulations. You are here now. But that was the easy part. The tough times start now. Every time you run out in this jersey everybody who has played in it before you will be watching you and judging you. And, more importantly, all those little kids that have trained to get to this place — like you had until today — they are all watching too.' I can't remember what my response was — it's all a bit of a blur, but I'd heard that when Glen Osborne got his tie and addressed the team after his debut against Canada earlier that year, the only thing he said was: **'You know the real good thing about this tie? Rushie hasn't got one yet!' That's the Oz I know and love.**

The other test I played in during the tournament was the one against Japan. Because we were expected to win it easily, the selectors picked only six test regulars in the side — Oz, Jeff Wilson, Robin Brooke, Zinny and Craig Dowd. There was a lot of talk before the game from outside of the team about the

Three tries against Japan in the 1995 World cup. Here I'm flanked by Oz (left) and Normie Hewitt.

number of changes and how we weren't really an All Black side. But we knew that if we had lost that game it would have been the All Blacks that had lost. We were the All Blacks that day. And like any test team that had played before us we carried all the expectations that go along with wearing the jersey. **Of course, we won easily (145-17) and I managed to grab three tries. Marc Ellis got six tries and was told off by Laurie Mains for being greedy. That's Laurie.**

Back on the political front, the New Zealand, South African and Australian unions had announced the formation of SANZAR and the plans for the introduction of the Super 12 and the Tri-Nations on the eve of the final. We saw comments in various media questioning the logic of signing a 10-year deal with News Limited. NZRFU chairman Richie Guy's critics said he was out of his depth. They mentioned the fact that he was a farmer and that he should never have been dealing with the suits from News Limited. But the fact is that South Africa's boss Louis Luyt was there and he was one of the richest people in the Republic and he had agreed to the same deal. So, from the outside looking in at least, it was a bit unfair to have a go at Richie. To me, Richie is a real rugby guy. I liked him. I respected him firstly because he had been an All Black and then even more for continuing to do his bit for the game at every level, well after his playing days. My impression was that he was never there for the trappings, but for the good of the game. We need more guys like him.

The day after the final, Richie Guy called us into a room and talked briefly about how well we had done as team. **He told us that anyone who played against the Wallabies in a few weeks' time as well as anyone who toured France at the end of the year would be paid. The figure that we were given was $10,000 and I remember thinking that was an awesome sum.** It was the first time that I would be given any money to play. I was so excited that at the time I didn't realise this marked the passing of an era. Amateur rugby — for the All Blacks at least — was over and we didn't even think about it — money does that to you.

Then Richie made what seemed to me was the biggest announcement of the day when he said that in 1996 anyone who played in the All Blacks was going to be paid $30,000. I couldn't believe my ears. This was unreal. That year at my law practice Copeland Fitzpatrick I earned $12,500. Remember, I had a deal with them that if I wasn't at work I wouldn't be paid and I was happy with that because I knew I had a job to come back to when I came home. **To hear from the big man that we were going to get $30,000 was incredible. It was explained to us that payments would be on a scale — more dollars for test players and a little less for the others.** I figured that I would probably take home about $15,000 at best. But the carrot was there to try and make more. All the boys were stoked.

We had to wait a couple of days before we could go home from South Africa. All the fish heads had gone home on their business-class flight, but no one had booked the All Blacks' flight. We had to watch all the Springbok victory parades and read the papers; it was torture. Pinetree called a meeting and told us to be in the team room at 10 am with our training gear. We weren't too impressed. The game against Australia in Auckland was still two weeks away and after a six-week World Cup campaign the last thing we wanted to do was have to survive a Laurie Mains training session. We could tell by the look on Laurie's face it was going to be a tough training to get the loss out of our system. We all filed in. We weren't the most enthusiastic-looking bunch of guys. We all had our boots with us and some pretty long faces as well.

Pinetree said, 'Look, we have to get this loss out of our system and there is only one way to do it.' The door swung open and they brought in a pallet of beer. We were there for the whole day. It was great. Everybody got into the mood of it. My job was to take people to their rooms as they fell over. In the end there were too many of them so I just threw them in the corner. There was a lot of hilarity, violence and nudity. It was a real masterstroke by Tree and Laurie. It snapped us out of the despondency.

The next day, a few of us — Robin Brooke, Mike Brewer, Zinzan Brooke, Fitzy and I — were invited to a WRC meeting. It was the follow-up to the original meeting I had had with them and Harty after the England semi-final. This time the meeting was at Harry Viljoen's place in Johannesburg. I was asked to come and have a listen because of my legal background. We met up with the WRC's Ross Turnbull and a few others and were told that most of the other unions had signed up with their scheme and that we were the last. He even said that the Springboks were in and that their captain François Pienaar had signed up most of the team. Later in the meeting, just as we were about to leave, Pienaar showed up and he confirmed that. We were impressed; so much so that we were a bit worried that if we didn't sign we wouldn't have anyone to play against. **Fitzy stood up and said that we would get back to them. He stressed that we didn't want to be rushed, the decision was too important for that.**

They then showed us the plans for the worldwide franchise competition, and then they talked money. They told us they had a big financial backer (we would later find out it was Kerry Packer) and mentioned that every player who had played in the World Cup would get $US750,000 over the next three seasons. They mentioned that the senior guys would get $US800,000 and the superstars even more. This was hard to comprehend. **The money was literally out of this world. On the way back we were sitting in the car quite pensively. It was hard to take it all in and I think we were all in a bit of a daze. While we were in the car — a brand-new Lexus — Robin Brooke in a deadpan voice said, 'I think I'll buy one of these.'** We all cracked up. We were all laughing, thinking that he was probably right. We would be able to afford it. Fitzy — because I was the lawyer in the team — asked me what we should do. I told him not to sign anything and then I said, 'That'll be a hundred bucks plus GST, thanks.'

When we got back from our WRC meeting we met with the rest of the team. The boys were as blown away as I was. But there was still that feeling that it was a little unreal and we weren't sure if it would get off the ground. We hoped it would but we didn't know if it could.

That night I was contacted by a rugby league agent about swapping codes. When I mentioned it to a couple of the boys I learnt that nearly all of the boys in the backs had had an approach. I was told that if I joined Super League — who were locked in a war with the Australian Rugby League — I could expect about $400,000 in the bank as soon as I signed. On top of that players could expect $200,000 a year once they had found you a club. I thought it was ridiculous. I hadn't even played the game but when I reminded them of that they said they didn't care about that. They were prepared to take the gamble that an All Black could pick up the game.

On the plane home there were lots of little conversations going on between the boys. Tree and Laurie stayed right out of it. The players knew that Rupert Murdoch of News Limited was bankrolling Super League and the SANZAR deal. We also knew that he was offering rugby players $30,000 a year and — thanks to the call from the agent — the league boys $200,000 a year. It seemed obvious which game was his priority.

Once back in New Zealand I went to see my boss Derek Dallow at the Davenports law firm about the WRC contracts. **The All Blacks had a meeting in Auckland the next day and I took a brief synopsis of what Derek had prepared for me. He had laid out the WRC contracts into layperson's terms so that we all knew exactly what was being offered.** I showed it to a few of the guys who were impressed by Derek's work and by the end of the week Davenports were the players' unofficial representatives. Derek stressed that all of the players should seek independent legal advice.

Over the next few days we had various meetings with Davenports and then we went to Wellington for a meeting with the NZRFU. They delivered a whiteboard presentation, putting the NZRFU's case, but it was an embarrassingly disjointed effort.

We left that meeting for a WRC meeting at Wellington airport. They had PowerPoint, video, the works. The difference between the two presentations was a stark reminder of just how professional the WRC set-up was compared to the NZRFU. I was totally impressed by the WRC. They stressed that rugby was a game for all shapes and sizes and, being rugby men, they were concerned about the future of the game. They told us that rugby was in trouble because of Super League. I remember seeing a video clip of Murdoch at the launch of Super League where he mentioned that in five years' time he thought there would be only one game played in the southern hemisphere and that would be rugby league. That alarmed us. **At that point I decided that, no matter what happened, I would be sticking with rugby.**

In terms of the decision that we were about to make, the big dilemma was the rugby unions. We knew we couldn't make this thing fly without being on side with them. Fitzy wouldn't give his All Black jersey away for any amount of money and we all felt the same, despite what a few others have said. So we had to get the NZRFU on our side. We told that to the WRC guys who said that the only people they wanted to get rid of was the IRB. They were confident that they could persuade the NZRFU to sign up with them. In hindsight, they probably should have gone to the NZRFU first. It would be interesting to see if the NZRFU would sign up to a WRC type of organisation now, considering how the IRB have treated them over the sub-hosting of the 2003 Rugby World Cup.

We knew the All Black jersey was owned by the NZRFU and we certainly didn't want to be playing in any other jersey. People would watch the All Blacks no matter who was wearing the jersey — the Baby Blacks in 1986 proved that. The New Zealand public would not care about a whole bunch of overpaid rugby players playing in a rebel competition. **It was like Fitzy told us: 'The public aren't coming to watch us. They are coming to watch the black jersey.'**

The NZRFU finally admitted to the presence of the WRC and suddenly our contracts went from $30,000 to $300,000 overnight. To me that was a little disappointing, because it showed me that the money had always been there, but the NZRFU were only willing to pay us the $30,000. That's all they thought we were worth only a few days earlier.

We realised that by promising us $300,000 each the NZRFU didn't have enough money for everyone else. **I think that might have been one of the factors for Jock Hobbs being shown the door by them soon after this 'war' ended.** He didn't care what it took to convince the All Blacks to sign with the NZRFU. I thought he did a great job for the rugby union.

Fitzy addressed the team and reminded us not to think with our pockets. He pointed out that while the NZRFU was offering us $300,000, a guy like Otago captain David Latta was going to get very little, if not nothing. Latta was one of those hard and tough grassroots rugby players who was never lucky enough to wear the black jersey but he was just as dedicated as any of us. Fitzy reminded us that we had a responsibility to everyone who played the game in New Zealand. That's what

Fitzy, who reminded us not to think with our pockets during the WRC negotiations.

people forget. They think the only thing we were concerned about was lining our pockets. But if that had been the case we would have signed with the NZRFU right there and then, with a guaranteed $300,000 for each of the next three years. **Fitzy stressed that we take our time before deciding what to do because our decision would affect a whole lot of people. It was much bigger, he said, than just the people in the room.**

There has been a lot said about how the young players within the All Blacks were railroaded at these meetings. I didn't notice them being pressured or brainwashed, although I do admit that they were probably a little unsure about speaking out because the All Black environment is a pretty intimidating one. It can make guys shut up, sit back and listen. It certainly did that to me when I first got into the side.

By now, rumours were circulating among players and press. Every rugby player I knew was giving me a call to find out what was going on. The All Blacks were all in the loop but the

WRC and the NZRFU weren't saying anything publicly. I was nominated by the powers that be within the All Blacks to go around the country and explain what was going on to all the provincial first-division players. **I jumped in a car, taking a WRC contract and an NZRFU contract with me, and I went to see various people dotted throughout the country.** I would arrive in a province and address anyone who showed up to the meeting. I showed them the WRC files and told them that the All Blacks were leaning towards those ones. I showed them the NZRFU ones as well so guys could see the disparity. I told them to contact their legal advisors and to contact me once they knew what they were doing.

I didn't know it then but I was being tracked by the NZRFU's Tony Ward and Richard Crawshaw, current and former managers respectively of the New Zealand sevens team. It was their job to find out where I had been and who I had talked to. As soon as I'd leave a meeting, they'd be organising to meet with the people I'd just addressed. Tony and I laugh about it now, but at the time there was a lot of pressure on everyone. I don't know how I would have reacted if I had run into them at the time. **These days Tony still gives me a bit of stick about the pro-WRC stance I took. He'll laugh and call me Judas. I just remind him that I am still wearing the black jersey and that if I wasn't committed to New Zealand rugby I wouldn't be here now.**

It was about this time that the team to play Australia was named. I wasn't in the side. The guys went over and they signed their WRC contracts after the test in Sydney. I signed my contract in Auckland. We had all signed under the proviso that the contracts would be held on trust at Davenports and not released until the whole thing had been confirmed. We didn't want our contracts out there until we knew this thing was going to fly.

One of the things I regret the most about the whole WRC controversy was a discussion I had with Brian Lochore at the NZRFU. He asked me to tell him which way the guys were leaning if it ever came down to a vote. I promised to call and tell him but with everything else that was happening I forgot to ring him. The next time I saw him he pulled me up about it. 'Rushie, you promised you would talk to me about it. You said you would ring me and you didn't. I am very disappointed in you.' I felt about two feet tall. **Letting down BJ was the worst feeling I had throughout the whole ordeal, because in my books he was the same type of bloke as Richie Guy — rugby was in his veins and all he wanted was the best for the game.** I can't say he was a childhood hero of mine because I never saw him play, but I had heard all the stories and I knew he was a man of mana.

While BJ was on the side of the NZRFU there was a guy on the WRC side who I had a lot of respect for. Geoff Levy, a South African, was the person that addressed the All Blacks at Wellington Airport. He was another guy with a real passion for rugby. He was articulate and came across as very professional and I'm sure the way he handled himself helped the players feel comfortable with what the WRC was offering. However, there was still no evidence of who the backer was, so as far as the players were concerned it was still a bit up in the air. Fitzy tried to put the pressure on Geoff Levy to get more information, pointing out that the All Blacks were starting to take a little heat from the public, the media and the NZRFU. Geoff reacted by depositing $US100,000 for each player into Davenports' trust account. **We were told that money was ours regardless of whether WRC went ahead or not. By doing that the WRC ensured that we had a little more confidence that they did indeed have a big backer behind them.**

A couple of days later we had a video conference, organised by the WRC, with the South African and Australian players. Basically it was set up for the benefit of the South Africans who were coming under a lot of pressure from Louis Luyt. As far as we were concerned the video conference was going to offer us peace of mind as well. Before the conference the Australians had said that they were all in, the South Africans had said they were all in and, by now, the All Blacks had intimated that we would sign the contracts and commit to the WRC once the NZRFU had come on board.

When François Pienaar didn't show up to the video conference we all looked at each other wondering what the hell was going on. **We thought immediately that the Africans had done a runner. Hennie le Roux was on camera saying, 'Don't worry about François. He is just caught in traffic.'** Le Roux was making noises about the pressure they were under from the SARFU but Fitzy and the Wallaby captain Phil Kearns reminded him that the Africans had signed contracts and said, 'You have to honour them. That's what we all intend to do.' Right then . . . that was the moment when I thought the WRC was doomed. The South Africans — who were the World Champions — had to be involved. What transpired was that Luyt had gone to each of them, asked them how much the WRC was paying them, and paid that amount into their bank accounts that same day. The money was speaking again. When it came down to a choice between mates and money, the South Africans took the view that you can always make new mates.

The provinces in South Africa still wanted to come aboard the WRC but once Kerry Packer, the main financier for the WRC, saw that the Springboks weren't prepared to sign he decided to pull the plug on the whole thing.

Within days the provinces within New Zealand signed deals with the NZRFU along with All Blacks Josh Kronfeld and Jeff Wilson. I certainly didn't blame them because at the end of the day they had to look after themselves. I remember at an NZRFU press conference — which Jeff and Josh attended along with a number of the top provincial players — they sat there talking about how committed they were to New Zealand rugby and the future of the game here. It's ironic that of all the people paraded by the NZRFU that day only Jeff and Ian Foster played out their careers in New Zealand. The rest ended up taking contracts overseas. Heck, John Leslie ended up turning his back on New Zealand and played for Scotland!

I don't blame guys for signing up to play overseas. Some of

the money they are offered is impressive. I have been offered massive contracts — one to play in France for $300,000 a year — but I have always turned them down. I'd be lying if I said money wasn't still a factor in keeping me in the game, but I like to think it's only one of the reasons. **The money I earn in New Zealand is good but it doesn't compare to what I could get in Japan or Europe. But at the end of the day the most important thing to me in rugby is the black jersey.** It was always my dream as a young fella to wear the black jersey and I would never walk away from that. No amount could compensate for the feeling I have every time I run out there wearing a silver fern on my chest. That's a priceless feeling.

The thing that disappointed me about Josh and Jeff wasn't that they signed with the NZRFU but that they didn't front up to the guys beforehand. In the morning they were with the All Blacks and that very afternoon they were on television announcing their decision to sign with the NZRFU. It felt like a real kick in the guts. We were all pretty good mates and all they had to do was look us in the eye and be up front about it.

I give Goldie credit for coming back and saying in his book *Seasons of Gold* that his only regret was that he didn't front us. Good on him. I congratulate him for that. **It was never about money for Jeff Wilson. He proved that when he took a year off in 2000.** And then, even though he was playing well enough to make the All Blacks in 2002, he pulled the plug on his career because he knew he didn't have the passion for rugby any more. It takes a lot of courage to leave the game.

When it was obvious that the WRC deal was not happening, Fitzy addressed the All Blacks at Wellington's Airport Hotel. He told us: 'Make your own deals with the NZRFU.' Hobbs' attitude was: this is the contract, it's not changing, sign it or leave it. They had us over the barrel but no one was complaining. We all signed — the standard contract was $200,000.

As for that guaranteed $US100,000 we were given by the WRC, we had to give it back. When it became obvious the

Jeff Wilson impressed me when he said in his book that he regretted he didn't front us before signing with the NZRFU.

WRC deal was dead we were told that we would be released from our contracts with the WRC but we would have to give the money back. Most of the guys accepted that but five guys sued and settled out of court. **The battle for the cash also had one of my team-mates' lawyers attempting to sue me, arguing that I had guaranteed the payment.** It was a ridiculous argument and one that never went to court but it was another sign of the power of money. It can corrupt people.

In my opinion, the whole WRC v NZRFU incident saved rugby. A lot of our boys would have been playing Super League if all they had been offered was the original $30,000 the NZRFU had put on the negotiating table. I certainly have no regrets about my role. A lot of people have bagged me for being a traitor and a turncoat, but all I will say to those people is I am still training, I am still running, and I am still trying to make that New Zealand sevens team. **Anyone who has trained with us will tell you that you need to be committed to New Zealand rugby to go through all of that.**

Credit needs to be given to the NZRFU, who didn't take any action against anyone in the All Blacks who had been involved in the WRC negotiations. They could have ended careers, they could have dropped players, but they didn't do any of that. Looking back it was a tremendous reaction on their part. There were no divisions in the team and when we toured Italy and France at the end of the year we were able to give Laurie Mains the perfect send-off with a 37–12 win in Paris.

Getting paid for it

BEFORE PROFESSIONAL RUGBY CAME along everyone was making money from the game except for the players. I'd been going to the Hong Kong sevens since 1988 and every year there were around 40,000 people there who had paid $300 each to get a seat. They sold tanker-loads of beer during the three days and the hotels were booked up months ahead. The airlines, merchandisers . . . everyone was making money. The New Zealand team meanwhile was getting $10 each a day. The tournament's sponsors would put us up in the flash Hilton Hotel but the problem was every time someone left you a message on your phone, it would cost you $5 just to clear it. To make matters worse, we eventually found out that the IRB was paying everybody the £20 ($45) a day allowance. **Every team was getting it except for us. I guess the NZRFU needed the money! It was the same for every top player.** Test matches would be sold out throughout the world, the NPC was a huge success but, again, very little if anything would trickle down to the players.

Things were so bad for us financially that I was on the look-out for any way possible to raise money to pay my mortgage. One day, when we were driving to the stadium I noticed that all these people were milling around the T-shirt stalls. When I had a closer look it turned out that all the shirts people were buying were ones with silver ferns or 'New Zealand' printed

Studying for my law degree . . . to the best of my knowledge this is the only picture of me ever taken 'over the books'.

on them. I figured we should get in on the deal so I bought a whole bunch of T-shirts, scanned our autographs on the back and made a few dollars for the boys. It was the only way to pay the mortgage.

At the time I was working as a lawyer at Copeland Fitzpatrick in Otahuhu and my boss Brian Fitzpatrick and I had a deal that if I wasn't at work I didn't get paid. **The last two or three years I worked as a lawyer I grossed between $10,000 and $15,000. Not a hell of a lot for a lawyer.** I tried cases in the High Court and District Court a couple of times. One of the District Court judges, Barry Morris, was a North Harbour fan. I'd walk into the court and we'd talk rugby. 'How 'bout that bloody Frank Bunce etc etc?' This would go on for about ten minutes. I could see the other lawyers getting annoyed but, hey, when the judge is one of the ones asking you questions you can't take sides with the lawyers!

I wasn't always the one having the last laugh in the courts, though. When I went to the High Court for the first time I fell for one of the oldest tricks in the book. I stood up in my gown and wig in front of the judge and introduced myself. 'May it please your honour. Counsel's name is Rush.' The judge didn't acknowledge me. 'May it please your honour. Counsel's name is Rush.' Still nothing. 'May it please your honour. Counsel's name is Rush.' Nothing. **Then one of the other lawyers told me to turn around. He said my wig wasn't on straight, so I adjusted it. When I turned around the judge said, 'Now, that's better, isn't it?' I started muttering to myself. I found out later it's a little thing they do to all the rookies.**

Without accommodating employers a lot of guys wouldn't have been able to continue to play rugby. Most of the time I would train before work, sometimes I would run at lunchtimes, and after work was when the bulk of training was done. Almost every day throughout the season I would be off work for an hour or two getting physio. You had to have a very understanding boss. If it wasn't for Brian I would have been struggling to make ends meet.

My wife Raina, who was working at the IRD, was the main breadwinner at the time. We didn't own a house and we were expecting our first child. In 1990 she started talking crazy about how I had been there and done that with my rugby. 'It's about time you knock rugby on the head and start thinking about your career.' I still had a few unfulfilled ambitions . . . I wanted to be an All Black. At the time I had only played for Auckland, New Zealand sevens and New Zealand Maori so I compromised. I kept playing rugby and asked my old man for the section at the back of his house in Otara and built Raina a house. **That kept her happy for a few years. Come 1995, though, and she said, 'Come on. You have been in the All Blacks now. You have done everything. Give it up and get your career going.** Let's get ahead for the children.' But overnight rugby went professional and she was kicking me out the door to keep training! To be honest, she has always been very supportive. When I was in the All Blacks — even when we were struggling financially — she was always there for me. She knew it meant a lot to me because it meant a lot to her and the rest of the family.

I left Copeland Fitzpatrick because I knew I wasn't bringing in enough work. I didn't want to be a drain on them. I went to work for Davenports on the North Shore, where Derek Dallow had offered me a job. That's where I was when all the WRC stuff came up. I had lots of heart-to-hearts with Derek. One of the favourite topics was my desire to go back to law after rugby. Derek would tell me that I had spent 30 years honing my rugby skills and for me to come back into a law office and not utilise those skills — in terms of playing and then coaching — would be a waste of my talents. **He told me to go and do my rugby stuff and when I get tired of it, to come knocking on his door. It was great advice and certainly gave me the peace of mind to go out and give rugby a decent crack.**

All of the players in those days worked. Nowadays at Harbour, for instance, half the guys work and half the guys are professional. You feel sorry for the guys that have to work a full day, but what the young guys doing that don't realise is that everyone used to work fewer than 10 years ago. You'd finish work, go straight to training for a couple of hours, go home and sleep. If you were a representative player, you'd train in the morning and repeat the process. They were tough times but everyone did it.

Club rugby was where we learnt to play footie, and it was the perfect training ground. I remember my first senior game. I was playing for East Tamaki against Manukau. We had a lineout, they tapped the ball down their side and I intercepted it between their lock and halfback, shot up the sideline, stepped the winger, and ran around the fullback. I saw this guy coming across the field. He had the angle on me and he was coming pretty quick, but the angle he was running on meant I knew that if I kicked the ball infield there was no way he'd be able

Being admitted to the Bar was a great moment — getting the great All Black wing, Bryan Williams, to do the honours was even better.

to beat me to the ball. So I put in a grubber kick and started to chase it . . . and boom! The guy hit me about three seconds late. That was the first time I met Frank Bunce. He looked at me and said, 'Forwards don't bloody kick, mate.'

In another incident that first game Maurice Roberts — an abrasive player who had played over 200 games for Manukau — smacked me between the eyes after one of the first rucks because I'd pinched the ball and said, 'Well, what are you going to do about it?' I figured I had better give him something back otherwise he was going to have a go at me all day so a couple of rucks later I gave him a short right hand. After the game he came up to me and said, 'Good on yuh, boy.' I learnt then that what happened on the field didn't have to spill over into the clubrooms after the game. It was a good lesson and a good introduction to club rugby.

You learn more about footie playing for East Tamaki than you would if you found yourself in an NPC squad straight out of school like a lot of the younger guys do these days. There are so many tricks to be learnt at club level. If Roberts had done what he did to me in a Super 12 game and got away with it, and then I smacked him at the next ruck, I probably would have been given a yellow card. A lot of guys wouldn't know how to react because they haven't been through it before.

Young players these days are a little softer when it comes to their mental strength and approach to the game. But I also believe they are better prepared physically. In many ways it's harder for the younger players coming through now, because there are a lot more things competing for their time. In our days the only thing we needed to worry about was getting out there and playing your football.

Professional rugby isn't about how much a guy gets in his pocket; it's about the attitude. In that sense the Auckland team of the late 1980s and early nineties was the epitome of what a professional outfit was all about. In those days, if you got to training half an hour early you'd be one of the last there. Grant Fox would have been there for an hour and every now and then he'd grab one of the young players and tell them that it was their turn to come early to catch balls while he practised his kicks. That was the era that I was brought up in. You didn't make mistakes. **If you dropped the ball in an Auckland training you felt like you had let the whole team down. They all looked at you and you knew they felt the same thing.** It wasn't just the young guys that would get that treatment either. If an All Black dropped a ball, in many ways, it was worse for them. They were harder on themselves than they were on us.

Rugby players, if you think about it, have got it easy. Look at the cricketers. If they make a mistake, they're back in the pavilion. They get slandered every time they make a mistake. But I have a lot of admiration for them. They only get one chance. When you look at the players they are playing against, in terms of sheer numbers, I think they do bloody well on the world stage. They have been professional a lot longer than us and I am sure that rugby can learn a bit from cricket in this country.

Having said that, every team that I have played in has had guys with the professional attitude, the type of guys that don't accept mistakes. But the great teams have 15 guys like that. And that's what was the great strength of that Auckland team — and the Canterbury team of today. From their coaching staff through to the reserves, they have a professional attitude. That's why they win.

Players train a lot more these days. Teams will assemble in the morning, train, have video sessions and train again in the afternoon before a weights session. **Rugby is treated like a job, which in a way is sad because I still play rugby for fun. It is a job, but I try to play for the same reason I always have — enjoyment.** I hope it never becomes just a job for me. People only work to make enough money so they can retire. I never want rugby to be that sort of thing for me. I don't want to *have to be there.* I want to *want to be there.* There's a difference.

I think in the professional game as well, the reasons for young guys to play has changed. For us, it was always about the challenge of wanting to be in the team. It's still the same these days in the sense of wanting to be as good as you can be. I am sure the guys wearing the All Black jersey at the moment would happily pull on that jersey if they weren't being paid, but there is that little thing called money. **For many young players the lure of the money is just as great as the lure of the jersey now.** They forget that there are only 15 jobs at the top of this industry and some of them are sidetracked by short-term financial gain. They lose sight of the reason they started playing the game — to wear that black jersey. That mentality has changed the game.

Another sad thing is that so many players opt to leave New Zealand for Japan or Europe far too early in their careers. I admit that nowadays it is harder for players to get lucky breaks. Because of the low profile of club rugby, for instance, unless you are in a Super 12 or NPC team you can be lost to representative rugby very early on. So those players that miss out early on in their careers bail. They leave New Zealand. The simple truth is we cannot afford to lose those players. **Our player base is shrinking. We can only hope that many of the senior guys that turn their back on New Zealand rugby return and put something back into the game.** The perfect example in that sense is Stu Forster. He's a tight bastard but after he finished with Otago and played in Ireland for a couple of years, he returned to New Zealand rugby and helped Hawke's Bay win the second division title. I know many of the youngsters in the Bay team learnt a lot from Stu (some of it even on the field). Now he's working for the union. We need a lot more senior pros like Stu in the game to come back and play that role.

To me, the biggest thing that has changed in the professional era are the fans. For the most part they are still die-hard supporters that want the best for their teams. But there is a large element out there now that expects entertainment. They demand victories because they have paid big money and they know the money is now going to the players. In the old days, they paid their money, the boys played and if they lost, well, it

Zinny Brooke and Arran Pene hold Stu Forster up for the camera. Stu will say he carried these guys often enough on the field.

was okay. They did their best. But today they know the players are getting paid a lot of money and they expect wins. Nothing else will do. The expectation of the public is much higher now. I don't think that just because a player is getting paid expectations should be higher. I don't care how much money you are getting, the fact is when Jonah Lomu is running straight at you, the last thing on your mind is how much you are being paid that week. You are thinking about a lot of different things at that moment.

You can also apply that rationale to the media as well. We all know that the game now has changed because everything that happens off the field is highlighted. That's just part of the territory now for players. Again, something in my era players didn't have to worry too much about.

When I had my car accident in 1998 I was stalked by the *Sunday News*. **A friend rang up and told me that there was a photographer parked outside my house. I didn't believe him. That sort of thing just doesn't happen in New Zealand. But, sure enough, when I checked, there he was, camped outside hoping to catch me driving while I was disqualified. He was there for two days.**

Media are quick to jump on players nowadays. They don't really worry about the people they criticise. You get a guy like Keith Quinn, who I have a lot of respect for. After we won the gold medal in Manchester he came out and said that the only reason I was in the side was because Gordon Tietjens didn't have the heart to drop me. That really annoyed me. I would have thought that with all of his experience he would know a thing or two about rugby by now. He wasn't at the training camps. He hadn't spoken to Titch, but I guess he's entitled to his opinion. The fact is I thought I had one of my better tournaments for New Zealand at Manchester.

It was interesting to see in a rugby magazine recently that Quinn and Grant Nesbitt got a bit of a serve from one of their own, DJ Cameron, who I believe is also a good journo. Well, they were onto DJ in the next issue like a ton of bricks. Not so much fun when you're on the receiving end.

I also had a run-in with Martin Devlin on Radio Sport. He rang me for an interview after we'd lost in Hong Kong. During the introductions he said I was past it and that the team had no heart (not a great way to elicit conversation!). I should have hung up there and then. I started giving one-word answers as a hint that I really didn't want to talk to him. In fact, I ended up saying that, but he kept on pressing. He might have thought it was funny, but if he was sitting in front of me, I would've clocked him. To his credit, he rang back and apologised. But it was too late as far as I was concerned. **They said it was good radio. I didn't think so. Funny thing is, I still think Marty is okay. His good mate Mike King keeps telling him I'm after him.**

I feel sorry for today's young players, though. Some of the things that have happened off the field during my time in rugby, if they had happened nowadays guys would be crucified in the press. They have to put up with much more scrutiny. In the old days it was just looked upon as guys letting off steam and having a bit of a laugh. Ah, the joys of touring. There's a chapter in that.

Mar del plastered

WHEN PEOPLE LOOK BACK at my career — if they ever do — no doubt the thing that they will associate me with the most will be sevens and, I guess, the Commonwealth Games. Two gold medals in two attempts with the sevens team have ensured that.

One of my proudest moments in sevens, however, came in 2001 when we won the World Cup, even though I was in a plane somewhere over the Pacific nursing a broken leg at the time.

I broke the leg in a game against England in Mar del Plata, Argentina. We had been pretty comfortable in our early game and it was our last pool game against the Poms. I really thought the team was on the verge of something special. We were playing so well. I played the first couple of minutes and then Karl Te Nana made a tackle and flipped a guy onto the ground and, somehow, they both landed on me and shattered my right leg. **My thigh bone had been driven through to the top of my lower leg bone and had shattered everything on the way through.**

In that instant there was no pain; it just felt numb. But then the pain kicked in . . . it was like nothing I had felt before. The game was continuing and all I could hear was Craig Newby yelling at me, 'Get up!' I'd left a hole in the defensive line and the English took advantage of that and scored. But I knew I was gone. I could see a big lump in my sock, which was either

Adios! The end of my World Cup campaign in Mar del Plata, Argentina, 2001.

swelling or a bone sticking out. It was a bone. **I was put on a golf cart and taken off the field. The driver must have been in a hurry because he did about 100 kph to the sideline. Every time we hit a bump it was like my leg was being broken again.**

When Wardie jumped in the ambulance with me we both knew that my tournament was over. We got to the hospital and I was just thankful that Argentina's team doctor had come with us because this place was third world. There was rubbish on the floor, tiles missing off the walls . . . the hospital was pretty average. I was pulled into a holding room and pleaded with someone to give me some drugs to take the edge off. Wardie went off to try to sort things out and a doctor came in with another patient. It was an old, old lady. She must have been 100 years old, just skin and bones. They wheeled her in next to me. We were about one foot away from each other and because neither of us could move we just stared at each other. I could smell her breath . . . I was convinced she was going to die right there in front of me. Then Wardie got back and asked what was going on and I told him to move her away from me. He gave her trolley a little push and about a minute later her family arrived. We wanted some privacy so he went to pull the curtain across. There was a big splash of dried blood down the side of the curtain. The place was a nightmare. I just wanted to get out of there.

Eventually the x-rays came back and they confirmed that my leg was broken and I was told that it was unlikely I would be able to play rugby again. I got my leg in plaster — from my hip to my foot — and they asked me if I wanted to stay in the hospital for a couple of days until the swelling went down. I was out of there so fast! I figured I could guts it out back at the Sheraton Hotel. I got some drugs into me and after that everything was goooood.

Back at the hotel, all the guys were waiting for me. They were a bit down and feeling sorry for me. I was rooming with Jonah and he went downstairs to get me some steak and chips — my first bit of red meat for a long time. **I felt a bit bad eating in front of the big fella. He could only eat the Titch diet: pasta and beans and shit like that. After a while Jonah couldn't take it any longer and he whipped downstairs and came back with some spaghetti and toasted sandwiches.** He stayed up all night to look after me.

Early in the morning, around 6 am, I heard a little tap on the door. It was the great Fijian player, Waisale Serevi. He had just heard that I had broken my leg and he wanted to come up and offer his best wishes. 'We really want to win this World Cup but we don't want to win it this way. I will pray for you. I want to see you back out there some day. I want to play against you again.' It was a special moment. Here was my biggest adversary in sevens just spending time with me.

In the morning I had to make the decision whether I would

I knew the big guy would do the damage. Here, Jonah poses with Karl Te Nana after securing victory in the final of the World Cup.

stay in Argentina and watch the boys or head home and have the operation. I spoke to our physio Kev McQuoid and rang the All Blacks' doctor John Mayhew; they both agreed I should get back to New Zealand and get the op done as soon as possible. A couple of hours later it was time to leave. I don't know why but I was feeling pretty chirpy. I guess I was resigned to the fact that it would be at least six months before I could even walk on the leg properly. **I just wanted to get home and get under the knives of Stu Walsh and Bruce Twaddle, two of the best surgeons around.**

I wanted to just sneak off, but the boys wouldn't have that. They wheeled me down to the bus by the lobby. In the sevens team — and the All Blacks as well — if you leave a tour you have to do a haka before you depart. If, for instance, we are on tour in England and when it's time to head back to New Zealand you decide to stay on in London, you have to do a haka. Your team-mates get to choose the time and place, and obviously they pick the most public place. So, as I was being taken down to the lobby I told Karl Te Nana that there was no way I was going to be able to do the haka. 'Whatever, bro. Rules are rules. Can't break the rules.'

They wheeled me to the lobby and I started saying goodbye to everyone. **It was okay until I started to say goodbye; it was an emotional time. And then they cracked out this haka. It would have woken up the whole hotel. The look on their faces made it obvious to me that we were going to win the World Cup.** I couldn't hold the tears back. It was one of the most emotional moments of my career. Before I got on the bus the guys all came up to me, shook my hand, and said a few words. They said they'd leave nothing in the tank. The big fella didn't say much. 'I can't promise you we are going to win but I can promise you I will run until I drop.' He had that look in his eye, which I recognised from minutes before the 1998 Commonwealth Games final. Jonah was determined that New Zealand would win the World Cup. Awesome!

I got on the plane with the Australian doctor John Best, who happened to be flying home at the same time. He looked after me so well it was embarrassing. I had someone on board in case anything went wrong. We had been flying for about an hour when we heard that Australia and New Zealand were set to meet in the final. Before he gave me my dose of sleeping pills and pain-killers I asked him to check with the pilot to see if there was any word on who won the Cup final. He came back with a big smile on his face and told me the Australians had clinched it. **'Oh shit! Give me the drugs mate. Knock me out.' The drugs started working almost immediately, and just before I was about to fall asleep he whispered, 'I was just pulling your leg. Your boys won it.'** But as I was falling asleep I didn't know which one was the lie. I didn't know we'd beaten the Aussies 31–12 until I woke up a few hours later. Then I heard that the big fella had scored three tries in the final. 'I'll run until I drop.' It was great. That news made up for all the pain I was in.

If someone had said to me before the tournament that the only way New Zealand would win the World Cup was if I broke my leg, I would have done it. The World Cup was the only trophy we hadn't won, and now we had it. When I got back to New Zealand, Doc Mayhew and the All Black manager Andrew Martin were waiting for me at the airport, which was a nice touch.

A day later, when the boys got back from Argentina they came to visit me in hospital. The trouble was they arrived only minutes after I had had a tube stuck up my privates to help me wee. I wasn't able to relieve myself because of the medication I was on so they stuck this thing into me and gave me some morphine for the pain. **When the guys came in I was a mumbling idiot. In the team picture I look like I'm drunk. Once that tube began to work I was literally pissed!**

There have been a lot of highlights since I first played for the New Zealand sevens team in 1988. But the fact is it's only the World Cups and the Commonwealth Games that people seem to remember. They forget about the tournament wins we've had in places like Durban, Dubai, Shanghai, Tokyo and

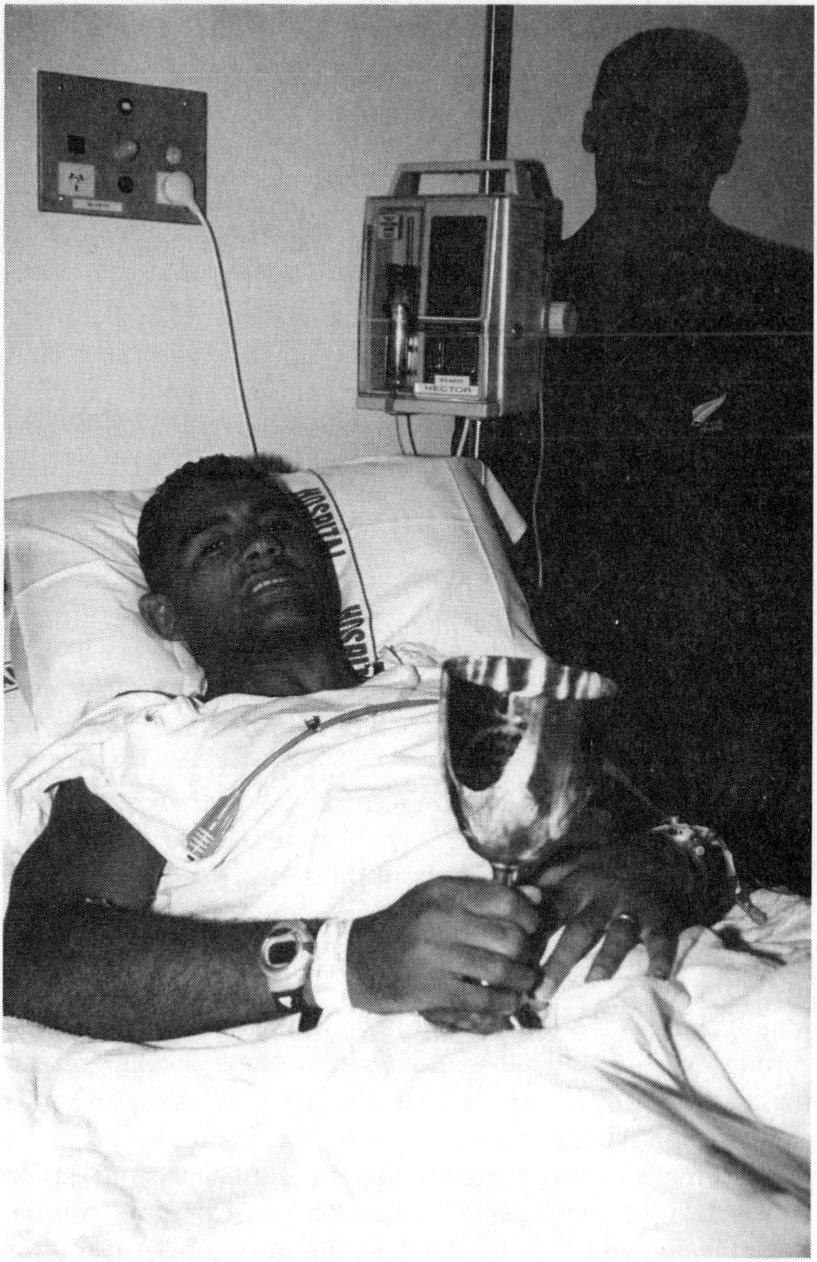

Back in Auckland and the boys — complete with the World Cup — paid me a visit in hospital.

London. Actually, since Gordon Tietjens took over in 1994 it has been New Zealand sevens' most successful era.

His record — and the team's — in the last three years is second to none. We have won the World Series three times, the World Cup and then the Commonwealth Games gold. In that time we have had a 92 per cent winning record. **The only tournament we haven't won in that time is our own one, at Wellington. That's a monkey we have to get off our backs.**

The success all starts with the management. Titch runs a successful company in Tauranga, Bay Engineer Supplies, and he manages his sporting teams along the same lines. It's interesting to watch him run the sevens team as a business and his business as a sports team. There are lots of parallels between the two. Like any team, the management is important and you have to have the right people in the right place. In our teams we've had Tony Ward as the manager, Kev McQuoid as the physio and, until recently, Keith Roberts as our fitness trainer. **Kev and Wardie are both young fellas that need to pull their heads in a bit — they're younger than me! I don't imagine that there are many teams where one of the players is older than some of the management staff.**

These guys have everything worked out to the smallest detail, but the great thing is that they are flexible and able to allow for changes, which is important when you are touring places like South America, France and the Islands.

Once we assemble — either at the adidas Institute of Rugby in Palmerston North or at our unofficial base at Mt Maunganui — we are put through fitness tests that include sprints over 40 and 60 metres, a phosphate decrement test (basically ten 40m sprints every 30 seconds, which sounds easy, but it ain't), a beep test and, depending on what sort of mood Titch is in, any number of shuttle runs. The shuttle runs consist of doing as many shuttles as you can in a minute. Sometimes we do one, sometimes we do five. Again, it sounds easy, but it ain't. After lunch on the first day we head to the gym and do our strength work. And, again, if Titch is having a bad day, it's back to the gym for another beep test.

The next day we'll start training, normally at 7 am, and have a 40-minute blowout. Then we'll have breakfast and be back out there at 11 am for the main session. There will be a lot of grid sessions and games against each other. We play tough too. **In fact, sometimes we can go through a tournament and not have as tough a game as we've had back at one of Titch's sessions. It is not uncommon for us to train for three and a half hours.** It's hard yakka, but I love it because there are some teams in the World Series that have a bit more flair than us and, at times, some teams can defend better than us on certain weeks. But there is no team in the world that is as fit as we are.

One thing Titch is extremely serious about is our diet. Up until a few years ago we weren't allowed any red meat in our diet. Now we are allowed to have it up until the Wednesday before a tournament. We aren't allowed anything fried — nothing. No potato chips, no bacon . . . not a sausage. We're not allowed fizzy drinks, ice cream or chocolate. Basically we are allowed to eat chicken, pasta and the lean meats. That's it. It's a boring diet but we're winning so we can't complain.

The tours are something else. I find the sevens tours a lot harder than the Super 12 tours. When you are playing for a team like the Chiefs you train once a day. Later in the week you button off as you build towards 80 minutes of hard, uncompromising rugby. In the sevens side, it is hard trainings every day; you are playing in hot and humid conditions, and you then play a string of matches over two days. It can be a real mental and physical test.

A typical tournament day starts with an 8 am wake-up call. By 10 am we are at the ground and by noon we are playing our first game. The next match will get under way at 4 pm and the next one at 7 pm. **Sometimes we'll play at 9 pm, depending on television requirements. It's a long day. A lot of times we won't get back to the hotel until 11 pm.** And it's not like you can sleep straight away. The adrenaline is still pumping through your body and it normally takes me three or four hours before I can

You can tell when Jonah's on the dress committee . . . 'freshie' night out in Singapore.

actually relax. The worst thing about getting back to the hotel on the first day of the tournament is the knowledge that you have to do it again the next day, and the games are, naturally, always going to get much harder.

The thing about sevens is that apart from Wellington, Hong Kong and the major tournaments like the World Cup and Commonwealth Games, the public and the media don't really take too much notice of it. I don't think you can underestimate its importance, though, because Titch has turned the team into a real breeding ground for young, talented players. A number of players have graduated from the sevens side to the Super 12 and even the All Blacks.

Sevens is a great classroom. A young player knows that when he is thrown in front of 40,000 people in Hong Kong he is either going to sink or swim. If he can swim, and make an impression, then he knows that the Super 12 scouts will take notice. It is a great

Rain, hail or sand . . . on Middle East sevens duty in Dubai. It's a great circuit.

stage on which to see what the young guys have got.

As a result of their success, each year we lose players that we have exposed to the international stage. The best thing about the 92 per cent winning record that Titch has built is that he does it with a new team every year. **If the sevens side has helped a player make a step up to the Super 12 or the All Blacks, we feel collectively proud.**

There isn't a tremendous amount of money available to the sevens guys. And maybe that's one of the reasons why we do so well. At the beginning of each new camp I pull the younger guys aside and say, 'We can't promise you money, because there's none. We can't promise you stardom, because there's not much of that, either. All we can promise you is a lot of sweat, long trainings, pasta and chicken. I don't know if any of you enjoy that, but that's the way it is. If you are here for the money and the glory you might as well walk out now because you won't fit in here. But, if you want to do all those hard yards and do what it takes, you have a chance to put on a black jersey.' Like all New Zealand's teams, before we play in the big games — like a Commonwealth Games final or at a World Cup — the thing we talk about is the jersey. That's what it's all about. I don't know much, but I do know that if you are playing rugby for any reason other than the jersey, you are not going to be successful.

We don't get a lot of recognition, although we did get nominated for a 2001 Team of the Year Halberg award. I wasn't too fussed about it, but when I got to the ceremony and saw who the other nominees were I thought we had a good chance of winning. It was great to talk to bowlers, cricketers, rowers, the basketball guys, etc and hear how hard they had trained to get there.

We didn't get anywhere near any of the awards. In fact, I think we came last in all the categories for which we were nominated. We were just happy to be there, though; to be nominated and recognised. However, I did think it was quite funny that we were one of the few teams or individuals who had actually won any competitions. I guess it's a sign of the politically correct times in this country.

Hart murmurs and Mains events

Coaches . . . sometimes you love 'em, other times you hate 'em. There is little doubt that the one coach people associate with me the most is Gordon Tietjens. But there have been others who have made an impact on me, as well as a former All Black manager of mine (whose comments have had to be edited for a PG16 book like this).

John Hart

John Hart picked me out of obscurity from an East Tamaki side to play for Auckland in 1986. It was a pretty nerve-wracking week all those years ago. He didn't say too much to me. He just pulled me aside and told me one or two things he'd like to see me do on the field. I remember his first address to the team. It was the first time I had been involved in a big team talk. We turned up for the game — a Ranfurly Shield match against Horowhenua — and I came in my No. 1s. That's the way it worked from under-16s up. **You always wore the suit and tie; it was a rugby tradition, or so I thought. It was pretty easy to spot the new boy when I walked in and everyone else had their tracksuits on.** There was no time to change so I ended up doing all the lineout drills in my suit and tie!

In the team talk Harty went right through the team and told

everyone what he expected of them. When he got to me, all he said was, 'Young Rush, just get out there and have a good time.' It was perfect. It relaxed me. **That's the thing about Harty: not only did he have a good appreciation of the game and how it could be played, but he was a very good motivator. He knew the right things to say.** He could talk you into selling your own grandmother and make you feel good about it.

Harty was somewhat of a perfectionist, always on the search for the perfect game. It was his dream. He wanted to be able to walk into the shed after a game and have absolutely nothing to complain about. And, amazingly, his Auckland teams of the late 1980s would have come pretty close to delivering that for him. Harty's Auckland team was, I believe, the best non-international team that the world has ever seen. The Canterbury team of the current era is not too bad as a provincial side. They are the best team in New Zealand — there's no doubt about that — but not many of their team are world class. That Auckland team, though, was stacked with guys who were the best in their positions in the world — John Kirwan, Joe Stanley, Grant Fox, Alan Whetton, Michael Jones, Zinzan Brooke, Gary Whetton, Sean Fitzpatrick . . . it was an incredible side. John Hart started all of that.

Laurie Mains and Harty came from the same school in the sense that they both were determined to get everything possible out of each of their players. **They did have different philosophies, though. Harty used to talk more about using your head. He'd meticulously go through game plans and make sure that everyone had a clear understanding of exactly what he wanted.** Then he would talk about the jersey, and what it meant.

Laurie came from the opposite angle. Having been an All Black himself, he talked about the jersey first. He used words like passion and pride. He'd recall famous All Black stories and try to motivate us that way. Only when that was done would he talk about the game plan.

Harty had a testimonial lunch last year and the likes of former Wallaby coach Rod Macqueen, former Springbok boss

If it wasn't for Harty taking a chance on a skinny kid from North Auckland, who knows where I might have ended up.

Nick Mallett and a host of players were invited, so it was a big deal. I knew someone that was going along so I quickly wrote a letter to Harty that I had been meaning to write ever since he was dropped from the All Blacks coaching job in 1999. **I thought he was treated very poorly after his side lost in the semi-final of the World Cup and I wanted to write to him that day, but I thought I would wait until the dust had settled.** Finally, I had the opportunity to write the letter. It was supposed to be a private note but before it could be handed to Harty someone had decided to read it out in front of the whole crowd.

'You picked me out of obscurity. Having the opportunity to start my career in that team instilled certain disciplines in me that have helped me in my rugby career no end. It was the best rugby team that I had been a part of and I am proud to have been just a small part of it. Don't worry about the lunatic fringe that have criticised you in recent times. There are lots of people out here who think you are a bloody good coach. I have always thought that the sign of a successful coach is that one day — when you have finished coaching — someone writes a letter like this, and then you will know you have made a difference to someone's life.'

I also added a PS: 'I'm still a little pissed off you dropped me from the All Blacks as early as you did!'

Laurie Mains

To me, Laurie Mains was right up there. I had tremendous respect for him right throughout my time with him in the All Blacks. **I'm not sure if the respect was mutual. I always had the feeling that he just tolerated me because I was one of Frank Bunce's best mates.** And, make no mistake about it, Frank was his boy. Frank could do no wrong. And he earned that respect from Laurie. Along with Robin Brooke, he played in every test during Laurie's four years in the All Blacks job.

I'll always have a ton of respect for Laurie because he was the first coach to pick me for the All Blacks. When I arrived at the All Blacks camp for the first time I was scared shitless of the

I'm sure my friendship with Frank Bunce helped me seal a spot in Laurie's All Blacks teams. Here I give Buncey a No. 1.

guy. At my training run we trained for about 90 minutes and then we did some fitness work at the end. He made us do about 100 down-and-ups — that's when you sprint for 10 metres, hit the deck, and then get up and do it nine more times, rest and then go through the whole process another nine times. It absolutely wrecked you. This was my first All Black run and there was absolutely no way that I was going to hold back. I gave it everything I had. Laurie was watching us all closely and was barking out encouragement — and the odd demeaning comment — at the boys. He came up to me during one of the breaks. 'Are you tired, Rushie?' **I didn't want to own up to being tired at my first All Blacks training so I said I wasn't. That was the wrong answer, obviously.** He stared at me with his hands on his hips and said, 'Never, ever bullshit your mates.' He sent me off to do the drill with the forwards and he wouldn't let me rest

Would you cross this man? Laurie Mains was a great coach and a real tough bastard.

afterwards because he wanted me to rejoin the backs and continue the drill. He came up to me again and said, 'Are you tired now?' I told him that I was. 'All Blacks are never bloody tired!' And he sent me off with the forwards again! As we were doing the drill, Stu Forster told me to 'say nothing'. So, after the drill, sure enough Laurie was waiting for me. I buttoned my lip and sure enough he moved on to his next victim.

Laurie was a tough bastard. He was so intense. You learnt very quickly to stay right away from him during the build-up to a match. If he caught anyone smiling on a test day he would blow his top. We all knew the rules. If you were a 'Dirty Dirty' — not in the test side — you knew to stay even further away from him. He had this ability to make you feel like you shouldn't even be in the same hotel as him at times. The Otago boys used to call him 'Lemons' because he always looked as though he had just had a big feed of them.

But, he got the results. The thing that made my respect for

him grow was that he changed midway through his tenure. In 1995, before the World Cup, we had a camp in Queenstown. He handed out a questionnaire that included questions like 'What do you think we are doing wrong?' And 'What do you think we can do better?' I — and a few others — thought that he was stifling the flair in the team so we all wrote that down. I tried to make the point that he had picked guys with certain skills that they had displayed in the NPC but when they got in to the All Blacks they weren't allowed to play that way. **At that period in the All Blacks, if you tried something you got told off for it. Guys were scared of having a go.** I thought that one of our major strengths was that we had a dangerous backline, so let's use it.

The next day at the camp Laurie addressed the boys. 'Right, we have all had a fair bit of input into this. We have been thinking of doing this for a long time but we didn't want to play our cards too early. We agree. We have to move the ball. We have the strength out wide. We've got the force to deliver it. My only reservation is that I don't think we are fit enough.' At that stage he eyeballed everyone in the room as though he was challenging us. 'So, we are going to be doing some work before this World Cup. Those of you who are up to it will be at the World Cup. Those of you who aren't won't be.'

He absolutely killed us at the training camp. Each day was a day of torture. All morning long the forwards would be doing contact drills. The backs wouldn't stop running. **We were worked so hard that at lunch a lot of us would have a sleep for half an hour in the changing room. Then, after a wake-up call, we'd switch roles and it would be the backs doing the contact work.** At the end of the day, we'd do fitness work! One day in Taupo he made us run 150 metres 26 times followed by 100 down-and-ups and then 30 ruck and runs, where a group of eight would sprint to a scrum machine, move it, run around a cone and hit the next target. The drills were so tough that a lot of the guys would be down to a walk by the end of the drill. But Laurie didn't care. He loved working us hard. It was all a part of his plan.

Shane Howarth was one who didn't survive the camps. He had injured his knee in one of the drills and tried to run through the pain but it got worse and worse as the day went on. Laurie went up to him and asked, **'Are you no good, Howie?' Shane said that the knee was no good. 'Well, go back to the hotel, pack your bags, and go home.' The boys couldn't believe it. Shane couldn't believe it.** He tried to take his words back and explained that the knee should be okay by the next day, but it was too late. Laurie had made up his mind. It was a reminder for all of us that he didn't tolerate any sign of weakness. There were no second chances in Laurie's world. By the end of that camp it wasn't about fitness anymore . . . it was just a mental test. The guys that were still there at the end were the guys who went to the World Cup.

It was during this time that Jonah and Laurie weren't getting along at all well. Jonah really struggled with the fitness side of things and Laurie didn't appreciate it. **The thing about Jonah is that he is never going to be able to run a three-kilometre time trial. He can't. He just doesn't have the physical ability to do that. But, you put a ball in his hand and he becomes a different man. He becomes a lethal weapon.** Rugby is not about running a beep test, and it's not about running three kilometres non-stop without a ball. Rugby is about having a ball in your hand, running around and running over people. And that's what Jonah is good at.

Jonah really struggled at the Taupo camp and Laurie thought he was just soft in the head and afraid of hard work. I knew that wasn't true because he'd been away with the New Zealand sevens side and I knew that when the stimulus was right, Jonah could, and would, do anything.

After the camp it was time for the Hong Kong Sevens and Jonah just smashed everyone. He was, along with Glen Osborne, one of the stars of the show. When he got back to New Zealand, Laurie told him that he could go to the Japan Sevens with Titch and the boys instead of staying in New Zealand and playing in the North v South All Black trial.

Reading between the lines at the time, it meant that Jonah wasn't being considered for the World Cup.

The big fella got very upset about it. **He rang me up and told me, 'I'm buggering off. I'm gonna sign for the Bulldogs. I'm going. Blow them all!' Then he hung up.** I rang his manager, Phil Kingsley-Jones, and we decided that we needed to do something in a hurry. I rang Titch and we organised a meeting with PKJ and myself. We knew we couldn't let Jonah go . . . we all knew that. PKJ had been on the phone to him calming him down. Next it was my turn to ring him. 'You can take off and sign up for the Bulldogs and get all the money and you'll be a sensational league player. But I think you are leaving some unfinished business here. Let's go down to the North-South game in Dunedin. Play one more game with the boys — me, Frank, Walter, Oz — play well and then go. Show these buggers what you have got before you go.' He agreed. They organised for me to room with him so I could keep talking to him. All the other guys tried to keep his spirits up as well.

Laurie — who wasn't coaching either team — came to see Frank and me to see if we could work it out. He wasn't in the habit of talking to Jonah himself. Once before a test match, Jonah was having bacon and eggs for breakfast and Laurie — who had been using me as a go-between — pulled me aside. **'What the hell is he eating? Go and sort him out.' I told Jonah that Laurie wasn't happy with what he was eating. 'Tell him to get stuffed!'** Laurie was waiting for me to tell him Jonah's response. The thing was, I wanted to be a test player and I didn't like the idea of returning that particular message, so I told Laurie that he was nearly finished the meal. I said to Laurie to just let him finish it and I'd talk to him later. Laurie gave me a serve and then stormed out.

Laurie is a pretty black and white character. There is no grey area with Laurie Mains. You do it his way or you don't do it. Unfortunately, that isn't the world we live in. Some people need to be talked to differently and Jonah is one of those people. If you go up to someone like Jonah and say, 'You are

Watch where you put that hand, mate! Laurie Mains often used me as a middleman between himself and Jonah when things got frosty.

going to do it my way or no way at all,' he'll respond by saying he ain't gonna do it. But, if you went to him and said, 'Jonah, can you do it this way because I feel that if you do it this way you will play well. **And if you play well, we're going to win,' Jonah would run through a brick wall for you. Frank and I explained that to Laurie. That Southern Man stuff just wasn't going to work with Jonah.** I reminded him that I had been on the sevens field with Jonah and I had heard the breath of opposing players being exhaled when the big guy ran into them. Until you hear that you can't appreciate the power of the guy. I also pointed out that I was busting my balls to make the test team myself and I knew that I was cutting my own throat by promoting Jonah, but I felt that he could be the difference between us winning the World Cup and not winning it.

To his credit, Laurie took it all on board. The big fella had a stormer in the trial. He was marking Jeff Wilson and he outplayed him. Goldie played well but the big fella was in a league of his own. After the game I went to Jonah and told him he had had a great game and said that next week there was another trial where he could prove another point. **'Nah bro. I'm off. You said one game. I've played it. I'm off.' At the after-match, Laurie came over to Frank and me and asked what he should say to Jonah. Frank told him to at least go over and tell Jonah that he'd had a good game.** Laurie strolled across the room and they had a discussion. After he walked off I went over to Jonah and asked him what Laurie said. 'He's trying to kiss my arse now.' We couldn't win!

Phil and the rest of us convinced Jonah to play in the next trials and the rest, as they say, is history. Overnight at the World Cup in 1995, he became the biggest name in world rugby. No one will ever forget his four-try haul against the English in the semi-final. But I can reveal that a few of the senior All Blacks weren't convinced that he was going to be the star of the show. Before our quarter-final against Scotland, Sean Fitzpatrick and Zinzan Brooke came to see me and expressed concern that Jonah hadn't been training too well. I went to see the big guy and told him that the senior boys didn't think he was switched on enough. I reckon you should show them what you can do, eh? **He put on his headphones and I could see his nostrils flaring so I knew he'd got the message. He destroyed the Scots.**

The measure of Laurie as a coach came later on in 1995 when we toured Italy and France. We lost the first test in Toulouse 22–15. Colin Meads, our manager, tore strips off everybody. In the midweek game before the second test we played the French B team. They hadn't lost a game for three years. The local papers were convinced this All Black side was on its way to three consecutive losses. Pinetree called a meeting. The first guy in the firing line was Tim Barry, who was touring with the team as Lion's representative. He was a good club player and was really popular with the guys. He trained with us and held his own. He was a bloody good tourist. 'Tim Barry, you can piss off.' After he left, Tree said, 'I will take the blame for that. I shouldn't have let Tim train with us. I shouldn't have let him into any of the team meetings. I blame myself. It's not Tim's fault. It's my fault. Now, for the rest of you pack of bastards. Laurie Mains: who the hell do you think you are?' Laurie was stunned . . . and annoyed. You could see it in his eyes. **'I was at the bloody test in Toulouse. I was with the French Minister of Police; we came to walk into the tunnel to get onto the field. We couldn't get there because the tunnel had been blocked off by the bloody All Blacks coach.'** Because the changing room we had been given was so small, Laurie had demanded that security block off part of the tunnel so the boys could change and warm up. He told security to let no one through. 'Not only could we not get through, the damn security wouldn't even let the French team through before the game for their warm-up. You gave them their bloody team talk!' Laurie looked at Pinetree and said, 'Fair enough.' Phew! We thought that was it. It wasn't.

'You forwards. Stu Forster and Simon Culhane have taken all the shit all week because of you bastards. You do your bloody lineouts and you clap when things go right. What are you clapping for? You're only doing your job!' All the forwards' heads dropped. **'You talk about blowing rucks . . . you couldn't blow a hen off its bloody nest.' The forwards were shrinking minute by minute.** 'I look at you guys and I have never seen so much skill in one team room in my whole life. I'll tell you something. In my day we didn't have half the skill of you boys. Not even a bloody quarter. But I tell you what. We were scared of no bastard. And you jokers were last week.' That really hit home.

Then he turned his attention to the backs. The night before he had been at a function where the topic of black wingers came up. Chester Williams, Emile N'tamack and Jonah Lomu's names came up at the function. 'Jonah you did bugger all last week. And last night I felt like getting up there and saying we have the worst one out of the three of them.' I had never seen anyone talk to Jonah like that. But he took it on the chin. Then Meads finished up: 'Right, let's get to training. These blokes are

Thanks 'Tree'. Your team talk after the Toulouse test in 1995 has helped me earn a lot of money on the after-dinner speaking circuit.

talking about whitewashing us. You midweek boys, it's up to you.' And he was gone. We had the best training run I have ever been involved in. We won the second test in Paris 37–12.

Laurie developed so much throughout his four years in charge of the All Blacks. **It's funny to think back at how distant he was with Jonah early on and compare the relationship they had after the French series.** At the end of the trip Jonah had joined Zinny and Robin Brooke and carried Laurie off the field. I have never seen that happen to an All Black coach. It was the perfect sign-off for Mains — a big win with a team that was united behind him.

Before the test at our last training run, after a big midweek win, Frank and Robin dropped three or four balls each. Laurie was ropable. He stood up in front of the team and said: 'Frank Bunce and Robin Brooke . . . you have got until 6 pm to tell me whether you want to play in this game. Because the way you trained you don't want to be there. I've got two guys on stand-by who would give their left arms to be there, so you come and see me before dinnertime.' Robin and Frank were the two guys who had played every test under Laurie and here he was threatening to drop them for the last one. Both of them went to see Laurie and got a bit of a telling off.

Earlier at the training Laurie called Oz across to tell him that he would be replacing Jeff Wilson in the team. **Oz reacted by sprinting across the field high fiving and yahooing. Laurie looked at me and said, 'I have no bloody idea how that boy has made it as far as he has!'**

That night at the captain's meeting — where no coaches are ever allowed to attend — Fitzy asked all the boys what Laurie had done for them. I got up and said that he'd made me an All Black and that was something that I would never forget. 'I owe him a big effort tomorrow.' I was ready to play the test right there and then.

On the morning of the test Laurie threw us a little bit. Normally the forwards go through their lineout calls and the backs walk through some moves at about 10 am and after breakfast you chill out until game time. In the spare time you go to the manager's room to pick up your jersey. But this time Laurie changed it. He called a meeting at 10 am and we all went into a room where he'd laid out all the jerseys on a table. **'This is my last test. I want to hand the jerseys out to you.' He called out every player's name. He handed over the jerseys and then said a few words about every single player in the room.** It was a very emotional moment. It was also a masterstroke. There was no way we were going to lose Laurie's last test. No way.

Peter Thorburn

A guy I owe a lot to in rugby is Peter Thorburn. He was the man who first selected me in the New Zealand Sevens side in 1988 and then he convinced me to leave Auckland and join North Harbour. He was a real character. A deep, deep thinker. He would always be coming up with all sorts of strange moves. In different NPC games we'd have 15 men in a lineout, a 15-man wall at a tap penalty, a 15-man scrum — things that

Brad Meurant (left) and Peter Thorburn . . . two North Harbour coaching stalwarts.

Buck Shelford. I played with him, against him and was coached by him. Awesome!

hadn't been seen before. He was one of the first coaches to really take the time to make sure his players were looked after off the field. He was old school in a lot of ways, though. He was hard and a coach I'll always have respect for.

Buck Shelford

I played with Buck Shelford in the New Zealand Maori side and he was my coach in my last seasons with the North Harbour NPC team. He carried the same mana that he had as a player in the coaching role. All the boys had massive respect for him. It could have been hard for him because, with guys like Frano Botica and myself, he'd played with us and now he was coaching us. But there was never a problem because we had far too much respect for him. I remember playing for Auckland Maori against the North Harbour Maori in the late 1980s and Frano and Buck were both in the Harbour side. **I was playing for Auckland and our coach came in to give his team talk. 'Buck Shelford. Boy! You fellas are in trouble. When that fella starts to run he's hard to stop. Don't know how you fellas are going to do that. Good luck, though.** And Frano. Boy! Those dancing feet. You are never gonna catch that fella. Anyway boys, good luck, eh. I'll see you at the after-match.'

When he left our captain said: 'Bugger it boys, let's do it for the coach!'

They're gonna hate me for this

Rugby has taken me around the world and brought me into contact with a raft of personalities. In my last book, *Gold Rush*, I jerked quite a few of the boys and they gave me a fair bit of stick for being so honest. I promised them all I wouldn't do it again but I just can't resist. It's time to get nervous again fellas . . .

BRAD MEURANT was never a big fan of me or of Glen Osborne, or Frank Bunce or Walter Little, or Peter Woods. It all stemmed from a game in his first year in charge at North Harbour in 1993. We had the wind in the first half and he came out at halftime to have a word with us.

'Come here you black bastards!' He looked pretty fiery so we all huddled up to have a listen to what he had to say for himself. 'When the bloody wind is behind you [and he held his hand up above his head and moved his fingers] and your hair is blowing like this, let's kick the bastard every now and then!' Then he stormed off. In the second half we ran everything and scored 40 points. He didn't talk to us for the next two years. For as long as I can remember he just named the team thus: 'And the backline — Ant Strachan, Warren Burton . . . Brown Brothers.'

The Brown Brothers. Me, Glen Osborne, Frank Bunce, Walter Little and Peter Woods. Brad Meurant loved us all.

GORDON TIETJENS is all about discipline, work ethic . . . that's Titch in a nutshell. He expects a lot out of us. **He expects us to work hard and you know he isn't asking you to do something he wouldn't do himself because he has a very strong work ethic.** If we are training at 7 am he would have been up at six working out in the gym. If training was starting at a more civilised hour Titch would have been to his office at Bay Engineer Supplies and done an hour's worth of work there before fronting up to put us through our paces.

It's a hard case watching him in public. If for whatever reason you are a little reluctant to stop and talk to people on a particular day, you just get in behind Titch. You are assured of a quick passage because he just pushes his way in everywhere. And he's not afraid to demand things. If he is on a plane and he doesn't like his seat, he'll make sure to change it.

On one trip, Titch wanted to change seats so he patrolled the cabin to find some unoccupied seats. He found three of them next to a lady who had put her bags in them to stop people from sitting down. She had obviously planned to stretch out after take-off. Instead of continuing to look for other seats, he just moved all the bags and sat by the window, put his earplugs on and went to sleep!

Titch has been touring for years and he knows all the tricks. No matter what hotel we are staying at, he will go into the room and sniff it. If he smells the slightest scent of smoke he demands a new room. So whenever we walk into a hotel now, our manger Tony Ward knows Titch will always come back downstairs to complain. Wardie has learnt not to wait. Now he just starts the process of getting a new room for Titch straight away because recently Titch has started complaining about views as well.

When Titch talks, you better listen. Here he gives the boys the message at the 2001 Sevens World Cup.

I have never known him to be happy in a hotel.

Once in South Africa, when the team were all suffering from diarrhoea, Titch thought he would be brave and wore white rugby shorts when we went out shopping. **He didn't realise it, but he had had a little accident. We were right bastards because we didn't tell him. He spent the next few hours walking around this big shopping mall with a big brown stain on his pants.** We thought it was funny at the time . . . until Titch took it out on us at training.

WE WENT to a mayoral function in Uruguay and in conjunction with the event they put on for us was the finish of a 10 kilometre running race. Hundreds of people were in the event and there were about 5000 spectators lining the streets. We got invited to watch the finish. We got there and sat down. Craig Newby and Justin Wilson must have got a little bored because they snuck around the corner, stripped down to their sandshoes and shorts and ran towards the finish line. **The Mayor, the President of Uruguay and all the other dignitaries rushed for their seats to watch the finish.** When we saw Newby and Wilson we all burst into applause and everyone around us thought that they must have been the winners. For the record, it was Justin Wilson by a nose. It was quite funny at the time but we got into a bit of trouble for that stunt. I'm not sure how they came up with the scheme. I must have turned my back on them for a minute . . .

WHEN I went away on my first trip with the New Zealand Sevens side in 1988 I invited my mum and dad to the farewell function. My old man, Merv, asked me to get him a beer. I showed him where the bar was and told him to go for it. He got himself a jug of Lion Red and he asked the barman, 'How much?' and the guy told him it was free. I didn't see my old man again that night. My father was a real character. He was always supportive of all of his kids. But, even though I knew he was proud of the things I have achieved in the game, he didn't like to show it. I remember one day I scored four tries for North Harbour. After the game he came up to me and said, 'What are you doing scoring four tries? You should be setting them up!'

The real strength in our family came from my grandmother. She had 13 kids — 12 of them were home deliveries. She brought up the family for a long time on her own because Papa used to have to come to Auckland to find work in the freezing works or on the wharves. **Whenever you went to her house she always had panakeke (bread) there for us. You never sat down at her house because she didn't like people not working. She hated laziness.** I got into trouble with her once when I was late for a game up at the school. I was supposed to be milking the cows but, because I was in a hurry, I had the idea of half filling the milk bucket with water. I thought it was a great scheme. She caught me. I couldn't sit down for a week.

TONY WARD is always joking about how there are too many brown fellas in the team, so when sevens rugby finally went professional he took the opportunity to have a bit of fun with us. The NZRFU had instigated three different types of contracts for the team: A, B and C. They were all dependent on how much time you had spent in the team. If you were in the Commonwealth Games or World Cup teams you'd get an 'A' contract and if you only played one or two tournaments in a year you were on a 'C' contract.

When Wardie was explaining the contracts to us he said that the 'A' was for the Aryan Brotherhood. 'B' was for the black arses, which were the Maori, and 'C' was for the coconuts. We all had a bit of a laugh, but Wardie had no idea that a day later the NZRFU's CEO David Rutherford would arrive at camp to explain the A, B and C contracts. I have never seen Wardie so white. He was looking at me, hoping that I wouldn't say anything to the big boss. I let him off the hook, but I got him back a few weeks later. The team was invited to the Waitangi Day celebrations at Government House where the Governor-

Tony Ward (right) and Craig De Goldi. Stay out of the pictures, Wardie . . . you've got Treaty obligations.

General hosted a tea party. We taped a sign to Wardie's back that said *Tino Rangatiratanga* (Honour the Treaty).

THE NEW breed of sevens player is a funny sort of character. Alan Bunting and Tafai Ioasa's big thing is to take three sleeping pills on a journey home and see who can stay up the longest. They did it on the plane at the beginning but then they got a bit smart and thought they would start doing it from the hotels before even getting to the airport. They haven't fallen asleep at the terminal yet; they just walk around looking dopey.

WE WENT to a function in Japan and they had a DJ pumping out the sounds. He asked for a theme song from each team. **They wanted to give us 'Men In Black' but we'd had enough of that song so Craig Newby and Craig De Goldi requested a song by Tupac Shakur called 'Hit 'em Up' in which every third word is an expletive.** They were on stage reciting the words. If only I had had a camera to catch the look on Titch's face. He was completely dumbfounded. He must really worry about the future rugby players of this country.

It's a good thing Titch didn't know me in my earlier days. When I was at varsity I was introduced to the Auckland nightlife by my cousins. **Every weekend for three years I was dragged along to a club called Cleopatra's.** We were playing rugby at East Tamaki and our coach Ron Reti always used to have a go at us for going out on Friday nights. Every Saturday morning he'd line us up and check our eyes and breath. We would always get away with it until he'd come to Alex Matagi. Alex had these huge eyes and he'd give us away every time because they were always bloodshot.

At the nightclub, none of us had much money because I was a student and my cousins had only just started working. We only had one set of clothes each. Between the four of us we'd share the clothes out and mix and match until everyone looked reasonable. If we went back to the club the next night we'd just swap clothes again. We thought no one knew, but it turned out most of the people at the club just felt sorry for us! **We didn't have a car so we used to get dropped off by Aunt Francis and take the bus home on Sunday mornings. Heading back to South Auckland we just used to pretend we were on our way to church!**

TUSI PISI and Chris Smiley, two of the new boys in the sevens side, made the trip to Japan this year. In the Japanese hotels they have porn channels on the televisions in each room but the private parts of the actors are blurred out. I walked into their room one day and they were both sitting there squinting. I asked them what they were doing. 'Bro, if you squint your eyes the blurry bits become clear. I tried it and it worked!' After that, every time I walked into anyone's room they were all sitting there squinting at the television.

JUSTIN WILSON is the new Glen Osborne of New Zealand rugby. He's not dumb — like Oz — but he did tell me that fifth form was the best four years of his life, which gives you a pretty good idea. He does some pretty stupid things. He has a habit of walking into closed glass sliding doors. He does it every tour. He's always losing things as well. Both he and Craig Newby made fools of themselves on tour in South America. **They were single at the time and they bought a phrase book so they could talk to all the young girls. They called it the Chicktionary.**

IN SOUTH Africa, we went to a lion safari park where we were told that the lions were pretty ferocious at feeding time. We thought that was awesome so we jumped in the cars and watched the keepers chucking meat to the lions. But the lions weren't interested. They didn't even move. We were pretty disappointed. We were in the van behind the Welsh team. They were obviously a little miffed with the lazy lions as well. They'd pulled up alongside them and the lions were just lying around the car doing absolutely nothing. Next minute you see one of the windows open and out comes a hand with a water bottle in it and he squirts this lion square in the face. The lion leapt up on the van, ripped the window wipers off and tried to break the glass. The Welsh boys were terrified, but at least we got to see some action.

AT THE nationals with the Harbour team I roomed with Tusi Pisi, Luke McCalister and Chris Smiley. Before the final day of a tournament I always like to have a shave, but I'd forgotten my shaving cream. **I asked the boys if they had any shaving gear I could use and Tusi said, 'We don't shave bro.' Jeez, I'm getting old.** Hell, I used to play with Luke's dad, Charlie, in the New Zealand Maori team in 1987.

JOSH BLACKIE is another sevens player who isn't a rocket scientist. He does okay academically but commonsense things tend to pass him by. We call him Lagi, short for palagi — because there aren't too many of them white fellas in the team. Once we were going from London to Wales in a bus and crossed the famous Severn Bridge. We explained we were going into Wales and told him to get all the passports ready for the customs check. He shot around and collected all the passports. Everyone was watching him do this and everyone knew we didn't need a passport to get into Wales. I told him that we could collect air points as well, so he'd better get everyone's air points details. So off he went . . . we were on a bloody bus!

I GOT into trouble once on a tour to Japan. We had a real young side over there for the tournament and the French coach instructed his team to get stuck into our young fellas. We knew that would be their tactics, but it was a bit over the top. **Craig De Goldi got head-butted and smacked the guy who hit him but Goldi was the one who got sent off. I was 'rested' for that game and I was fuming.** We won the game, which was a bit of a bonus, and as we were walking off the ground, a TV camera was stuck in my face: 'What do you think about the sending off?' I said that it was better to get a red card than wave a white flag. TVNZ's Keith Quinn and all the other media boys hooked into me for that.

CRAIG NEWBY, on his first trip away with the sevens side to Dubai, got injured and didn't play in the tournament. So he hooked up with another of the injured boys, Rua Tipoki, and they hit the turps. It was the last day of the tournament and while the rest of the boys went back to the hotel to relax for the seven hours between games, those two stayed at the ground to look after our gear. By the time we got back to the ground, they were hammered. After the final, which we won, Newbs got all emotional and started crying. As soon as I saw the tears I knew that the story was going to end up in this book. **I went up to him and said: 'There is something we have to sort out right now. There is no crying on rugby trips.' He thought I was serious and started crying again!** Hanging out with Rua Tipoki was always trouble.

ONCE WHEN the Mongrels sevens team went up to Singapore for a tournament, my club team, Takapuna, went up as well. For some of them, this was their first rugby trip abroad and they got a bit happy at the bar and decided to strip down and run on the field during the final. As most people know, in Singapore there are very strict laws about things like that. The authorities cane people they find guilty of vandalism and it wasn't that long ago that they did the same to anyone with long hair. **And there are our boys doing a streak on the cricket ground in the middle of town. The cops were trying to find them for the rest of the time we were there.**

The day before, one of the young guys had gone shopping and he ended up paying $30 for a Rolex watch from some guy on a street corner who had taken him to a tiny little shop. Before he'd even got back to the hotel the bloody thing had broken so he went back and the guy that had sold him the fake watch explained that his was not a proper shop so the cops wouldn't interfere. Our man came back to the hotel and told us what happened. We thought that was no way to treat people and decided to send along the 'Jerk Squad'.

A few of us went looking for him and, sure enough, a guy came out of an alley and offered us the chance to buy a watch. Our sole mission was to rip off as many watches as possible from this guy. I'll give him his due . . . he watched us really carefully. I would try and distract him so the other boys could lift a watch or two, but it wasn't really working. Then he showed me another watch and I looked at the boys and gave them the 'get ready' signal. He was saying, 'Very good watch. Very good watch.' I asked him if it had a luminous dial on it so I could read it in the dark. 'Yes. No problem. You can read in dark.' I said I wanted proof. **So he turned the lights out . . . we ran out with a few watches. Like he said, the cops wouldn't interefere. Oh yeah, one of the Jerk Squad was a cop, and top rugby player, but he shall remain nameless.**

A COMMON thing to do when you are on tour is to 'do your business' in anyone's toilet except your own. On one tour there was a phantom crapper — no one could figure out who

Me and Seymour once again ready to carry the young fellas . . . this time in rickshaws in Hong Kong.

was causing all the 'damage'. Finally, though, some of the boys caught him. They planned on outing him at the team's court session but knew that they would need some evidence. So they got some of the toilet paper and 'deposits' he'd left in the room — he would never flush — and put it in the safe in the room for safe keeping until the court session. On the field, we went on to win the tournament and in all the celebrations we didn't have time for a court session. **When we checked out of the hotel the 'evidence' was still in the safe for the next hotel guest to find. The hotel promptly cancelled their sponsorship of the sevens tournament.**

TO HELP pass the time one year Walter Little, Glen Osborne and I decided to do a diving course. There was no problem with the theory part of the exam. Well, not for me, anyway. The second part was multi-choice. I finished with about 10 minutes to go and I saw Oz just motoring down the page.

I said, 'Bro, you can read quick.' He said he hadn't ticked an 'A' for a while and carried on answering the questions using that theory. Then we had an oral test. One of the questions was, 'What should you do when you get down to the red zone on your tank?' The correct answer was that it was time to head up to the surface. **They asked Oz. He said, 'It means that you've only got time for one more sack of kinas. So swim real fast.' I think Oz was getting bored with the test by then.**

I HAVE to tell another story about Gordon Tietjens. It's my favourite one about the guy. We were staying in a low-budget hotel in Chile and Titch's pillow had gone missing from his room after a team meeting. He was convinced that Dallas Seymour and Owen Scrimgeour had taken it. Later in the afternoon, at training, he had caught these same two players imitating his running style (it's a bit unorthodox because his knees have had it) and that really sent him over the edge. **When we got back to the hotel he called a team meeting and said to the boys, 'If my pillow isn't back in my room after dinner, there will be trouble.' After dinner there were about 50 pillows outside his door.** He wasn't amused. So he called a meeting with Dallas and Scrimmo and asked me to attend as well. He tore strips off them. He told them that he caught them imitating him at training and Scrimmo said, 'Fair enough, Titch. You caught us. Sorry, mate.' Seymour, though, was just plain embarrassing. Instead of owning up he just kissed Titch's arse. 'Titch, I have far too much respect for you to do something like that.' It was shocking. He hung Scrimmo out to dry. The funniest thing, though, was that once Scrimmo and Seymour had left the room, Titch found his pillow behind his bed.

A LOT of people like to take shots at Jonah Lomu. They question his work ethic and some even question his desire to play rugby. Both arguments are ridiculous. Last year, when I was injured, I travelled to the UK with the big fella while he played for the Barbarians. With an All Black season on the

People are always taking shots at Jonah. But if they took the time to ask anyone who knows him, they'd get the real story.

horizon I was hired to help with his fitness — the All Black coach at the time, Wayne Smith, knew the value of a fit Jonah Lomu. We'd run in the morning — and I'd thrash him — and then we'd go to the gym in the afternoons and he'd thrash me. It was great to hang with the Barbarians team. Even though I wasn't in the team I was given all the gear. It was a great trip to be a part of . . . except the grief I got from Robin Brooke who was in the Baabaas side. Every time I got on the team bus I would hear, 'Who is that guy? Can someone get him off the bus? He's being a real nuisance. I think he's stalking me.'

Our visit to England coincided with the Twickenham Sevens. And after injuries had ripped Titch's squad apart he rang me to see if Jonah would go on stand-by for the team. Jonah jumped at the chance. I have always respected the big guy. He's a good mate of mine and I totally rate him as a rugby player. But when he accepted Titch's invitation he grew another notch in the respect stakes.

Jonah had an All Black trial to play the following week in New Zealand and most players would have wrapped themselves in cotton wool. He'd taken a whack on the knee in a Baabaas match and it was swelling, but it didn't matter to him. **He was in the UK earning some good money with the Baabaas and he knew he wouldn't earn a cent playing for Titch and the boys, but that wasn't even a consideration.** He said to me, 'When I get the chance to put on a black jersey, it goes on.'

The New Zealand team had a tough first day but when Jonah arrived on the second day and walked into the changing room you could see the whole spirit of the side lift. Here he is, the biggest name in rugby, putting his team and country first. Jonah didn't have his best day in the black jersey, but it didn't matter. His presence lifted the side and we won the Twickenham Sevens. It was a gesture I'll never forget, and neither will any of the young guys in that room.

The boys in the latest band

Gordon Tietjens has the Midas touch. He has made a career out of his ability to pick players from relative obscurity and turn them into Super 12-level stars. He has put a number of players on the road to greatness in the fifteens game which has, inevitably, meant a high turnover rate of players in the sevens sides. As a result, some of the boys in the sevens team these days don't have the profile that players of the last decade had. Anyway, here's an introduction to some of the guys from this year's team who have contributed to our three consecutive World Series wins since 2000. In time, some of them will go on to greater heights, despite the stories I am about to tell.

Craig De Goldi

One of the great workers in the side is Craig De Goldi. Up until the Cardiff tournament a few weeks before the Commonwealth Games he had never been out of the team. One of the best times we had together was when we played for an invitational side up at the Middlesex Sevens at Twickenham. Instead of playing against the Fijians, Goldi and I played with them. We never really hit our straps but we didn't have to. We won the tournament pretty comfortably.

It's not often I get to play with Serevi, but Craig De Goldi and me experienced that rare opportunity at the Middlesex Sevens.

A proud West Coaster (you'll be amazed at how many of them there are around the world), he was poached by Auckland from the great Ngongotaha club in Rotorua. Very rounded person, as his musical tastes range from reggae through rap music to heavy metal. He'd be the ideal person for the music committee but most of us can't stand even a little of that heavy metal crap. **A lot of people call Goldi 'Horse' — and it's not because of the way he runs.**

Chris Masoe

Back in the old days, Samoans who arrived in New Zealand were given the name 'Fob', which stands for 'fresh off the boat'. These days though we use Fop — fresh off the plane. That's what I call Chris Masoe. He is one of the strongest fellas I have ever seen playing footie. **If you go into a tackle situation with him, nine times out of ten he will be the one who comes away with the ball.** One of the Aussie boys put a bit of the dirty stuff on Chris during a game this year but after Fop sorted him out at the after-match function he didn't have any more trouble from the guy. (His brother Maselino is a world-ranked boxer.) Runs in the family. A lot of guys give Chris a hard time about his English, but I always say his English is a hell of a lot better than our Samoan.

Tafai Ioasa

Tafai Ioasa — or Blowfly because he is one of those guys who is always hanging around you. He never leaves you alone. It's like he's afraid to spend time on his own. He slipped off the scene a bit towards the end of the season but he is probably the most gifted ball player among the forwards. **He's a great friend of Stu Forster — one of the young guys that Stu has taken under his wing and completely wrecked.** Not as tight as Stu yet, Blowfly is quite happy to spend his cash. But, it's like Stu says, 'Give him time.'

Damian Karauna

Damian has one of the better nicknames in rugby — Bum Bum — because he has a good 'boot' on him. He is one of the leaders of the team. Gets on well with all the boys. At the trials he always wants to play for the underdog team and more often than not he turns them into a better team than the so-called stronger team. He's a little bit lost these days without his sidekick Owen Scrimgeour, whose sole aim was to be the most hated rugby player in New Zealand. By all accounts he pretty much succeeded. I liked him for the fact he was that way. Bum Bum is a real good team man. He's in charge of the music for the boys, as well as being our Fines Master. He enjoys bossing the young players around. He has deserved that role because he has had to work hard for everything he has achieved.

Damian Karauna . . . hard on the field and enjoys bossing the younger guys around.

Josh Blackie

Josh is a guy with a lot of talent. He's a big unit. Titch was convinced that we lacked a bit of size up front so 'Lagi' was brought into the team this year to add some intimidatory bulk to the side. He's a good boy but I'm not sure how tough he is. At one of the trials he dislocated his shoulder and we had to move on to another field while the ambulance officers stabilised him. Later in the year one of the Samoan boys dislocated his shoulder and he just walked off the field. **When Josh did it he was lying on the ground screaming like a bitch. He needs to harden up a bit.** That Southern Man thing is obviously a myth.

Alan Bunting

Alan got his break in the sevens side after a stand-out year for the Bay of Plenty in the NPC last year. He's one of the fittest players in the side. That's what a year in the Bay — being coached by Titch, of course — will do for you. He's a proud kid so he won't like hearing this, but his room-mates are always complaining that he has a habit of farting during his sleep. Sort it out, eh Buntsy!

Craig Newby

Craig is another player whose only tournament was the Commonwealth Games. **He first came into the team in 1999 as a fresh-faced, pimply kid out of Rotorua Boys High School. We didn't have a bed for him at his first trial so he had to sleep on the floor in my room.** He has come a long way since then. Newbs — who plays with me at North Harbour — is proud of his record at the sevens nationals. He keeps reminding everyone that he has played the tournament three times and won three times. A couple of years ago, when he was captain, we beat Waikato in the final and when we were back at the hotel getting ready to go back to Auckland, coverage of the final was just starting on TV. We all sat down to watch. They showed Newbs being given the trophy and the commentator said, 'There's Craig

Craig 'G Man' Newby has Karl Te Nana in support as he attacks for New Zealand at Manchester.

Newby, the North Harbour captain . . . on paper anyway.' He was absolutely gutted. We all cracked up and poor old Newbs just walked out of the room. **Sometimes we call Newbs 'G Man'. He doesn't wear a G-string but if he did, and he wore it backwards, it wouldn't matter.**

Rodney So'oialo

Rodney So'oialo's only tournament this year was the Commonwealth Games. For a guy who hadn't played since the Super 12, he went bloody well. Because of an ankle injury from earlier in the year, his first run for months was with us at the trials. He gutsed it out, which is probably the thing that convinced Titch to pick him. As a player, he has the potential to be an All Black. He just needs to put his

Caught! Anthony Tuitavake and Rodney So'oialo check out the flash cars at Manchester United training . . . from behind the bushes.

mind to it and believe in himself a little more. Rodders loves playing in the physical games. The harder the better. It's an island thing.

Dallas Seymour

My old mate Dallas Seymour led the team to Malaysia and Singapore this year after I had to pull out of the trips because of injury. I have no doubt that those two tournaments — two of the gutsiest efforts from the team — were the turning points for the side. Seymour and I both started playing for the New Zealand Sevens side back in 1988. He hasn't played a whole lot recently because he has been involved with the Crusaders set-up in the Super 12. He still has a lot to offer. **He's a great guy to have in the trenches with you. You know he is going to put it on the line every single time.** He's a great role model for the boys in terms of them learning from his training and work ethic. We have a saying in our team, 'When the boots go on, switch on'. Seymour takes that to the limit. He is the consummate professional in that sense. His major downfall, however, is that

Dallas Seymour. A great player and great mate, although he struggles with the fact that his wife is more famous than him.

his wife is more famous than him. Another downfall is that he was the captain of the side in Singapore when the boys had a big brawl with the Samoans. Seymour started it. It was a terrible scene. Shocking stuff. Not what we want to see on international rugby fields. Shameful. It would never have happened on my shift.

Amasio Valence

Amasio Valence is our playmaker. When he is on form he is the best sevens player in the game. **Moji is the only player in the world who has the ability to upset Fijian captain Waisale Serevi. I love watching those two go at it; I think Serevi probably sees a lot of himself in Moji.** I feel a bit sorry for Moji because it must be hard for him to play against his countrymen. Sevens is a religion in Fiji, much the same way that the All Blacks are something of a religion to New Zealanders. He invariably gets

Amasio 'Gretzky' and me . . . he's always skating on thin ice with Gordon Tietjens.

a hard time from the Fijian boys. In one game I heard them yelling out a name to him. I asked him later what it meant. 'Traitor!' I always say to Moji before games; 'These are your brothers. You need to play your hardest because they will be asking the question of you.' He always responds with a big game. **Despite being one of the stars of the team, he is always in trouble with Titch.** On a few occasions he has come very close to being thrown out of the camp, so close, in fact, we have started calling him 'Gretzky' because he was skating on thin ice. His list of misdemeanours includes missing training, missing tournaments, playing club rugby when he shouldn't, and getting caught at KFC stores.

Jared Going

We call Jared 'Sos' (Son Of Sid) — he hates it. It's a shame that Sos never saw Sid play for Northland or the All Blacks. Sid was the best player in the world when I was growing up. Sos is a bit of a pretty boy. I went out with him once in Whangarei. He likes to think he owns the town and, judging by what happened that night, he's probably not too far off the mark. Although, I do remember a lot of people asking him who his good-looking mate was. Sos is a real talent. He has played every position in the backline for Northland except for halfback. **But when I look at him I see an openside flanker, because he's a shitty bugger; he gets stuck in and he can run all day.** I reckon he plays for the best family team in rugby, but I'd like to see the Goings go up against the Osbornes. With Bill and Glen in the backline, along with the Parkinson boys, it would be a good test for the Northland boys. The game couldn't be on a Sunday, though, because the Goings are Mormons — except for Sos, who picks and chooses when he celebrates the Sabbath.

Ross Martin

Little T-Rex — Ross Martin — made me so happy this year when he made the team. Like Craig De Goldi, he would have been at four 50-man camps held after the national championships and this year he finally cracked it and made it through. I was really proud of him. His season was affected by injury but he'll be back. Another Rotorua boy. He likes to hang with Goldi a lot but we try not to hold that against him.

Hayden Reid

Hayden 'Newsboy' Reid loves his hair. Up at Hong Kong he started wearing it in spikes and when I introduced him to a room full of people **I mentioned that his mother used to go out with a cockatoo. He wasn't impressed with me.** Newsboy loves to talk. He is always talking. He never stops, and he asks the stupidest questions. 'Rushie, what do you think about when you watch the sun coming up?' What sort of question is that? I told him, 'I think of how I wish it would piss off so I could get back to sleep.' I don't think that was the answer he was looking for. He's a good tourist. Always up for a laugh. I always knew that he had a good side to him and when he deserted Otago for North Harbour he played at my club, Takapuna. It confirmed that he was indeed one of the good ones. The other name we have for him is 'Reido' and recently one of the boys added 'file' to the end of it.

Anthony Tuitavake

Anthony has won the coveted nickname 'Marmite', because he's black and because he's smooth. He had a couple of solid games for Harbour in the NPC last year and was invited to the sevens camp. By his own admission, he didn't want to come because of the training, but I'm sure now he's glad he took on Titch's sessions because he's got a gold medal to show for it. Got into the Commonwealth Games squad ahead of Newsboy and Justin Wilson. I put him on the music committee this year because he is a young guy, but he likes old school tunes. He is one of the Massey Mafia along with Tusi Pisi and Chris Smiley. I think there's a little love triangle thing going on there.

Karl Te Nana

Karl is one of the senior members of the team now and over the last two years has been the best sevens player in the world. One of KT's real strengths is that he is a great team man. He makes the young guys feel like they belong straight away. He treats everyone the same. We are lucky in the sevens side that the guys who have been around for a while are all pretty good at welcoming the young fellas into the fold. **There's no real secret as to how we do it; we just take the piss out of them as often as possible and as quickly as possible.** But once training starts, a guy like KT, who may seem to be a carefree type of guy, works his butt off. I had to introduce him at a function once in Hong Kong. He had his hair in dreads and he had beads in it. 'It's okay to be different, to stand out from the crowd, but after seeing you in the showers the other day, you didn't have to get the Stevie Wonder thing happening down there as well, did you?' KT captained the side when I was out of action for nine months with my broken leg. He did an average job. I knew the boys were happy to have me back.

Joe Rokocoko

We call him 'Mic' because, being long and slender and sporting an afro hair style, he looks like a microphone. One of the real talented guys to come through this year, Joey is fast. Real fast. He is the perfect example of what the sevens side can do for you. He was a star in fifteens as a schoolboy so we knew there was a little bit of talent there. We invited him to our 50-man camp. It's a full-on camp with a lot of hard sessions followed by a number of games. Joey will admit that he struggled. He would do one run and he'd be gone. He knew that he had a long way to go to get to the levels where he needed to be. **Halfway through the year Titch decided that we needed a game-breaker, someone with the X-factor. By the time of the Cardiff tournament at the end of the world circuit, he was our best player.** Every time he got the ball

Karl Te Nana and hairstyle . . . kids, this is what happens when you don't wash your hair.

in his hands he would run around guys and just run away from them. It's a pity he broke his leg while he was playing for the New Zealand Colts because he would have had a gold medal hanging around his neck. He would have been an absolute sensation in Manchester. He'll have his chance in four years' time.

Anthony Koonwaiyou

Anthony is affectionately known as 'Coon', which is a politically incorrect term in certain circles. If I was a white guy in South Auckland I probably wouldn't yell that out while I was standing in the middle of the street. **This kid is an exciting talent with speed to burn. Once he works the stamina into his game he will turn a few heads.** He's great to train with. He keeps me feeling young because he has so much enthusiasm. He is so young, in fact, that when I first played in Hong Kong in 1988 he was only five years old!

Jason Tiatia

Jason 'Pretty Boy' Tiatia is the first guy I have toured with who has been approached to do a modelling shoot. **When we were in Hong Kong last year he was asked to do some modelling, so in the week leading up to the tournament he was off getting make-up put on and striking different poses.** I'd have to say that the pictures were shite, but he actually looked the part. (I wonder if Anthony Tuitavake, Tusi Pisi and Chris Smiley would have been impressed?) Pretty Boy faded away a bit this year and was desperately unlucky not to make the team at the end of the year. He's the type of player overseas clubs would love to get their hands on, but I'm rather hoping he stays, because he still has a lot to offer the team.

Nick Evans

Nick is another of the youth brigade Titch has brought on board this year. **He plays for East Coast Gays in the North Harbour competition. He has played for New Zealand in Australian Rules so he**

has a lot of skill. His first tournament for us was in Brisbane and he held his own against guys like Wendell Sailor and Mat Rogers — not bad for a guy playing his first international sevens tournament, and only the second sevens tournament of his life.

Brad Fleming

One of our speed guys, but always injured . . . I'm sure he's made out of porcelain. Had one injury-free season and was outstanding for Wellington. Met a guy once who said we had a mutual friend in Brad Fleming. He said he'd spent the night

Brad Fleming and a golden smile. He looks up to Karl Te Nana so much he even copied his hairstyle.

with him in prison in Dubai. Apparently he cried like a baby the whole time. Sorry, Brad. Couldn't help it.

Justin Wilson

Justin played the first two sevens tournaments this year with a stress fracture in his back. That speaks volumes about the man. He would be a great centre in fifteens, but is continually played out of position on the wing. He has the potential to go all the way in the game but just needs someone to give him a break. One of the funniest guys you could wish to meet, although I can't relay any 'incidents' because I don't want to inflate his already gigantic ego.

Joseph Tauiwi

The late Joseph John Tauiwi was, along with Peter Woods, one of the unsung heroes of the New Zealand Sevens team in the 1990s. He wasn't well known by the average New Zealand rugby fan, but within the sevens side between 1994 and 1997 we knew he was one of the main reasons we were in the middle of a great era for the team. We called him Kutu. He had natural talent. He was one of the best readers of a game that I have played with. He was a real hard case too. If he wasn't moaning about something it must have been time for the gear to be handed out because he was always first in line — a real Maori boy. Earlier this year we heard that he had cancer. I saw him at the Taupiri Sevens and he had lost a lot of weight. I gave him a bit of stick about how skinny he was and he couldn't stop laughing. He had a big smile on his face, just like he always had when we'd arrive at a tournament. He played in 14 tournaments for New Zealand. Kutu always thought he was going to beat the cancer. I thought he would too. But, eventually, things got worse. I saw him in Auckland Hospital a few times. He was moaning about the food and the chemotherapy. But he was still smiling. They buried him in his New Zealand Sevens blazer at his mum's marae in Katikati. Haere ra ehoa.

Joe Tauiwi did the black jersey and his whanau proud.

My supporters

IF GOOD HUMOUR IS the health of the soul and sadness its poison, then I must be the luckiest guy around. Humour has always been a big part of my life, thanks to my parents Merv and Unaiki.

My old man is a real character. Born and bred in Belfast, he was working by the time he was 12 years old. Before that, his parents would send him down to the local train station to shout abuse at the trains going past. **The idea was that the train drivers would get so annoyed that they'd throw coal and spuds at him and his mates. He would collect it all up, take it home and get a pat on the back.**

The old man — who was adopted — never really got on with his parents, and with The Troubles between the Protestants and the Catholics coming to a head in Northern Ireland, he and a group of his mates decided that they'd had enough and decided to catch a boat to Australia.

A week later he showed up at the docks raring to go — not having told his parents — and he was the only one there! Being the stubborn bugger that he is, he decided to take the boat anyway. The first stop was England where he began work as a painter before joining the navy. After his time in the service, he carried on out to the Antipodes.

He arrived in Wellington and never left. Legend has it he

got on the piss and missed the boat to Australia. Thank God for that — I might have ended up a Wallaby!

The old man is 71 and is still working as a painter. He can still beat any of us when it comes to painting a roof . . . and we have tried to beat him many times.

Being an Irishman, he was often thirsty — indeed, he drinks for the both of us. **He is not an alcoholic, though, because, as he says, he has never been to a meeting in his life.** Whenever he feels like it, he stops drinking for a year and then, to the very day, he'll start again. I believe he was on the wagon when I made the All Blacks for the first time. Mum said he got off it quickly and was pissed for a week. He shouted the first keg. My grandfather shouted the second keg. After that, they just kept taking turns.

That wasn't the biggest party he ever had, though. **When my parents got married the party went on for two weeks. Mum and my grandmother left after three days!** The old man said they had to call a brewery truck to come and get the empties because no one could get into the back of the house. They took away 190 dozen on the first trip.

Mum used to play netball at the courts in Auckland's Khyber Pass and the old man was, and still is, a soccer man . . . in his words, 'a real man's game'.

He has never played a game of rugby in his life, but he's an expert. He's never wrong. I don't know if any of the All Blacks teams he's selected would win any games but they'd have had some great parties. My old man would always pick Frank Bunce and Walter Little because he agreed with them when they said, 'You got a poof for a son because he doesn't drink.'

Mum is obviously responsible for the Maori side of the family. Her father is Ngati Kahu and her mother was Ngapuhi. We grew up in Matangirau where my grandparents were also born and raised. My dad never really got on too well with the Maori side of the family because, according to him, most of them were 'useless bastards'. I think he has chilled out a bit over that in recent times.

Growing up with him watching us play rugby was, at times, embarrassing. The old man didn't give a hoot who was watching. He would swear his head off at us and every second or third word would be an expletive. In turn, Mum would be swearing at him to leave us alone!

I know it is a cliché, but the fact is that I would not have had the success I have had in rugby — or life for that matter — if it wasn't for the support of my parents. They were always there for us kids . . . whether it was to watch us play rugby, box, play tennis or when we were in Maori culture groups. Their support paid off too, because all my brothers were good footie players.

My two younger brothers (Bru and Honky) both played in the age-grade North Auckland teams, with Bru playing for the seniors for a couple of years as well. **Honky did really well considering he had a toe lopped off as a youngster by my cousin Raymond. They were chopping wood for the copper and Raymond's aim was a bit astray. Nevertheless, it certainly helped us out when it came to Christmas presents.** Honky got tow trucks for years afterwards. My two older brothers (Putti and Lawrence) got hitched pretty early and rugby just wasn't the priority for them that it was for the rest of us. There is no doubt, though, they could have played rep rugby as well.

Some of my most fierce games were against my brothers on the back paddock outside my grandfather's place. Putti — being the oldest and strongest — was the only one not crying by the end of it.

My sister Huia played netball for the local teams. I thought she was going to be a real problem for the family after an incident with puppies. Our dog Mutt had some puppies that Huia decided she would take for a swim in the creek. She ended up drowning the whole litter and when we found her she was pretending they were little steamboats. Lawrence, a real animal lover, was distraught.

The biggest lesson Mum and Dad taught me was about

At home with my VIPs. Left to right: Martyn, me with Brady, Blair (back), Robert, Natalie and Raina.

support. They never put pressure on us to do anything we didn't want to do. It's a lesson that I will hopefully pass on to my kids.

My two eldest boys — Martyn and Blair — are playing in the under-9s at East Tamaki and my daughter Natalie is playing for her school netball team. The two youngest — Brady and Robert — are getting beaten up in our family games on the front lawn at the moment, just as we used to. They should turn out all right.

I am glad that my kids have had the opportunity to watch

me play, although to them I am just Dad rather than an All Black. If there is a hero in our house, it's certainly not me. It's their mother.

Raina supported the family when rugby was an amateur game. While I was off touring the world, spending 150 days away from home each year, she was in Auckland raising five kids. So, everything I have achieved is basically because of her support. Thanks Raina.

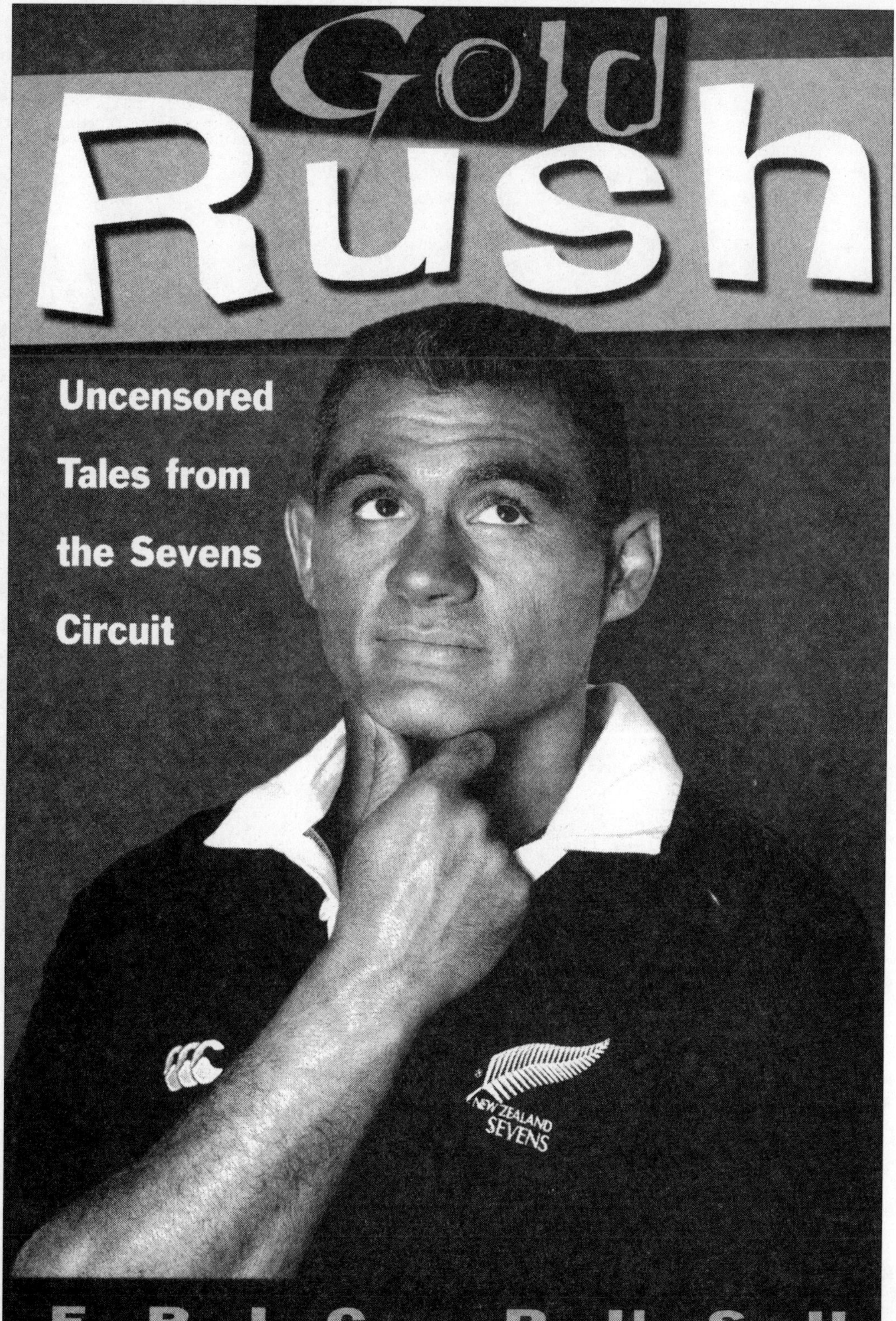
Gold
Rush
Uncensored
Tales from
the Sevens
Circuit
NEW ZEALAND
SEVENS
ERIC RUSH

Foreword By David Campese

THE GREATEST THING ABOUT my 15 years in provincial and international rugby is the number of great characters I've come across on my travels. Eric Rush is definitely one of them. In preparing to write this foreword I tried to think of ways to describe him, and it wasn't easy because there is so much that makes up Rushy's character.

When you get to play against him and meet him off the field, Rushy is very similar to myself in that we try and enjoy ourselves as much as we can on the field as well as off the field.

In the '90s, it's clear to me that too many people play the game for the wrong reasons. Many are motivated by money and many probably think they deserve to get what they're being paid.

When you look at a guy like Eric, you see a man that gave more to rugby than a lot of the new breed of players are giving back to the game. Long before professionalism came along Rushy was already a true professional.

Like many of us from that era, he dedicated his life to rugby, even though he wasn't getting paid to play the game. It didn't matter that his bank account suffered because he was playing the game he loves. You have to be a special type of character to have made the sacrifices that players like Rushy have made.

When Rushy first came on to the scene it was obvious to me

David Campese: When Rushy eventually retires it will be a sad day for rugby.

that he was a player worth admiring. On the park, he set a very high standard for himself. You never saw a game in which Rushy was playing where he wasn't playing to his ability. Like me, he hates losing, but unlike many of the new breed of professionals, he could accept defeat.

The time to measure the depth of a person's character isn't when he's standing on the podium at the Commonwealth Games with a gold medal hanging around his neck. People always show their true character when things are tough . . . when they've taken a few hits. Rushy was always able to have a bit of a laugh – win or lose. That's how he has become one of rugby's great personalities.

Obviously 1998 was a defining year for Rushy. The highs were awesome and the lows miserable. But no matter how bad things can seem one day, as you go through life, the highs have a way of superseding the lows. That's why I'll never worry about Rushy because through it all you know that he will emerge with a smile on his face.

When Rushy eventually retires it will be a sad day for rugby. Throughout his career, whether he was playing sevens or playing for the All Blacks – playing flanker or on the wing – he proved that you can be highly skilled and be the focus of the team, but still enjoy yourself.

When Jonah Lomu came on the scene, as big and as strong as he was, it was the death nail for players like Rushy and I. Almost overnight, the skill factor that our games were based on wasn't as highly regarded as raw strength.

I like to think there is still room in rugby for players who have flair, players who are unpredictable and players who entertain. Unfortunately, coaches these days are so concerned about winning they have forgotten how the game is meant to be played.

When fans go to a rugby game they want to be entertained. They want to see the skill of an Eric Rush and they want to identify with a character like Eric Rush.

But the fans' enjoyment is slowly being squeezed out of

them with the emphasis in the Tri-Nations and Super 12 only on winning. When I was playing for Australia, of course I wanted to win. Of course it hurt when we lost. But regardless of the result, rugby was fun to play.

I think the younger generation of rugby players should have a look at the themselves and ask the question, "Why do I play?" If the only answer they can muster revolves around money, then that's sad. Rugby is the world's greatest game and you should be playing it for the love of the game. Having come towards the end of my playing career I know that the awards and the money mean very little once your boots have been hung up for the last time. Unless the emphasis in rugby is put back on the enjoyment factor, rugby and its young professionals could find themselves on a scrapheap before long.

One of the reasons I am so happy to contribute to Gold Rush is because it's vital that a person like Eric Rush is allowed to portray the camaraderie and the friendships that rugby can provide.

Rushy was, and still is, an exceptional footballer. His skills have been well documented and in 1998, in case you hadn't realised it before, his strength of character was there for all the see.

His ability to lead New Zealand to rugby's first Commonwealth Games gold medal was as much a tribute to an inspirational captain as it was a celebration of rugby's coming-out party.

Some may have been surprised at Rushy's ability to block out the pain of a broken hand, or his mental strength to focus on his team, while privately still being torn over events in August. To know Rushy, though, is to know what a competitor he is.

And through it all – the All Black tests and the sevens successes – he is as down to earth as the game itself. If young players in New Zealand want a role model, then Rushy's it. He has never been too big to sign an autograph or talk to the fans.

He understands the responsibility that players carry for the game.

It was always a pleasure playing against Rushy, and it was always a challenge. I remember playing in the Paris Sevens in 1998 and Rushy was running down the sideline. I caught up to him and said, "I've got you Rushy." He smiled at me, put his foot down, and scored the try.

Rugby is fun when characters like Eric are around. I hope this book goes some way to reminding people of the importance of that enjoyment factor in rugby – a part of the game that is slowly disappearing.

Thanks for the memories, Rushy . . . and don't forget to send me a free copy!

David Campese
Sydney, December 1998

Golden Games – The Diary

Now that I'm getting on a bit people start asking me what the defining moment of my career has been. There have been lots of highs and lows – on and off the park – but when it comes to highlights it's hard to go past the sevens gold medal at the 1998 Commonwealth Games in Kuala Lumpur. It was a two week journey that ended in triumph, but along the way there was literally plenty of blood, sweat and tears.

SUNDAY 30 AUGUST

AS SOON AS I ARRIVED at the Waipuna Lodge in the Auckland suburb of Mt Wellington I could sense a real level of excitement. The sevens team had been getting together for tournaments all year. But this one was different because we knew we had our top team available and there was a real edge in the side because everyone knew we were taking away 15 players but that only ten players would make it to Kuala Lumpur. That didn't detract, however, from the buzz of being involved because no one had been to the Commonwealth Games before so we were all going into the unknown.

There was quite a disjointed start to the camp because

several of the boys were missing. The All Blacks – Jonah Lomu, Joeli Vidiri, Christian Cullen and Caleb Ralph – were still making their way back from Sydney where the All Blacks had lost 19-14 in their last test of the year, while Roger Randle was still at home with his wife Kelly who was expecting their second baby.

The boys who had assembled spent the afternoon watching North Harbour's NPC game against Counties. I wasn't playing because of my broken hand. The best thing about it was watching coach Gordon Tietjens . . . he was worried that Rua Tipoki would get injured. It was Titch with an itch – he just couldn't sit still. Actually, it was hard to concentrate on the game. I couldn't stop thinking about what lay ahead of us.

MONDAY 31ST AUGUST

Nothing could have prepared us for the hype that we all felt when the ABs arrived. When Jonah, Joeli, Cully and Caleb joined the team everyone – including the guys who had been around the traps for a while like Rua – couldn't hide their enthusiasm. **When Jonah walked into breakfast Rua looked at me and said, "Shit! Look how big he is!"** He was big, too. Poor old Cully looked like a midget standing next to the big fellas. It was interesting seeing Amasio sitting next to Jonah. Only the day before he'd been watching him on television playing a test against Australia and now he was in the same team and sharing the same dreams. You could see the awe in his eyes.

Our first training session was real sharp. Even the ABs, who had just lost their fifth test in a row, couldn't hide their enthusiasm. Christian looked good. He was quite surprised at the speed in the squad. Jonah also looked real sharp. He talked the whole training and ran well. Four years ago he would have been dead after one of Titch's trainings but not now . . . it was almost as though we wanted to stay out there. Caleb looked like he was cruising but that's because he's got three lungs. Poor old Joeli let it slip that he couldn't sleep the night before. Not because of jet lag, though. He was worried about Titch's training, and what it was going to do to him!

After training Jonah took me to his barber in Penrose. We were almost late for the bus to the airport but I didn't want to break Jonah's ritual of getting a haircut before each trip.

Eventually we joined Singapore Airlines' cattle class. Jonah stayed down the back with the boys. He didn't have to because he is a VIP with them. It didn't surprise me because Jonah's always been a good team man. The most memorable thing about the trip was that Rua reminded me, on more than one occasion, of his farting qualities.

As soon as we got to Singapore Jonah was recognised and mobbed. Not Cully, though, because, he says, "I'm not 6'5" and black. Just a little white boy who blends in."

Once we'd checked in to the Boulevard Hotel we had a team meeting and I put the acid on the ABs about leading from the front. I also said no to any 'back seat' mentality – a rugby tradition that sees the experienced guys sitting at the back of the bus. I didn't want any superstars in the side. Everyone was on the same level because everyone would need to contribute the same on the paddock. Then we talked about focusing not on the final outcome, but on individual and team performance.

Even at this early stage there was a real sense that all of New Zealand was behind us. The only sort of adverse comment was coming from the NPC coaches, and that was fair enough. Every coach is judged on his results and obviously if Mac McCallion is missing Jonah and Joeli, that's a huge gap in his team. The same thing applied to Wellington which had just paid out a lot of money for Christian. I'm sure Graham Mourie would have been pleased if he'd never heard of the Commonwealth Games! But, to me, Titch was under the same sort of pressure. He was going to be judged on his results as well. But regardless of the feelings of some of the NPC coaches there was never any doubt the NZRFU got it right when they made everyone available for the Games. The day a provincial jersey takes precedence over a black jersey is the day that money and professionalism have gone too far.

TUESDAY 1ST SEPTEMBER

THE DAY STARTED WITH a pool session at Singapore's PE College. **Titch being Titch didn't take long to do something stupid. He walked into the women's changing-rooms to get his togs on. No one said a word till he came sprinting out the door, red as a beetroot.**

On the astro turf hockey field, we played five on five touch and soccer games. My team cleaned up which inevitably meant we had to put up with Owen Scrimgeour moaning for the rest of the day. Then we did stride-outs. It ended up being a real good blowout.

After training we went for a quick look around the shops. You can always tell the boys on the good contracts. Scrimmo and Brad Fleming were spotted in the bargain bins looking for their 'Bad Boy' clothes. Cully bought white undies. He says women love them . . . but he warned the boys only to wear them on the occasions when you know your lady is going to see them, otherwise they stain too easily.

We trained again in the afternoon. A few of the boys were crook in the guts. My only worry, though, was the hand I'd injured before leaving New Zealand. I remember thinking I might have to ease off it for a couple of days.

WEDNESDAY 2ND SEPTEMBER

AT BREAKFAST WE HAD to weigh-in to make sure everyone was eating and drinking enough. Jonah checked in at 125kgs – I guess he'd been eating enough! Then we headed for the PE College and the weight room. Titch demanded the guys work hard and he got a good response. We were doing a circuit and Scrimmo and Dallas Seymour were right behind him. Every time we changed machines those two would use the machine Titch had just been using. Titch being Titch put the weights up when he was done. Pride, however, wouldn't let Scrimmo and Dallas adjust the weights down to a respectable level so they struggled through the session on these incredible weights.

Before the "cull" . . . the full New Zealand Sevens squad in Singapore prior to the Kuala Lumpur Commonwealth Games.

Titch was pissing himself watching them struggle.

Back at the hotel I called a players only meeting to discuss what we wanted to do that night. Titch isn't usually too keen on letting the boys out when we're on tour but because we were going to be away for a while I convinced him we should have some time to go out, just to help keep everything in balance. He agreed . . . as long as it didn't affect training the next day.

Before lunch we had another meeting because Titch wanted to know how the team wanted to be told which five players would miss out on the trip to the Commonwealth Games. The options were to be told individually or in front of the team. There was a real serious mood in the room. I said everyone in the room was training well and that Titch had said he couldn't name his team at the moment. Scrimmo eased the tension when he said he could suggest one name for the team. Then all the boys came up with ideas on how Titch could deliver the news – a red ribbon on your door; no blankets on your bed; no place set at lunch; bags in the foyer when you got back from training;

boarding pass at lunch . . . there was lots of kidding but you could tell that everyone was nervous about the final selection.

In the end we decided that Titch would tell the players individually the night before they were due to go home so they could get on the piss.

We had lunch at the exclusive Singapore Cricket Club, which was built in 1852. There were lots of local officials there and one of them told me that it cost $80,000 to get a certificate to enable you to buy a car in Singapore. The country's average wage is $30,000. That would mean only Jonah and Cully would have cars in this team! Rua and Caleb were wearing their shades at lunch – obviously having a sleep. **Titch leaned over to me and said, "Did they go out?" He's got a nose for that sort of thing, has Titch.**

We headed back to the hotel and that night we suffered through Titch's toughest training run of the trip. The boys really struggled. Everyone was reduced to a walk at some stage. Cully's heart rate was measured at 192. His highest rate in the past had been in the low 180s.

THURSDAY 3RD SEPTEMBER

TITCH ALMOST HAD A scrap at reception before we left for a speed session at SCC. Some irate Oz tourist was doing his nana at a young receptionist. The Ocker asked Titch what he was looking at, and if he had a problem. Very diplomatically, Titch told him that if he carried on in the same manner he might be in need of surgery of some sort. The Aussie went real quiet when Jonah and Dallas walked past and asked Titch if everything was OK.

At training Titch matched up guys who were competing for places. There were some real intense boys this morning. It was blisteringly hot as well – something like 35C and humid. **I got matched with Jonah and got caned, although I came back into it as the big fella got tired.**

We headed back to the hotel and into the pool. There wasn't much talk on the bus till the air conditioning kicked in. After today we had all our drivers trained to have the air chilled before we got on the bus.

We were only allowed to have a light lunch because Titch had warned us that the afternoon training would be the hardest yet. The guys fronted for the team meeting before training as focused as they would have been for a test match. Titch didn't disappoint. We went for two hours. It was so tough it felt like we didn't have a break. Cully managed to get his heart rate up to 194. When he could catch his breath, Caleb told me he'd forgotten how hard sevens trainings were. Bruce Reihana admitted he actually thought about hitting Titch a couple of times – something Dan Parkinson and Dallas did to each other. Everyone was on edge.

The training session turned out to be an an exercise in mental toughness. Titch knew what he was doing. He knew a training session like that would bring the team closer together. I was quietly confident we would do real well after seeing how determined everyone was.

The planned night safari at the local zoo was canned because it was too late and the guys were knackered. Cully said the bears went to sleep at 8pm anyway . . . Monza (Tony Monaghan) believed him.

Brad and Cully, who are sharing a room, have started arguing. They argue about the remote, tidying up their room, the bathroom and everything else. I think they've decided that if they don't talk to each other they will get on OK. They'd be stuffed if the TV broke.

FRIDAY 4TH SEPTEMBER

BREAKFAST AT 8AM. GOT sent back to put on a collar. No fun when you're on the 20th floor. No cornflakes left when I got back.

It was an easy day of training. We had a weight session. Everyone was laughing at Jonah. He bicep curled my bench press weight (not saying much).

After lunch I went shopping and bought a CD player and

Jonah's got a smile on his face, but his big mate Joeli got quite snaky during this visit.

speakers because I was sick of watching CNN in the hotel. I only bought them because Caleb said he'd buy them off me at the end of the tour for threequarters of the price. As soon as I paid for them he dropped it to half price. Typical. He can't help it, I suppose. With a face like his he'd have to be a bit of a crook.

After dinner we went to the night safari and had photos taken with the snakes. Rua got his taken with a big python on his back. There were calls of "Which one's the snake?" and "Caleb, Get off his back" from the crowd. **I tickled Joeli's leg with a piece of long grass and he leapt five feet in the air and screamed. Everyone cracked up. Lucky there was a big crowd around; otherwise he'd have killed me.**

After the night safari we had a night on the town. The owners of one bar bought us a couple of free rounds and then put the acid on us to do the haka. We should have seen that coming 'cause nothing's for nothing these days. So we did the haka and brought the house down.

An obnoxious, drunken Pom was hassling some of the boys. Scrimmo saw what was going on and started talking to him. Within minutes Scrimmo had gotten him to shout us drinks. Scrimmo promised to return the favour in New Zealand (hoping he wouldn't come, of course) but in the event that he did, he gave him his phone number: 0800 SCRIMMO.

Then we headed to the Hard Rock Cafe. **Titch was trying to copy the barman throwing handles around but he smashed the glass on his very first attempt.** Seeing we couldn't impress the staff with our handiwork behind the bar, the DJ demanded we did the haka. The boys didn't want to and the DJ announced we wouldn't do it because we couldn't dance. Jonah took this as personal insult and went up and did it. The crowd went wild and joined him. I guess it shouldn't have surprised me that everyone knew who he was.

SATURDAY 5TH SEPTEMBER

AFTER AN EARLY START we were on the bus by 10am on our way to a coaching clinic with kids at Padang. Jonah, Brucey, Amasio and I took the under 13s. We thought we'd made them run hard but Titch, who had the under 19s, had made two of them throw up and had the rest doubled over. He just can't help himself. He had a big smile on his face.

Before the afternoon training session I went to the hospital to organise an x-ray on my hand. It looks like it did the day I broke it. After discussing it with Titch he decided that we would make a last minute decision about it just before the

Games. In the meantime I was to train as usual . . . but was told to stay out of the contact stuff. Despite not being 100 per cent fit, the day ended on a bit of high for me. Our training at the Ministry of Education grounds was awesome. Everyone was real determined and there were good, positive vibes in the squad.

SUNDAY 6TH SEPTEMBER

HAD AN 8AM WAKE-UP call from Hodder Moa Beckett sports editor Warren Adler about completing this diary – he was a bit worried I wasn't doing it because the last book he'd worked on was Frank Bunce's *Frank Confessions* and, by all accounts, Buncey was the worst organised 'author' Warren had come across in his three decades in sports journalism. Warren was so worried about Frank not keeping a diary on an end-of-year All Black tour, he arranged free cell phone time for Frank to call New Zealand and leave his diary on an answerphone. Frank was supposed to call every couple of days. As it turned out, Frank left only two short messages in five weeks – both were to tell Warren not to worry!

After breakfast it was off to Sentosa Island. We'd been given the day off before our final training session before the squad was named in the evening. **We spent most of the day at the water slide park. All the boys were going hard on the slides. I went down a couple of tubes in tandem with Jonah. Bad move; too much momentum.**

We met the Aussie netballers. They all wanted photos with Jonah so I acted as photographer. I didn't know it then, but I'd be taking a lot of photos of Jonah over the next two weeks.

Titch got lost on his way back to the bus. Don't ask how . . . out the front gate, turn left, bus right there. Titch turned right, caught the monorail right around the island and eventually found the bus. It makes you wonder, doesn't it?

In the evening everyone was quiet and tense before our training at Singapore PE College. We played against a SCC team. They were quite useful because they were unorthodox and they showed up a few weaknesses which was good.

Back at the hotel I joined Titch, our trainers Keith Roberts and Kevin McQuoid, phyisio Annette O'Connor and our manager Ross 'Thursty' Thurston at the selection meeting. There was a lot to discuss. The meeting ended at 2.30am.

MONDAY 7TH SEPTEMBER

D-DAY. TITCH MET with each player individually and told them whether they'd be going to the Commonwealth Games or not. The unlucky ones were Scrimmo, Dan, Tony Monaghan, Brad and Rua – although Rua would stay with the team until I had a final fitness test in KL.

Learning who was in and out was probably the most emotional moment of the whole trip. The guys that were staying had to attend a function but someone had mentioned what time the unlucky five were leaving. There was no team call made but every single guy in the team was in the foyer to say goodbye. I got down there and I looked around and there were tears in all the players' eyes – not just the guys that were going home. It was a really emotional moment. We ended up talking about that moment a few times in the next week.

Someone made the comment that Titch had earnt his money. He admitted telling the players they weren't going to the Games was one of the toughest things he'd ever had to do as a coach.

They all took it pretty bad, too. A couple of them, who weren't heavy drinkers, told me later they got slammed on the plane ride home. When I saw Scrimmo a few weeks after the Games he told me he couldn't even bring himself to watch the Commonwealth matches. It was too painful for him because he knew he could have been there.

Our training session that afternoon was the worst I'd been involved with in 11 years of playing sevens. We were lethargic, there was lots of dropped balls, no one was working and no one was talking. Jonah and Joeli got worse and worse the longer the training went. Titch was furious. At one stage he said, "It's not to late. The other players are still at the hotel. If you think you're not good enough, come and tell me before they leave so I can put someone in the squad who wants to train." I knew he was talking about bringing Monza into the 10 because he'd always run unitl he dropped. All the confidence built up during the last week was gone in one training session. Titch was real quiet afterwards. That usually means he's really pissed off.

Back at the hotel I had a go at the boys. I was quite negative. I just couldn't figure out what had gone wrong. Was it because the team had been named? Was it because we had to work harder at training because all of a sudden there were only 11 of us instead of 15? Were we overtrained? Was it the heat? The humidity? I didn't know, but what I did know was that things were going to have to improve quickly.

That night we went to a function with the Australian and Welsh teams. **There was a charity auction where each team provided an autographed ball and jersey. The Oz ball went for $2000 and the jersey for $7000. The Welsh got $3000 for their ball and $5000 for the jersey. Both of ours went for $12,000 apiece!**

TUESDAY 8TH SEPTEMBER

BY 6.30AM WE WERE on the bus to KL. We were met by New Zealand's Director of Athletes Services Peter Miskimmin. We were given our accreditation and he took us on our orientation. There was huge excitement in the team. We were finally here.

On the bus Peter warned us about losing focus. He'd played hockey at the Los Angeles and Barcelona Olympics so we took in what he was saying but we didn't realise until we were in the village what he meant about the distractions. All of us were just staring at these awesome looking athletes, wondering what events they were all in.

It was interesting because at the start of the week you could see the nervousness in everyone. It didn't matter if they were gymnasts or boxers – everyone was raring to go. We were too, but because we hadn't been in this position before, I think we were more easily distracted. **Even when we went to lunch we'd sit there for two hours perving at all the women and after a while you started getting worried because you started looking at the men as well because their physiques were so awesome.** You see these guys walking past in their bike pants and you can't help but be impressed! Some of the sprinters . . . man! Even New Zealand's Chris Donaldson. I'd like to chuck some boots on him. We asked him if he wanted a game on the wing but he reckoned he couldn't catch. I can't think of anywhere else we could have spent two hours having lunch.

It was a great to see guys like the West Indian cricketers and the top sprinters but it was just as good seeing some of the New Zealanders for the first time. We'd be like, "Hey, there's Trent Bray, that awesome swimmer" or "look, look, there's Rowan Brassey and Millie Khan." It was great but we had to keep reminding ourselves why we were there.

We weren't thinking about the gold medal at this stage. We really tried not to focus on that because if you look too far ahead, that's when you trip over the thing that's in front of you.

We walked through the village to our block. The whole New Zealand team was in the same building. Our rooms were three levels below ground with the netball girls in the wing opposite us and the hockey girls above us.

After moving into our rooms it was off to the training ground. Kenya was playing the Bahamas when we got there and they stuck around to watch us have another shocking training – dropped balls, no spark and no talk.

When we got back to the village **Jonah was mobbed. I couldn't believe how many people recognised him.** Eventually we made it back to our rooms. Rico Gear, Bruce, Joeli and Amasio were with me while Cully, Jonah, Caleb and Roger drew the short straw and had to room with Dallas. The rooms weren't too bad, although every time the hockey girls would go to the toilet, Joeli and Amasio would have to run for cover because the pipes leaked into their room. It could have been worse, though; it could have been the boxers living one floor up! It was obviously Amasio's first time in a nice apartment. I walked in on him having a shower . . . only he wasn't using the shower. He was using the extension from the toilet that is normally used for spraying your, well, you know.

Then it was off to the official function where Les Mills welcomed the team and Graeme Miller was named flag bearer. At dinner I sat with Brett Leaver from the hockey team and the hurdler Zion Armstrong. Brett's an old mate from Otara. His brother Mark used to be in my class at school. They gave me a few tips on village life. I remember feeling like the new kid on the block.

Titch called a meeting when we got back to the apartment. He reminded us about staying focused. He also banned ice cream from our fridges. **The day ended with me walking in on Dallas and Julie Dawson snogging in the foyer. The netball girls had obviously arrived from Darwin.**

WEDNESDAY 9 SEPTEMBER

I SLEPT LIKE A log and only just made it to breakfast for a meeting. A few of the guys were actually late and Titch was seething. Despite this, we had one of our better trainings in the morning before heading back to the village. Once again Jonah was proving popular with the female English athletes.

I always knew he'd be a worldwide superstar. I remember once when the All Blacks were on tour we were in the back streets of Sicily. We went shopping and we walked into this jeans shop and the three girls working there just mobbed him. **I remember thinking, "Shit, this guy is famous."** If you get recognised there you'll get recognised anywhere. So I kind of knew what would happen to him when we got to the village but I didn't think it would be on the scale it was. Everyone knew him. Everywhere we turned people wanted their photo with him or an autograph.

Obviously a lot of good things have happened to Jonah because of his fame but, to be honest, I don't think I would like to change places with him. I certainly couldn't handle it as well as he has. He has had to pay a price for his fame. He's got no privacy anymore. **One Christmas he wanted me to go shopping with him. He said he'd come and pick me up so I waited around for him. It was nearly midnight before he arrived. It turned out he wouldn't shop any earlier because he didn't want to get hassled.** People can say that it doesn't take much to sign a piece of paper but the thing is Jonah has to remain cheerful the whole time. The first autograph is no problem but by the time the 50th person asks, you can imagine that he's got just a bit tired of it. But Jonah has a great attitude. He's always reminding himself that each time someone asks for an autograph it's the first time they've met him so he's always making an effort to smile . . . even if it's the hundredth time he's had to sign his name.

Before our practise game against Malaysia I decided to get a pain-killing injection for my hand. I screamed my head off. As I walked out of the doctor's office some little gymnast was laughing at me. Real embarrassing. I was just glad none of the boys were around to see it.

At the training Malaysia made monkeys out of us. They scored the first two tries. In the end they got four and we got six. Titch was pulling what is left of his hair out. **We played with no urgency, no stamina and no confidence. The defence was non-existent.**

Titch went across to thank the Malaysian team for playing us so I called the team in. No one was saying anything. They were just staring at the ground. I decided the only thing to do was to crack a joke. So I said, "That f---ing showed them!". Everyone started chuckling. I don't think Titch was too impressed when he came back and found us laughing. He went quiet again . . . the Malaysians were smiling. They had their shirts off and were strutting around as though they'd won the tournament. That got us laughing again.

Titch and our trainer Keith Roberts gave me a fitness test. I passed. I was in the team.

THURSDAY 10TH SEPTEMBER

THE DAY STARTED WITH another early training. Titch worked us real hard. Malaysia didn't want to play again because a team had pulled out of the competition so the draw had changed. Because the hosts could pick their pool, they picked us. Obviously they rated their chances after yesterday's effort. Finding that out picked us up. It gave us a lot of motivation. We couldn't wait to play them.

In the evening Cully, Caleb and I went to watch the men's hockey team draw 3-3 against South Africa. A few of the boys played cards on the balcony and noticed some African boxers run past – again and again. I think they did about 40 laps of the village. Someone should have told them athletes could use the bus service!

FRIDAY 11TH SEPTEMBER

NO TRAINING BECAUSE THE Games start for us tomorrow.

The highlight was the opening ceremony. It was awesome. All the teams assembled in the gymnastics stadium next door to the main stadium. It was a good photo opportunity. The boys got lots of photos with the netball team and, of course, Jonah was popular again.

As we made our walk to the stadium, crowds were lined up all the way. Everyone was screaming 'Lomu!' We were towards the back of the New Zealand team with Chris Donaldson, Zion, the boxers, the swimmers and the cricketers. We lined up in the tunnel and **we heard the announcer in the stadium say "New Zealand" and the whole team, 200-plus of us, just roared. It was a totally unique experience.**

Jonah and me pose with a few of the New Zealand boxers just prior to the Games march past.

It's hard to explain what it was like walking out on to the track with 100,000 people cheering. We were just all proud to be wearing that Silver Fern.

SATURDAY 12TH SEPTEMBER

EVERYONE WOKE UP LATE. No time called for breakfast but that was still no excuse. **Titch went to breakfast by himself. I'm guessing he was pretty angry.** We had a pool session at 10am. Titch gave us a lecture and I had a talk also. We had to start being hard on ourselves.We had lunch and left for the ground but it was real hot in the stands and uncomfortable. Thursty organised a hotel for us nearby – an inspired move.

We played Sri Lanka at 5pm and cruised to an 80-0 victory. It was a good win because we kept the foot on the pedal. The hunger that had been missing for most of the week was back. The black jersey does that.

After heading back to hotel, we jogged back to the ground for our 9pm game against Malaysia. The boys were really focused and hungry. We won 53-0. A good result, scoreboard wise. The boys punished them physically in the contact situations because of the training debacle. It was good fun.

We headed back to the village but we had to leave Amasio behind. He had to pee in the bottle for the drug testing and couldn't do it. After an hour or so we got tired of waiting and told him to catch the next bus.

SUNDAY 13TH SEPTEMBER

MOST OF THE DAY was spent trying to relax before our 5pm game against Tonga. We struggled early but came away to win 41-12. It was a good result because it brought us back to earth a bit. We headed back to the hotel to rest up for our game against the Bahamas. We learnt that we had to score more than 10 tries to avoid Fiji in the quarters or the semis. The boys went real hard and we ended up getting 13.

Back at the village we had a team meeting. We talked about having the opportunity to create history but we were mindful of taking things one game at a time. We needed to focus on performance because we knew if we did that, the results would come. **Before going to bed we got the draw. We had Wales in the quarters. Too tired to be nervous.**

MONDAY 14 SEPTEMBER

FINALS DAY: MAYBE IT was too much nervous energy but everyone fell asleep on the bus on the way to our hotel. We jogged to the ground and took care of Wales 38-14. They got two tries, though, which wasn't good.

I broke my hand again. I hadn't strapped it properly probably because I got carried away in the build-up. We headed back to the hotel to prepare for the semi-final against Samoa. I warned the guys it would be tough, even though

Samoa hadn't played that well up to then because they always save their best for us.

It turned out to be a real tough game. We were behind most of the way and got in front right at the end. At one stage it looked like they were going to score a late try but **Rico and a few others got back to shut it down. We'd been saying all week that big defence wins tournaments and we were proving it.**

We headed straight back to the hotel, even though we only had a hour to go until the final.

I thought about not starting because my hand was useless. It was just up to Titch whether he wanted to put me on first. He decided I would go on and just go crazy and when the Fijians got tired we'd bring on Caleb because he's got the legs. My hand never felt right – either in Singapore or KL. But it's amazing what adrenalin does. As soon as the tournament started I was able to get on with it. When Wayne Smith was coaching the sevens team a few years ago he came up with the saying, "boots on, switch on". Once the boots were on, I forgot about the pain.

The saying is pretty apt for sevens because you have got to relax when you're not playing. It's not like a 15-a-side game where you can build up all week and then after 80 minutes you can relax. In sevens you usually have a game in the morning, one in the afternoon and then another in the evening, so you've got to be able to switch off in between.

At the hotel, the boys were definitely switched on. Usually when we warm up for a game, Dallas and I start it off. But at the hotel **Jonah was in the corridor before us so I knew he was ready. He couldn't wait to get to the ground.** It was a good sign.

In the changing-shed before the game I thought I'd try and rev him up a bit. I remembered that after Fiji won the Hong Kong Sevens earlier in the year a reporter asked them if they thought they would have won if Jonah had been playing for New Zealand. And one of them, I can't remember who it was, said that he thought Fiji would have still won because Lomu is only good for one or two runs a game. So I told Jonah the story. **I told him how they thought he was useless after a couple of runs. And his nostrils flared up. I'd never seen him so worked up! You could see the fire in his eyes.** He put his headphones on and he wouldn't talk to anyone after that. I tried to talk to him about a penalty move we had sorted out and he said, "Bugger the move! Just give me the ball!"

Now that Jonah was fired up I thought I'd try and get Joeli a bit worked up. I told him how a few years ago, when Fiji didn't pick him in their sevens team, that one of their officials described him as "as useless as tits on a bull". His nostrils went out, too, and you could tell he was ready to tear those Fijian boys apart.

By this stage I was feeling pretty happy with myself so I walked around the changing-room to see who else I could pick on! I told a few more stories to the boys just to help motivate them. But, to be honest, **everyone was up for it anyway. We were one game away from a gold medal. We owed the Fijians for what happened in Hong Kong.** Titch talked about Richard Crawshaw – our long-time manager who had died of leukemia in July. There was heaps of passion in the boys. We couldn't wait for kick-off. When Zinzan Brooke was playing sevens he used to talk about being white hot in the stomach and ice cool upstairs. That was what we needed now. If we could control our aggression we could create history.

Before kick-off I had a real good feeling about the game. I just knew we were going to win after what had happened in the semi against Samoa. We won that game because of our defence. When Rico made that vital tackle towards the end there were three other guys with him. I figured if we were prepared to bust our guts on defence like that no one could beat us. The funny thing is that throughout the tournament we hadn't played very well. The only game we played really good sevens was against Sri Lanka. But I still felt good about the final because we were working hard on defence and big defence wins tournaments.

The atmosphere was unbelievable when we went on the

field. There were bus loads of New Zealanders there from the village. Jonah was awesome. For the first time in 11 years of playing the Fijians you could see fear in some of their eyes when the big fella got the ball.

And when the final whistle went and we'd won 21-12 there was a feeling of complete joy. It was totally different from anything else I've ever experienced. All year we'd been talking about winning at the Commonwealth Games.

When you win Hong Kong it's worth $US180,000. But that doesn't mean anything when you compare it with winning a gold medal. So there was a real feeling of relief . . . a bit like the feeling you get when you're in a winning All Black team. That's why the All Blacks don't react with the unbridled joy that we had in KL because every time you put that black jersey on you have to win. In the ABs it's the fear of losing that drives you rather than the joy of winning. There was a lot of relief when we won the gold, but we were able to be much more emotional about it because of the occasion.

People have told me since that the scenes of joy when we won were some of the highlights of the Games. We did the haka in front of all the stands. The crowd were loving it. We were, too. We actually forgot that there was going to be a medal ceremony. We were told to put our track suits on and assemble at the podium. Dallas suggested we do what the 1972 Olympic rowers did – join hands and lift them above our heads once we'd got our medals. That went down well with the boys. They called out "New Zealand" and we stepped up onto the podium. **Man! What a great feeling. I could hear Jonah and Dallas sobbing next to me. Some people reckoned I was crying but . . . it was just sweat.**

One of the best moments was looking at our trainer Keith Roberts. He'd trained a lot of Commonwealth and Olympic Games athletes in the past but none of them had made it to the podium. Six months before he told us that we would be good enough to get the gold. I remember looking at him and he had tears streaming down his face. He was so proud of us and we

Winning gold was a real team effort – trainer Keith Roberts (left) and coach Gordon Tietjens savour the moment with me.

were so happy for him after all the work he'd put in as well. Then these ladies started walking towards us and they were carrying out medals. They were glowing. The only sad part about the night was that Keith, Kev, Thursty and Titch didn't get medals. They all deserved to be standing next to us.

There was more emotion when we got back to the changing-shed. That was the time when **I started to think about my family and all the things I had to overcome to make it on to the field.** We knew that all of New Zealand would have stayed up to watch the final and that was a real humbling feeling. It wasn't just about rugby anymore. We'd won New Zealand's first gold medal of the Games.

By the time we got back to the village it was about 2am. We'd made a decision not to celebrate too much because we knew that a lot of the New Zealand athletes still had to

Jonah, me and Dallas Seymour pose with our medals under a banner made by some of my aunties.

compete. But when we eventually got to our rooms we got a bit of a shock. The netball girls had decorated the corridor with messages, balloons and posters. That really made us feel like part of the team. I don't think any of the boys took their medals off that night. There were a lot more hakas, lots of singing and a bit of nudity. It was great night . . . the kind of night you never forget.

TUESDAY 15 SEPTEMBER

AT 9AM WE WERE still up singing and bullshitting. **Jonah got the clippers out after breakfast. No 1s for everyone.** Seemed like a good idea at the time. I thought I looked okay, but not too sure about some of the other fellas.

Everyone was congratulating us at breakfast. The downside

Sevens heaven . . . the golden moment in Hong Kong.

of the whole gold medal experience came when Roger, Bruce and Titch had to leave to go back to New Zealand for their NPC commitments. I think New Zealand rugby missed out on a great opportunity by not letting the boys stay for the duration of the Games. Every other team, with the exception of the English, stayed and supported their teams. I know that Jonah came in for a bit of flak by staying on, even though his knee was puffed up. I think that was a bit unfair. **We all should have been able to stay and support the people that had supported us because there's no doubt that we all came away with the feeling that as rugby players we have got it pretty good nowadays.**

The comment was made within the sevens team that the swimmers and the runners and some of the other New Zealanders were real athletes. They make a lot more sacrifices than we do. A lot of them end up owing money just so they can compete. It's their sense of achievement that drives them. You couldn't help but be inspired.

Jonah, Dallas and I made up for the other fellas being back in New Zealand by supporting as many of the Kiwi athletes as possible over the next few days. It didn't matter if they were winning gold, silver or bronze, making a final, or just competing. It was a great time to be a Kiwi.

On Song In Hong Kong

THERE'S A SAYING ASSOCIATED with the Hong Kong Sevens – if you get bored, you turn around and watch the rugby!

Not because the rugby's boring, but because there is so much happening in the stadium that sometimes the sevens, especially on the first day, struggles to match the entertainment in the South Stand. And depending on who you are touring with, life back at the hotel can be just as colourful.

There are plenty of rules to learn when you're on the road and the first one that was passed down to me when I first made the trip to Hong Kong in 1988 came courtesy of Johnny "The Shu" Schuster. He was an experienced All Black at the time and I was a bit nervous when I was told I'd be rooming with him. **When we got into the room he looked at me and said, "First lesson, boy . . . take everything." He opened up his bag and started taking everything from the room – the hair dryer, the robes, the towels, even the hangers!** Then he said, "Do you want any of this stuff?" When I said "yes" he told me to go to one of the other rooms and strip the joint!

Straight away I was at ease. I realised that the players in the team – even though guys like John Kirwan, Terry Wright, John Gallagher, Shu and Zinzan Brooke were heroes of mine – were all good fellas. They wanted to win, no doubt about that, but they knew how to have a laugh as well.

To me, the biggest buzz of the trip was playing with those guys. I had never even thought about playing sevens for New Zealand until right before the final of the nationals at Pukekohe a few weeks earlier. I'd made my debut for Auckland in 1987 when I played one game at the nationals, but in 1988 the Auckland coach Maurice Trapp made me a regular in the team. **Before the final Maurice told me 'they' would be watching me. It took me a while to work out that the 'they' he was talking about were the New Zealand selectors.** We won the final and I was feeling pretty pleased with myself but when I got back into the changing-room Maurice told me he thought I did enough to make the team. I'd forgotten there was going to be a team selected! Then Nick Botica – Frano's dad – told me he thought I'd done enough as well. Oh man! I was so nervous. All I could think about was Scottie Pierce. He'd played awesome sevens the year before but didn't make the New Zealand team. I didn't want to go through what he had to.

In a few minutes we were all in the clubrooms and they read the team out. I didn't hear any of the names . . . you never do when a team's being read out. You just listen for your name. Then finally – it was the last name read – I heard "Eric Rush, Auckland." I couldn't believe it. I was in the New Zealand Sevens team. All the players were rushed into a side room where the coach Peter Thorburn and manager John Sturgeon gave us a little team talk. I don't remember anything they said. I was standing there in a dream.

I was in a bit of a dream when we got to Hong Kong three weeks later as well. I was just blown away by the place. Then we were dropped off at **our hotel – The Hilton! I'd never seen anything like it. But, as the saying goes, I hadn't seen anything yet.**

The atmosphere at the Hong Kong Stadium is unbelievable. If you're a rugby player or supporter, and you haven't experienced the Hong Kong Sevens, then you haven't lived through the ultimate rugby experience.

It's the crowd that make the Hong Kong Sevens what it is. Sure, the rugby players on show are the best in the world but

Another tough day at the Hong Kong office – physio David Abercrombie, Terry Wright, Kevin Putt, John Schuster and me.

without the crowd and the atmosphere they generate it wouldn't be half the event that it has become.

Basically, it's a three day party . . . a very good party. You know how sometimes when you arrive at a party and you're quite excited about it but when you walk in the room everyone is real quiet? Well, Hong Kong is like the party you go to and when you arrive everyone is dancing and ready for a great night.

There's lots of drinking going on. The bars stay open the whole weekend so places like *Joe Bananas* and the *Bull and Bear* are always jam packed with fans. **But in my 11 years of going to Hong Kong I have never seen a single fight. Not one. That would never happen in New Zealand.** Imagine if a couple of hundred boys had a few drinks one afternoon. All it would take is one fella to say something nasty about another and it would be all on. But not in Hong Kong. The crowd are a good natured bunch. They support their teams with a lot of passion, but once their team is out, the underdogs automatically get their support.

Without a doubt the star of the show is The Pie Man. He's more popular with the crowd than any of the players. He's a big fat English guy. **He's got a stomach on him that makes Richard Turner look like a slicker version of Terry Wright.** I've never seen a stomach like it. Every year about 30 people show up with Who Ate All The Pies? t-shirts and he's always wearing his I Ate All The Pies top. Whenever the TV cameras are on him and he appears on the giant TV screen, the whole crowd starts yelling and he stands up, off comes the shirt, and he eats another pie. He spends more time signing autographs than watching the rugby.

One thing you are always guaranteed of in Hong Kong is a few streakers. The crowd love it when someone makes a dash across the field and, of course, the security people loathe them. One year when we were preparing for our quarter-final, a streaker ran right through the middle of our drills. He ran to the other side of the ground and dived across the line as though he'd just scored the winning try. About 10 security guys started chasing him when he headed back towards us. We should have chucked a black jersey on him because he showed a pretty good side-step and great fend to some of the fellas in the chase. He ran through us again and then dived into the crowd. The security guys were determined to get him but within 30 seconds about 50 guys had taken off their shirts to throw the security guys off the scent. Then they started singing, "Whe're's the streaker," taunting the poor security fellas.

Obviously a lot of the stunts are inspired by the giant TV screen in the ground. In 1997 a couple was caught having sex in the back of one of the stands. The crowd loved it but I'm not too sure what the couple thought about it!

One of the great traditions is for people to propose marriage on the screen. A few players have done it over the years and one year Scottie Pierce decided he wanted to get engaged to

Who ate all the pies? Take one guess!

his girlfriend Jane. He wasn't sure if he wanted to make it so public though, but we encouraged him to go through with it. "Yeah, great idea Scottie. Go for it! It'll be great. She'll never forget it. She'll love it." **He was really excited about it when it happened but we thought we'd make him a bit more nervous so we were like, "Bloody dickhead.** What did you do that for? What a stupid idea." The funniest thing about it was she wasn't even in the ground when the proposal was posted. She'd gone shopping!

There is generally a really good rapport between the players from different teams. This usually shines through on the

Sunday night when after all the finals are completed the Hong Kong Rugby Union puts on the players' dinner. One of the best was in 1990 – even though we'd lost the final to Fiji. Every year the organisers invite a few teams to do a skit. We always just sing a song before doing the haka. The stand-out performers that year were Will Carling and his English Barbarians. **They hired a beautiful model to M.C. their skit and she told everyone that the Baabaas had organised a beauty parade. You can guess how all the rugby boys reacted to that.** We were cheering and getting ready for a great night. The M.C. introduced the first lady and out walked Will Carling wearing a bikini! What a let down.

I couldn't even go up to him and tell him how bad he looked because I was banned from talking to him by the other English fellas. We'd played the Barbarians in the semi-final and beaten them 24-6. I scored a try when I chased a kick from Zinzan and picked it up just before Will got to me, so his team-mates told me to turn my back on him every time he came up to me because that's all he'd seen of me all day.

A few of the boys knew what was going on so they played this game with him. It was a stupid game but at the time it seemed quite funny. Basically you had to go up to someone, mumble something, and when they asked you what you said you shout as loud as you can, "Get F---ed!"

Poor old Will had to deal with it all night. He's a good fella, though. I owe him a lot actually because the following year, when he was captaining England, he got a call from the Barbarians wanting to know if I was good enough to play for them in a match against England at Twickenham. **In those days only one non-test player was able to play for the Barbarians and, thanks to Will, I got the call.** I was pulled out of an Auckland B team trip to Wellington and the next day I was flying to London with Ian Jones, Richard Loe and Joe Stanley.

When we got to Twickenham on match day I went out on to the ground with the other Barbarians just to soak up the atmosphere. After a while the English team came out and I saw Will out of the corner of my eye. I wasn't sure if I should go and say anything to him. In the end I didn't . . . I thought I should just remain serious and focused. A minute later he came up to me and mumbled something. I was about to say, "What?" but then I realised he was trying to catch me out by playing "Get F---ed?" I just laughed at him and he walked off swearing and muttering to himself.

That eased the tension for me for a while. Just before kick-off, though, I was real nervous. I was about to run out on to Twickenham – 'the home of rugby'. David Campese could tell that I was feeling it a bit so he said, "Stuff it, man. Just play sevens. That's what I'm gonna do. Just chuck the bloody thing around. Who cares if we win or lose?" England won the game by two points and I was named Player of The Game. A week later we played against Wales at Cardiff Arms Park and won and I was awarded Player of The Game again. Then there was **all this talk about me playing for Ireland. I qualified because my old man's Irish. But, hey, a Maori boy wearing green socks? I don't think so.**

Will was just one of the international superstars who showed up in Hong Kong regularly. It wasn't until my first Hong Kong experience in 1988 was over that I realised how lucky I was to be a part of the whole thing. The Australian team boasted names like Campese, Simon Poidevin and Michael Lynagh. I was so focused on trying to impress my own team mates that I didn't take much notice of any of the other teams until I was looking back at the tournament a few days after the final.

I used to idolise a lot of the international guys. Being a flanker at the time, I had huge respect for guys like Poidevin and the great Scottish No 7 John Jeffrey. Then one night I went to a club called 1997 and the two of them were **arm wrestling . . . hanging upside down from the rafters above the dance floor! Hong Kong has that effect on you. Everyone is doing crazy things.**

Shu's party trick was to confuse the locals with a little toy he used to carry around with him everywhere. It would make all these different sounds. His favourite thing to do was to cue up the sound of a mobile telephone ringing. We'd be sitting in a busy airport waiting for a flight and all of a sudden this phone would ring. He'd let it ring a few times and then he'd take off his shoe and start talking into it. "Hello . . . I thought I told you not to call me on this number!" You'd look at the expression on peoples' faces and you knew they weren't sure if he was taking the piss or not.

And, of course, wherever there is beer there's always someone willing to spike someone's drink. That happened in 1989 when the English Barbarians spiked our drinks at the Sunday dinner. I don't know what they put in it but **Zinzan was the worst affected. He almost went into a coma. Ambulances were called to the hotel and everything.** Shu had had some of the same drink but he was just pissed. He was running down the corridor of the hotel breaking all the lights outside each room. It would be an understatement to say that the staff at the Hilton hated us.

The most innocent laughs from Hong Kong usually come courtesy of the Papua New Guinea players. A lot of them have never been in a big city before, let alone a place like Hong Kong. Normally on their first day the players spend hours just riding the lifts. Up and down, up and down, just laughing. They've never seen lifts before!

One of the great things about sevens is that it brings the best out of all the boys – on and off the field. When you play fifteens there's always so much pressure . . . especially in the All Blacks. **There's pressure to win in the sevens team as well, but the difference is we're still able to enjoy ourselves because the atmosphere created by the fans is so infectious** – something not all coaches appreciate.

I don't think Gordon Tietjens could believe what he saw in his first year in charge of the team in 1994. Titch's coaching philosophy is based around discipline and, as far as he's concerned, that means strictly no alcohol. So, you can imagine his surprise when we got to the *Bull and Bear*, ordered his

Happiness is being in Hong Kong . . . and beating Australia in the final!

lemonade and turned around to see the boys having a beer. He was livid. He was even more upset when a few of the boys decided to stay on after the rest of the team headed back to the hotel. The next morning he came to see me and said he couldn't believe the guys were drinking beer. He didn't want to say anything to them but told me, as captain, I should. So I called them all into my room. I said, **"Look boys, it's easy for me to tell you guys not to drink because I don't drink. But Titch isn't happy."** The ring leader was the senior All Black Graeme Bachop and he agreed on behalf of the team that they wouldn't drink for the rest of the week. Then he looked me straight in the eye and said, "If we win, you're going to get pissed with us." I figured if that's what it takes to stop the boys from drinking I'd go along with it.

A couple of days later we played Australia in the final and won 32-20. I'd forgotten about the deal but within seconds of the final whistle going Bash grabbed the front of my shirt and said, "You're with me tonight!"

Mess with Gordon Tietjens at your peril.

It was the first time I'd ever drunk. All the boys were ganging up on me, handing me drink after drink. They didn't realise that I was chucking every second one in the pot plants. The boys were upset that I was still on my feet . . . **I don't think a lot of them even knew where their feet were! At 7am the next morning Bash was in terrible shape. He was standing in the foyer of the Hilton Hotel, walking around in circles.** He had no shirt on and his tie was around his head. Every time one of the hotel staff tried to help him he'd start yelling. He wouldn't let anyone touch him. In the end we had to carry him to the lift. A couple of hours later we had to go down to breakfast. I'd never seen an uglier sight. All these rugby fellas were sitting there with food falling out of their mouths. The only ones that were well behaved were the guys who'd fallen asleep on the tables!

Titch has relaxed a bit since those days. He tends to let the boys out every now and again to enjoy themselves but the boys know not to push him. If they have a late night and it interferes with their training the next day it's a pretty good bet that player won't ever wear the black jersey again. Titch sets high standards and he expect his players to be the same.

I remember his first training session with us in 1994. I thought he was a bloody maniac. He worked us so hard. He wasn't happy until everyone was walking at training. Usually players are laughing and talking before a training session but when we fronted up for our second day with him everyone was nervous and quiet. I remember thinking that he was working us hard because he wanted to stamp his authority on the team after taking over from Wayne Smith. But, five years later, he's exactly the same. I don't have any doubt that the reason why we've been so successful with Titch is because he works us so hard. In 1993 we lost in the semi-finals against Western Samoa – the first time a New Zealand team hadn't made the final since 1985. A year later, when we won it, none of the games were as hard as Titch's trainings. None of them.

I like the idea of going into coaching when I hang up my boots and there's plenty that I've learnt from Thorbs, Smithy and Titch that I'll take on board. Thorbs was a great man manager while Smithy was a meticulous planner. It continues to amaze me that with all of these awards that are given out every year Titch still hasn't received a nomination for Coach of the Year. People like to heap a lot of the praise on the players when we're winning but there's no doubt **Titch is the guy that brings it all together. His real strength is identifying young talent.** He could pick someone out of Manawatu and say, "Watch that boy." I'd ask Titch what the player's name was and he'd say, "Christian Cullen." A few weeks later Cully was in the team for the 1995 Hong Kong Sevens. He played one game for us and 12 months later came back and won the Leslie Williams

Trophy when he was voted Player of the Tournament – all this before he was in the All Black squad. Since Cully there's been a heap of other fellas who Titch has promoted. Guys like Jonah Lomu, Caleb Ralph, Rua Tipoki, Roger Randle and Rico Gear all have Titch to thank for where they are today.

The master stroke of Titch's career in charge of the sevens team came as soon as he got the job. He made us play with a sweeper. The only other team using the sweeper system at the time were the Fijians.

When I look back at the success we had in Hong Kong before Titch and the sweeper system – we'd won it in 1989 and made the final in 1988, 1990, 1991 and 1992 – I can't help but be amazed that we were able to do so well, because without a sweeper the opposition only have to break one defensive line instead of two.

The change definitely helped us. We had immediate success in 1994 when we beat Australia in the final and we followed that with two wins against Fiji in the next two finals.

There's little doubt that sevens has been good to me . . . especially considering that in the early days I just saw sevens as a way to get fit for fifteens. But that changed when I made that first trip to Hong Kong in 1988. Zinzan was the captain and he was as competitive as they come. He used to say to us, "We aren't going to lose. We're not going to f---ing lose!" That was his team talk! But he led by example. **He was the sort of captain that you really wanted to follow. The boys would have laid down in front of traffic for him.**

Unfortunately we weren't good enough to win that year. We lost to the Australians 13-12 in the final. But Zinny was good about it. He told us to remember what it felt like to lose the final. "We'll get 'em next year," he said.

And, sure enough, we did. We beat Australia 22-10 in the final. It was an unbelievable feeling. I remember walking off the field with John Gallagher and he told me that winning Hong Kong was a better feeling than winning the World Cup. You can't get a better compliment for the place than that.

Of All Blacks And Chicken Wings

HONG KONG HAS PROVIDED many highlights and one of the most memorable came in a hotel room! In 1992, after we lost to the Fijians 22-6 in the final, I got a phone call. New All Black coach Laurie Mains was on the other end of the phone and he told me he and his selectors – Peter Thorburn and Earle Kirton – wanted me to play in the up-coming All Black trial.

I'd played all my fifteens rugby as a flanker at that stage but Laurie wanted me to play on the wing. I said "yes" straight away and hung up and went into a bit of a panic. Winger? I didn't know anything about being a winger. Poor old Terry Wright got a good old ear bashing on the way home because I didn't even know where a winger should stand.

When I got back to New Zealand I went straight down to the trials in Napier, and had quite a good game although Grant Fox was getting pissed at me because I kept asking him where to stand (I still didn't know!). I was marking Lolani Koko who was about six foot five and 18 stone. **I had to look twice at him when he first ran at me because I thought he was wearing sunglasses . . . actually, they were his nostrils!**

I did enough to be named in the shadow team to play the All Blacks that weekend but because I pulled my hamstring in the last minute of the first trial I decided I'd better pull out. Doc (John) Mayhew came to see me but I told him not to bother even looking at it because I knew it was pretty bad. But he told me he needed to have a look at it because **Laurie was considering me for the All Blacks. When I heard that my heart almost came through my skin.** I couldn't believe what he had just said. I just told him to fix me up quick.

He gave me physiotherapy and I had a fitness test the next day. But it was no good. It didn't come right in time. I was the most disappointed I'd ever been in my life. I headed back to Auckland convinced that I'd missed my chance. I watched the trial on television and the shadow team ended up beating the All Blacks. I couldn't help thinking that I could have been a part of that.

I missed out on the All Black team to tour Australia and South Africa but I was given the consolation of a place in the New Zealand 'B' team. Even though my hamstring was still a bit suspect, I played against England 'B' at Hamilton. Tony Underwood made a monkey out of me in my second game on the wing. I had a couple of good runs but I learned a few lessons as well.

When we headed back to the hotel we watched the All Blacks play New South Wales and there was a big scrap and Paul Henderson got sent home because he'd broken his hand. I remember as we went to bed we had heard that Paul was coming home and our flankers at the time were Dallas Seymour and Mark Carter. We ran a lottery in the team as to who should go, and we entered our names in it.

Anyway, the phone went at three in the morning but I couldn't be bothered answering it. Then there was a knock on the door. I was rooming with Timo Tagaloa who, like me, was pretending to be asleep because neither of us wanted to get out of bed. Then the door slid open and it was Thorbs. Poor old fella. He wears big thick glasses – he's pretty much blind at the best of times. **But in a dark room with two black guys, you could forgive him for having trouble seeing.** Anyway, I watched him walk around feeling his way with his arms. Then he grabbed the first foot he could find and said "Get up. Get up!

Congratulations you're an All Black." He'd grabbed Timo's foot and within a second he was up on his feet bouncing around on his bed in his lava lava, yelling and screaming. It was awesome. I was so happy for him. Then Thorbs says "Oh, you are Rushy aren't you?" Then I realised I was the new All Black and I started yelling and screaming. **Poor Timo just collapsed on his bed. Man, I felt sorry for Timo, but that was all swallowed up in the emotions of me making the All Blacks.**

Two hours later I was on a plane to Australia and within hours of getting to Canberra I was told I'd be playing the next day against A.C.T. Before my first team meeting I was shitting myself. I was real nervous about meeting Fitzy as he was one of the old guys in the Auckland team.

I'd made my Auckland debut in 1986 but it was never a united team.

People always ask me what it was like to be a part of such a great team but, in reality, while Auckland was beating everyone, it was almost as if there were two teams within the one. There were the All Blacks – guys like Gary Whetton, John Drake, John Kirwan, Terry Wright, Steve McDowell, Joe Stanley and AJ Whetton – and the rest of us. In my five years with Auckland, Gary Whetton never even spoke to me. Guys like Michael Jones, Zinzan Brooke and Robin Brooke weren't accepted as part of the group until they made the All Blacks. After being in the team for a while I could appreciate why Auckland was hated so much around the country. **There was a real arrogance to some of the players. But, you can't take anything away from them because that Auckland team was the best team that I have ever seen.** They won everything and they won everything with style. I left Auckland to join North Harbour in 1991 without ever really making it in Auckland. So when it came time to meeting Fitzy – now the All Black captain – I didn't know what to do.

Before I even had a chance to think of something to say, Fitzy came up to me. "Welcome to the club, Rushie." That meant the world to me coming from someone like him. Then the whole team came over and congratulated me. I was on cloud nine.

I couldn't sleep the night before the game. I was rooming with Graeme Bachop and he knew what was going on so he thought we should go and find all the brown fellas. So we went to the physio room and there they all were – Michael Jones, Frank Bunce, Walter Little . . . if they had a bit of brown blood in them they were there. None of them were injured. It's just that in those days you had to pay for everything so they'd always go to the physio room to book-up videos and order room service!

I'd heard about the tradition of receiving your All Black jersey from the manager in his room but apparently it didn't apply this time . . . not for a midweek game against the A.C.T. **I went into the changing-shed and the jerseys were just pulled from a bag and tossed to the players. Mine came flying across the room and landed on the bench. I grabbed it and hung it up and just stared at it.** I looked around the room and all the boys were going through their normal pre-match routine. The props were looking quite calm, the flankers looked like they were getting ready for war and the backs were warming up by throwing a ball around and practising their sidesteps. I slipped my jersey off the hook and took it into one of the toilets. I was so excited. I had my first All Black jersey. I started rubbing the Silver Fern all over my face. This was it. My dream of being an All Black had come true. I don't think I could believe it, even at that stage.

I went back out and joined the other boys who by this time all had scowls on their faces. I hung the jersey back up because I wanted to savour the moment. I put my tracksuit top back on and was jogging round the room thinking about what I had to do. Then, a couple of minutes later, just before we were going on, Frank came in and asked me if I was ready. I told him that I'd been ready for this game for 20 years. **I was about to walk out into the corridor to get ready to go on to the field and he said, "You better put your jersey on, mate!"** I was just so pumped up for the game that the jersey was still hanging on the hook!

With Dallas Seymour (left) and Andy Earl after a midweek match for the All Blacks in South Africa, 1992.

The game was an awesome experience. I ran out there, scored a try and didn't make too many mistakes. It was only my third game on the wing and it was for the All Blacks. After the game Laurie and Earle came in and said that they were going to make a winger out of me. They told me I'd had three games so the time for excuses were gone. I was a winger now and that was that. From now on, there was no room for error.

I had to wait another three years before I got my first test cap. I went on the tour to England and Scotland in 1993 but it wasn't until the World Cup in South Africa in 1995 that the next part of my All Black dream came true.

The occasion was our World Cup game against Wales at Ellis Park. Jeff Wilson and Jonah were on the wings and I was on the reserves bench. I was so excited just to be on the bench because it meant I got to keep my test jersey. The boys were going great and then Jonah almost scored a try (another one!) but he got a bit of a knock. Laurie told me to warm-up straight away and I flew down to the sideline. Jonah was limping back and I didn't know it but Laurie had phoned Doc and told him to get him off the field and save him for the next game. But Jonah, like the rest of the All Blacks, hates coming off. He was telling Doc to leave him alone, but then he looked up and saw me at halfway. **I must have looked real keen because as soon as he saw me, he walked off. Frank and Walter had their hands up and I was just running around high-fiving everyone!**

The first time I'd seen Jonah was when I was playing touch in South Auckland. One of our guys made a break, and Jonah was on our side of the field, and the next thing I saw was a big black guy taking off to catch him. He was big, but boy was he fast. I was like, "shit – who is this guy?" I had a couple of cracks at him but he was picking me up easy and I was thinking he would make an awesome sevens player. I talked to him after the game.

"Ever played sevens?"

"Nah."

"Do you want to go on a sevens trip?"

"Oh yeah. Where to?"

"Singapore."

"Oh yeah. When do we leave?"

"Next week."

"Choice, bro."

Jonah was still at school. He was only 16 but he could have made the team that year if he had wanted to. He eventually made it to Hong Kong in 1995 where he was absolutely awesome.

When Jonah first got into the All Black team Laurie couldn't talk to him. Laurie's from the old school. He's very honest. There's no grey area with him. Everything is either black or white. His attitude is, "you do it my way, or you don't do it at all." That's how it is with him. You always know where you stand with Laurie Mains.

Jonah has never been the greatest trainer. Not many of the

Polynesians are. They don't like the hard training, but when you put a ball in their hands on the paddock . . . that's another story. We had these killer training camps before the World Cup in 1995 which were not really about getting fit. It was more a mental thing. Guys were pulling out all the way through. They'd get to the sideline and Laurie would ask what the problem was. I remember Mark Cooksley and Shane Howarth complained about hamstring problems. Laurie responded by telling them to get back to the motel, pack their bags and go home. They didn't just get sent to the sideline they actually got sent home. **They had legitimate injuries but Laurie wasn't pissing round with anyone at the camps.**

At the next camp Cooksley came back and got another injury, and the poor guy kept running through it. Laurie got stuck into him, asking him what the hell he was doing playing through the injury and poor old Rigger didn't know what the hell to do. We had been training all day. We'd have to run twenty-five 150s, 100 down and ups, ruck and runs . . . the whole lot. Jonah just didn't do well in them and Laurie didn't think he was mentally tough enough. Jonah, being quite a moody guy, wouldn't respond to Laurie's 'black and white' mentality.

After the camps Jonah was selected for the Hong Kong Sevens. **Gordon Tietjens knew what Jonah was capable of, and he knew how to get the best out of him. He never demanded anything from Jonah. He just asked for it.** Jonah responded and was the star of the show, joining Glen Osborne and myself as the only New Zealand winners of the Leslie Williams Trophy, awarded to the best player of the tournament.

When we came back to New Zealand Jonah was named in the North Island team to play the South Island but he was also told that he was in the sevens team to go to Japan which meant that he'd miss the two All Black trials which were on at the same time. That meant he wasn't in the frame for the World Cup.

I was still on a high after winning Hong Kong and he rings

me up and says, "Bugger them. Bugger them, man. I'm off to league." I said, "What are you talking about, boy?" He said, "They bloody dropped me, the bastards; they bloody dropped me." He put Phil Kingsley-Jones on the phone and he confirmed that Jonah had been told to go to Japan. Then **Titch rang up and asked if I'd heard from Jonah. He'd heard that Jonah had quit and that he'd signed to play league.** Between the three of us we persuaded him to go to Dunedin to play the North-South game. I just told him to go down there, have one more game with the bros and then take off. "Come and play with Frank, Walt, and Ice and then go." He agreed. I knew if we could get him to Dunedin that would buy us a little bit more time to convince him to stick with rugby.

When we got down to Dunedin they roomed me with him. Laurie came to me, cause he wouldn't talk to him, and said, "What the hell is wrong with this guy." Frank and I told Laurie that he had to talk to Island fellas a different way than he'd talk to anyone else. If you're "in your face" to a guy like Jonah, he'll just switch off. But if you go to him and say, "you're the man, this team really needs you", he'll win the World Cup for you. I told Laurie that if he left Jonah at home, he could be leaving the reason for winning the World Cup behind. I told him that at my own detriment because I was a winger and I was cutting my chances down by saying that Jonah should go. But I honestly believed if we didn't take him we wouldn't win the Cup. Laurie responded by saying, "But I can't talk to him. I can't f---ing talk to him!" If Jonah was eating some fatty food **Laurie would come to me and say, "Rushy, what the hell is he eating now? Go and tell him to watch what he's eating."** So then I'd go off and tell Jonah this, and he'd just say to tell him to get stuffed!

Laurie would always come to Frank or I to talk to Jonah. We told him that he had to be more complimentary to Jonah to get the best out of him. Jonah needs encouragement. Laurie made an effort after the North-South game. Jonah was angry as hell that day and he killed everyone in that game. He was marking Jeff Wilson who played okay, but Jonah was on fire. Jonah

"Rushy, what the hell is he eating now . . ."

came off the paddock and Laurie said to him, "That was a bloody good game, well done." I went up to Jonah and asked him what Laurie had said and Jonah was like, "Oh, stuff him, he's just trying to kiss my arse now". Laurie couldn't win!

The New Zealand selectors named him in the 'B' team for the next trial match and told him not to go to Japan. **He ended up playing awesome rugby in the next two trials and made the World Cup team . . . and we all know what happened there.**

I wasn't involved with the All Blacks during the struggles of 1998. My involvement with the team finished in 1996. I played four tests that year – three as a replacement – and was part of the midweek team on the historic, series-winning tour of South Africa. But from the outside looking in, the one thing that really seems to be missing from today's All Blacks is a sense of fun.

When I got into the All Blacks in 1992 I was surrounded by All Blacks from the old school. The jersey meant everything to them. Mike Brewer came up to me before my first game and asked me if I was willing to piss blood for the jersey. He told me afterwards he'd only said it because Mark Shaw had said it to him before his debut. The players were full on. It was all about winning, but when the game was over they'd hit the beers. It's all about a tour balance. You can't expect the players to be full on all the time.

Laurie understood that. He'd let the boys relax. He'd never join in, though. In that sense he was pretty aloof. I was shit scared of him. **You learnt pretty quickly to stay away from him on the day of a game. The Otago boys used to call him 'Lemons' because he always looks like he's just had a big feed of them.** He was a real tense fella. He loved that jersey so much; it was the bee-all and end-all. Everything he did was geared towards winning.

Towards the end, he chilled a lot, especially during the World Cup. He got on a lot better with the guys. Frank Bunce was his boy. He loved Frank. Frank got away with plenty. He could do no wrong. I sometimes felt that because Frank was my best mate, Laurie felt like he had to put up with me. That's what it felt like, anyway!

After the World Cup in South Africa we had three tests to play – one against Italy and two against France – before the end of the international season and the end of Laurie's reign as coach. He was as relaxed as I've ever seen him on that tour. One night we were at a restaurant and, because we weren't allowed to eat meat, we all had to order the fish. But it looked horrible. The only fish I eat is snapper and I don't know what sort of fish was on the menu but when I saw it I knew it wasn't snapper! I went to see Doc Mayhew to see if I could order anything else and Laurie asked me what was wrong. After I told him he said I could have a steak. **All the boys were dark. They started calling me Eric Mains after that.**

The thing about Laurie was that he was never too big to

Butter wouldn't melt in our mouths . . . me, Frank and Oz.

admit he was wrong. After we'd been beaten in the first test at Toulouse he copped a serve from our manager, the great All Black Colin 'Pinetree' Meads. When we arrived at the ground for the test we were put in a dressing-room which wouldn't have been more than a couple of metres across. **Laurie was furious when he found out that the French were in a beautifully spacious room with spa pools.** When his demands that we were put in a better room were turned down he blocked off the entrance to the room. The door was right by the entrance to the playing field so it turned out the French had to go the long way around when they tried to warm up before kickoff. Because Laurie had issued strict instructions that no one was to get past, Pinetree and the Minister of French Police couldn't get into the shed before the game either.

Back at the hotel, Pinetree had a few choice words for Laurie. "Laurie, I got a few things to say," Pinetree started. "Laurie, who the hell do you think you are? You stopped the French from getting on the paddock to warm up. You gave them their bloody team talk!"

You could have heard a pin drop but Laurie's old school, too, and he respects people that have been there and done that and he has a great respect for Pinetree. "Point taken, Pinetree," broke the silence.

Then Pinetree let rip into our forwards. **"You guys talk about blowing rucks . . . you couldn't blow a hen off it's nest!** Poor old Stu Forster and Simon Culhane, they get the blame for the loss, but it was you bastards. In my days we had a forward pack that didn't have one quarter of the skills that you guys have got. Not one f---ing quarter. But I tell you what. We weren't bloody scared of anyone. And you bastards are!"

That set the tone for a pretty ferocious week of training. There was heaps of motivation to win that second test . . . revenge, the jersey and for Laurie. It was his last test in charge. On the morning of a test the normal thing to do was for the forwards to go through their lineout moves and the backs to go through their backline moves before going to the manager's room to get your jerseys. But Laurie made us go to the team room where he had all the jerseys lined out on the table.

As he handed them to the players he thanked us for all of our support. **When he was talking to Jonah the big fella had tears in his eyes - that's how far those two had come.** It was so emotional for all of us. We were ready to play the test right then and there. It was obvious to see how much Laurie meant to us when the Brooke brothers carried him off the field after we won the test later that day.

John Hart was a very different coach. Both of them are great coaches, there's no doubt about that. They just have different ways of motivating their players. Laurie always talked about the importance of playing from the heart, and then the jersey, and the importance of playing smart. Harty would talk about the importance of playing smart first and then he'd talk about the jersey and the heart. They had slightly different approaches, but with the same end result. It's a small thing, but when you've been an All Black, the jersey comes before everything.

Mongrels I Have Met

I'M PRETTY LUCKY MY rugby career coincided with the first few years of professionalism. I've been able to jump on the gravy train and make up for all those years I played rugby and lost money. Because of all the sevens I was playing, in the early '90s I was only able to earn about $12,000 a year – not great money for a lawyer. But while it's great to finally get paid for playing, I wouldn't give up the amateur years for anything.

You'll never hear me complain about those early years because, while my bank balance wasn't getting any bigger, I was able to play sevens in places like Uruguay, Argentina, Chile, Bahrain, the United Arab Emirates, Samoa, Fiji, the Cook Islands, Australia, Japan, France, Spain, Israel, the United States and the United Kingdom.

And **at the centre of most of the mischief on those tours was Lindsay Raki.** By the time I met Raki he'd already played his last game for the New Zealand Sevens team – in Hong Kong in 1987. He'd made a name for himself as a feisty, attacking fullback with Counties and made his NZ Maori debut in 1985. My first tour with him was in 1988 when the Maori team toured France, Italy, Spain and Argentina.

The team was stacked full of great players. There were lots of guys who had been, or were going to become, All Blacks – fellas like Buck Shelford, Hika Reid, Arthur Stone, John Timu,

Frano Botica, Jasin Goldsmith and Robin and Zinzan Brooke.

The thing to do on that tour was to **have challenges with your team-mates and the loser would have to be the other fella's slave.** Raki had a goalkicking competition with Frano and lost. Frano decided to work Raki pretty hard . . . it started on the team bus.

"Boy," Frano said.

"Yes, master."

"Get the boys a drink."

"Yes, master." (Raki handed out drinks to everyone on the bus. A few minutes later we stopped at a restaurant for lunch.)

"Boy, get me a banana sandwich."

"Yes, master." (Raki went out to the kitchen and couldn't find any bananas.)

"There's no bananas, master."

"Well, go and buy some!" (the team decided the slave shouldn't have to pay, or things might have gotten out of hand. Frano gave him a 100 Franc note – about $NZ60.)

Ten minutes later Raki came back with two huge boxes of bananas – 100 Francs' worth.

"You arsehole!"

"Nothing's too good for my master!"

We didn't know it then, but the friendship Raki and I struck up, would lead to many sevens trips over the next few years. One of our most popular destinations was the Uruguay Sevens.

Nowadays, the official New Zealand Sevens team plays in Uruguay but when we first started going in 1992 we were very much an unofficial New Zealand team. I'd been the year before when Frank Bunce and I had played with Jason Little, John Eales and Darren Junee. Because of the success and popularity of the 'Anzacs', the organisers decided to invite the official teams from Australia and New Zealand in '92. **They rang me and I told them not to worry about going through the NZRFU because I could organise the team myself. I rang up a few of the boys and pretty soon I had a team.** I'd be joined by Frank, Glen Osborne, Dallas Seymour, Ant Strachan, Richard 'Pod'

Mongrels all! From left, Junior Paramore, Ant Strachan, Oz, Frank and me. In front, Richard Turner and Lindsay Raki.

Turner, Junior Paramore, Peter Woods and Raki.

On the way to Uruguay we flew on the same plane as the Australians. They were sitting up in first class in their No 1 clothes while we were up the back wearing jandals and t-shirts. We gave the Aussie coach Bob Dwyer a bit of a hard time. When I walked past him I said, "Hello Bob." Then Ant said, "Hello Bill." Raki chipped in with "Hello Brian" and soon all of the boys were taking a go at him.

Before the tournament started we had to attend a press conference and they introduced me as the captain of the All Blacks. I explained to them that we weren't an official New Zealand team and they asked me what we called ourselves. **Before I had a chance to answer, Raki leaned over my shoulder and said, "They call us The Mongrels."**

It was probably an apt name because at times we acted more like mongrels than we did rugby players. There were two rules when you were a part of The Mongrels. The first was that you never took any money with you on trips . . . the first thing we learnt to say in each language was: "What do you mean we have to pay?" The other rule was that we were only members of a team when we were playing . . . at every other moment, it was every man for himself.

We didn't see daylight for our first two days in Uruguay. We learnt pretty quickly that the nightclubs didn't open until 2am. So we'd go out for dinner at about 6pm, head to a few of the bars, roll into the clubs at 2am and then stumble out for breakfast at 6am. **A couple of times, as we were heading back to the hotel, rolling drunk at 8am, we'd pass the Australians coming out on their way to training. "Hello Bob", "Hello Bill . . ."**

After a couple of nights out on the town we thought we should get a bit serious and organise a training, so before we went to bed one night we'd organised for our tournament-supplied driver to pick us up at 10am. So, sure enough, the phone rings at 10am and Raki answers. "The boys are a bit tired, come back at noon." The phone rings at noon. "Come back at 1pm." The poor guy waited all day and we didn't even end up training.

In a way I miss The Mongrel days. When rugby turned professional the NZRFU took over the responsibility of sending teams to sevens events around the globe. But even though we weren't an official team, **The Mongrels had a bit of success. I wasn't stupid when I picked the teams because I knew if we won the events we'd be invited back the following year.**

Even in Uruguay in 1992, when the boys were drunk more often than they were sober, we were too good for the Australians and we beat them in the final. The biggest battle during that trip was trying to avoid being jerked – "jerk them before they jerk you", Raki used to say.

It was all out war between the fellas who were divided up between two apartments. Upstairs were Raki, Frank, Woodsy, Oz and Dallas. I was downstairs with Pod, Ant and Junior. The guys upstairs were throwing fire crackers and water bombs at us, and one night it got too much for Pod. He stormed

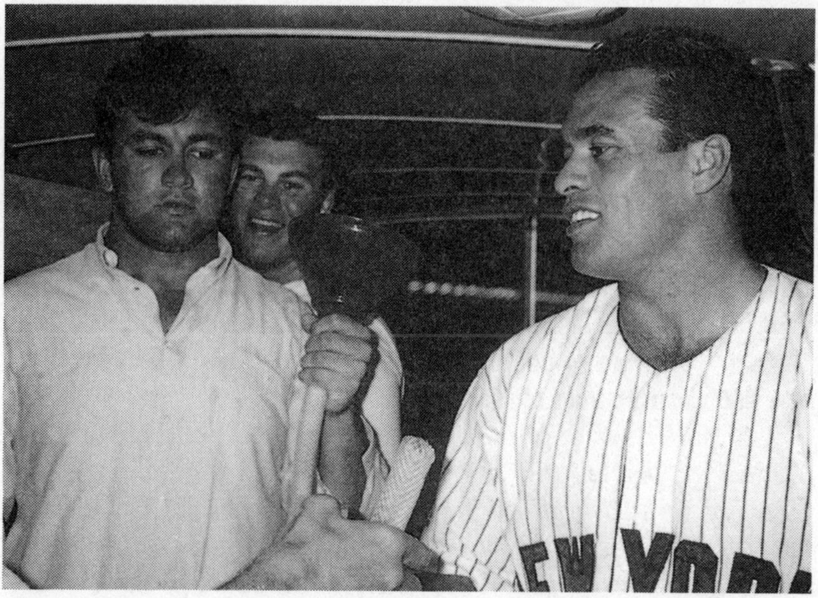

Mongrels Richard Turner and Lindsay Raki about to re-fuel prior to take-off.

upstairs, ripped the phone off their wall and pretty much destroyed the place. It was the only time in Mongrel history that we broke anything. The owner of the apartments was upset but the boys did the right thing and brought her flowers the next day. By the time we left she was doing our dishes for us and actually asked us to stay longer!

It was a memorable trip for another reason as well . . . Raki got jerked! As the captain of the side I was responsible for giving the players their reimbursement money for their visas to get into Uruguay. I handed the money for the five people in his apartment to Seymour, but seeing as though Raki was in the toilet at the time, the other four fellas split the money between them. For the rest of the tour Raki kept asking me where the money was and I kept telling him I hadn't received it. **Six years later he still rings up saying "I'm going to get yous . . . no one rips me off, bro."**

Raki never liked parting with money. When The Mongrels were in Hong Kong on a stopover, Raki, Pod and Frank bolted from a taxi when they were dropped off at the Stamford Plaza. The driver ended up chasing the three of them into the hotel's kitchen. Pod and Frank hid behind the bread trolley but Raki ended up being surrounded by kitchen hands and the driver. Never one to back down from a challenge, Raki, calling on all his knowledge of the martial arts (i.e. absolutely none), struck his best Bruce Lee pose, looked his attackers in the eyes and said, **"What's your style? Mine's the drunken man's style, and he started doing all these fancy moves, with all these little guys jumping backwards and forwards in front of him." The silly thing was the taxi fare only came to $3.00!**

Raki, like the rest of us, hated being jerked. Raki always had to have the last laugh. On our way to the Portugal Sevens one year, Raki and I stopped over in Los Angeles for three days. On the last day we decided that we wanted to go to Disneyland and we asked the owner of the backpackers' place where we were staying if we could come back and have a shower at the hotel before heading out to the airport. He said that would be fine but when we got back later in the day we were told we weren't allowed to use any of the facilities because we'd already checked out.

Well, this made Raki pretty dark. We went to the airport and made our way to the gate where we had to wait for our flight to New York. "I'm still pissed off, bro," he said. Then he had an idea. He wanted to go back and phone the hotel. I put up a bit of a fight but Raki was determined.

"Sometimes you have to go that extra mile to put the best jerk on." So Raki found a phone and rang up the hotel. With his best Asian voice, he put the jerk into action. **"Hurro. I just arrive with Phillipines' Boy Choir. I need room for 23 people. Please send van. Also, you must bring trailer for tuba."** Within a few minutes four vans had arrived – the last one with a trailer for the tuba!

Along with Uruguay, another popular place to visit was the Middle East. The Mongrels used to go there every year. We'd start in Bahrain and then work our way to United Arab Emirates for the Dubai Sevens. The association with the area began in 1990 in Hong Kong after New Zealand beat the Arabian Gulf team by a then-record 54-0. After we played our final against Fiji, we went out on the town with the Gulf team. They couldn't believe that the 'All Blacks' wanted to hang out with them – little did they know the only reason we hung with them was because they were buying the drinks. We ended up having a great time and they invited The Mongrels to play in their sevens tournament.

Two months later, business class tickets arrived along with $1000 each for spending money for our transit time in Singapore. Eventually we got to Bahrain and, predictably, the first stop was a bar. Bahrain is an unbelievable place. One of the sponsors of the tournament was Gulf Air and, because Arab women aren't allowed to work, the airline hire women from all over to work as hostesses. This, of course, went down well with the boys because **the place was crawling with all of these unattached young girls. The perfect place for a rugby tour.**

Part of the deal for getting the trip was that while we were in Bahrain we played for the Warblers team in the local sevens competition. After the ex-pat Kiwis in charge of the team got us liquored on the first night, we had to attend the Warblers Dinner the next night, the Gentleman's Dinner the following night and then a good old fashioned pub crawl at the end of the week. It was pretty clear early on that sevens was going to be secondary to the drinking.

At the Gentleman's Dinner it was a tradition that every member of the team addressed the guests. **At The Mongrels' first-ever Warblers dinner, Raki stood up and gave a now famous speech.** It was all about what he and his mate got up to in Scotland. Apparently, they were both trying to pick up the same woman, but both got rejected. Their answer to this rejection involved, let's say, a fairly basic sort of revenge. Anyway, there's Raki, in front of 2000 people, telling this story saying, "Shit, it was funny!" I had my head in my hands. When I looked up all I could see were all these naval officers with shocked looks on their faces.

The next year the Gentleman's Dinner organisers decided it might be safer to let just one member of the Warblers address the guests. Because Frank had just returned from the World Cup with Samoa, we let him take the mic. Frank has never been a great man with words, so he stood up, told a dirty joke, and asked if there were any questions. A Welsh guy started heckling him and Frank diplomatically said, "If someone doesn't shut him up, I'll go down there and bash him." Kiwis were banned from the microphone after that.

The pub crawl on the final night would always start at the flashiest bars. You normally couldn't even dance at them. They were the sort of places where the rich and famous went to pay $30 for a Coke. **As the night went on, the places we'd visit declined in standard. Our last stop was Louis' Bar – a place with a dirt floor.** The boys were in fine form by this stage . . . something the room full of Indians didn't appreciate.

Raki got things going when he stole one of the local's bicycles from outside and started riding it through the bar. The little Indian fella who owned the bike started the chase as Raki rode around knocking down tables and chairs in the process. Eventually he got the bike off Raki, and we got booted from the bar.

There is no way any of the locals would have got away with half the things we got up to. They still have a "chop your hand off" mentality if you're caught stealing. One time Frank borrowed one of the Warbler's Mercedes and lost it in the middle of Bahrain. They found it two days later, with the windows wound down and the keys still in the ignition . . . in the exact same place Frank had left it. The locals wouldn't touch it because they knew the consequences.

While we were treated really well by the ex-pats, most of the Arabs looked down on us. **I was talking to the wife of one of the Warblers at a bar one night and this Arab fella came up to her and said, "Leave him. I have more money than this man."**

Raki never really got along with the Arabs. He had a distinct dislike for the arrogance that some of them had, and one time in

Raki wasn't much for making friends with the locals . . . this excursion got us thrown out of a Bahrain night spot.

Singapore he saw an opening. He told the boys to start the car while he waited in the lift. He saw an Arab man walking by and bolted out of the lift. **As Raki ran past him, he ripped off this fella's head-dress and headed to the car. But just as he did it, a group of Arabs were walking into the hotel and they caught and bottled him. Raki ended up having to go to the hospital to get some stitches in his head.**

There were a lot of people in the waiting room and Raki was told by one of the nurses to go and join the back of the line. Our manager/beer taster Mark Thompson said, "He is severely injured." When he was told again to go to the waiting room, he collapsed on the ground and started screaming as though he was in agony. A nurse escorted Raki to a doctor's room and left him there. Straight away Raki was on the ground screaming again. A doctor showed up and immediately stitched him up. As soon as he was done, Raki stood up, said, "Thank you very much" and strolled out smiling at the people still in the waiting room.

Trouble was never very far from Raki. One year a few of The

Mongrels were invited to the Cook Islands where invited players are divided up amongst the local teams. Raki was put into the Tupapa side. **He went to the first training, was late to the second training and didn't show up for the third training. He told us he wanted to be the first invited player that was hated by his team.**

The Tupapa players were known as the Men from the Mountains because of the location of their village. They played well in their first game and a few of the boys were talking to Raki after the win. He reckoned that by the end of the tournament we'd be able to hear "Tupapa, the Mountain Men" chants from the crowd.

The team continued to play well and, sure enough, the crowd were yelling out "Tupapa, Tupapa". Every time he heard it he'd look around at us on the sideline and shout, "The Mountain Men". In the final, Tupapa played the Waisale Serevi-led Police team. Tupapa were beating them when Serevi's team were attacking on the 22m and Raki intercepted a pass. There was only one guy to beat and Raki, who was looking at us when he was running down the field, threw a pass to his support and the defender intercepted it and scored down the other end and Tupapa lost the final. The whole crowd let out a groan. The only people you could hear screaming were Stu Forster, Simon Tremain, Peter Woods and me. **We were rolling around on the floor of the stand laughing. Raki wouldn't come and talk to us after the game. When we left the airport the next day, he was the only player whose team didn't come to see him off!**

Without a doubt the highlight of my overseas experiences with the New Zealand Sevens team came in 1998 when we visited Jerusalem. It was one of the most incredible weeks of my life. I'm not a religious man but at the time, and even now when I think about it, the hairs on the back of my neck stand up. There I was, a Maori boy who grew up in Otara and Kaeo, walking on the same streets that Jesus Christ walked on. It blew all of us away. We were taken to Calvary where Jesus Christ was crucified, went into the manger where Jesus was

Haka at the Wailing Wall – it was only after our Jewish hosts gave us the green light that we went ahead.

born and to the Garden of Gethsemane where he spent his last night and where they had the last supper.

It was great having Waisiki Masirewa there with us. His religion is important to him and he was able to describe the significance of everything we were seeing. We were hanging off his every word. He'd say, "You guys don't realise how lucky you are because there are so many millions of people in this world who would give their left arms to be where we are today."

It was an incredible few days for the boys. On that trip we'd been in London looking at the Tower Of London, in Paris at the Louvre looking at the Mona Lisa and then in Jerusalem, looking at the same ceiling that Mary and Joseph would have looked at the night Jesus was born 2000 years ago.

Money can't buy those sorts of trips. It's times like that when you realise just how lucky you are to be a rugby player with all the

got a sports psychologist down to talk to the boys about about mental imagery. After the session, Peter Thorburn asked the boys what they thought and everyone was saying it was great until Thorbs got to Todd. "It's all bullshit mate. You just run, tackle, run and tackle some more."

Norm Berryman

He's never been known as a great trainer. He loves his fast foods and fizzy drinks which aren't allowed in Titch's teams. **Because he was banned from eating all that fatty stuff when he was in the sevens camp I don't think he was too excited about the game.** He didn't last through training one day and Titch asked him how he was. Norm answered, "I would have spewed if I was able to eat anything." Hugely talented player and one guy who enjoys rugby on and off the field. A great tourist – would have made an awesome Mongrel!

Frano Botica

A real talented sevens player, fifteens player and league player. Frano was one of the best sevens players I've ever seen. He had all the skills and awesome speed. His only downfall is that he looks like me. My kids mistake him for me and his wife has admitted their kids do the same sometimes. I just wish I had his bank account! Frano's problem is that when he's had a few he likes to take on the big fellas in the team. **I've seen him take a few beatings trying to get to the back seat.** In All Black teams, only the most experienced players get to sit at the back of the bus. But occasionally a young cocky fella will try and join them. I've seen more injuries occur on the bus than on the field.

Mike Brewer

Everyone talks about Buck and Fitzy being the guys that epitomise what it is to be an All Black. For me, Bruiser is in that category as well. He was an uncompromising fella on the field, but always loads of fun away from the paddock. His aborigine accent is awesome.

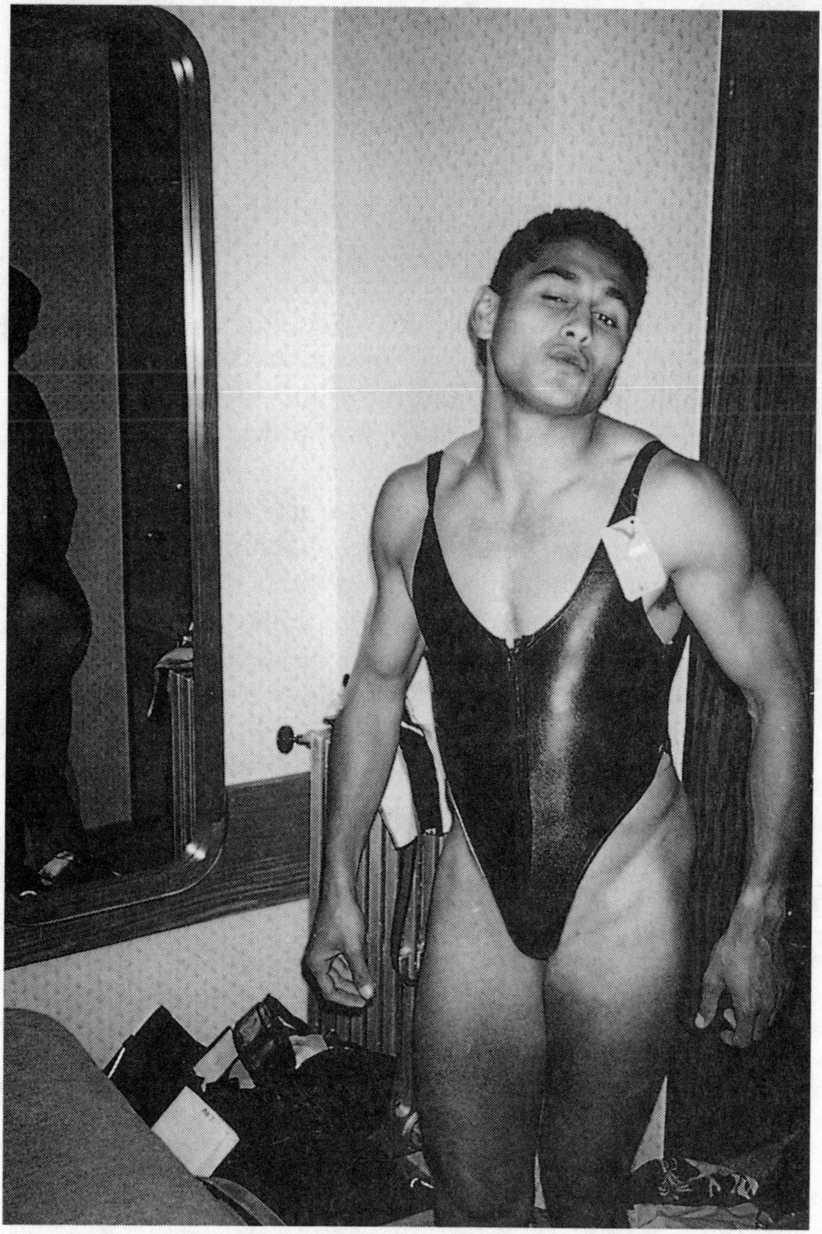

If you've ever wondered what some of the All Blacks do in their spare time, here's the answer. Frano Botica models a swimsuit Zinny bought for his girlfriend in France (nice bikini line, Bots.)

Robin Brooke

One of the things I am proudest of in my rugby career is that I was the one who gave the big fella his nickname Moose. He never liked it and he used to get annoyed with me every time **I called him Moose. "Why do you call me that?" he'd complain. Actually, I don't know really . . . it's probably because he looks like one.** Moose once played in a sevens tournament with The Mongrels in Singapore and when the boys were watching the tape of one of the games later on, we couldn't believe what we were hearing. Moose scored a runaway try against one of the bunny teams in the draw and the commentator said, "I was talking to Robin Brooke earlier in the day and he revealed that he had run 100m in less than 11 seconds." Eleven seconds! It takes him that long to get out of the starting blocks. Moose has also got a terrible habit of getting nude. It doesn't matter if it's in his room, on the bus or driving in the car. I don't know why . . . maybe he thinks it will make him move faster! When we were in Fiji once Moose took off all his clothes as we drove from Nadi to Suva. I've also seen him playing tennis in the nude with the head of a big company, whose name and firm shall remain nameless! Speaking of locks and nudity, on an Auckland rugby trip to Masterton, Mata'afa Keenan and Rudi Kapeli were having a spa and decided to play a game of squash. **Neither of them could be bothered getting dressed so they played in the nude.** Fortunately, the gym was closed to other patrons. Rudi, who of course wasn't wearing any shoes, slipped and got his toe stuck under the door. Mata'afa, who thought he was trying to help, opened the door and poor old Rudi's toenail was ripped off. If that wasn't bad enough, it turned out there were video monitors on each court and the staff at the reception desk were having a great laugh.

Zinzan Brooke

His real name is Murray. He has admitted to me privately that he regrets changing it to Zinzan. In fact, I think from now on

Zinzan? Murray? Whatever . . . he's still my mate.

we should show him the respect he deserves and call him Murray Brooke. Murray was the type of player that always led by example. He had a great rugby brain on him. He would do things that other guys wouldn't even dream about. Murray was a real competitive bugger off the field but occasionally he'd surprise us with a good Samaritan deed. When we were on tour with the Maori team in Spain one year Murray decided to help a motorist who was trying to get out of a tight parking space. To help the motorist out, Murray got Moose, Frano and I to push a van that was parked in front of it out of the way. **It must have been in gear or something because as we were pushing it the engine switched on and it started to stutter down the street.** Robin and I were rolling around laughing as Frano and Murray tried to stop the van. It ended up crashing into a shop window, but not before it had scraped the sides of three other cars. As we were running away, wearing our All Black-issue t-shirts, Murray was shouting out, "Hide your fern!" The thing I like most about Murray is that he's just a good old Maori boy. He never pretended to be anything else. Despite his fame and his success, he was always happiest when he was just one of the boys.

Olo Brown

The big boy has played in the Singapore Sevens a couple of times and **for a while he was a regular at the Papatoetoe Sevens. No doubt that sevens experience has helped him become such a mobile prop.** For a quiet fella Olo's got himself into a few funny situations on tour with the All Blacks. In 1995 we couldn't find him the morning after one of the tests but I had a sneaking suspicion I knew where he was. Sure enough, he was one floor up in the hotel in the corresponding room. The only thing was that the room was occupied. Apparently, in the middle of the night he was banging on the door of this young French couple and when they opened it he turfed them out. The couple were quite good natured about it, seeing as they were in town to watch the test, but it was quite funny to see Olo in this room surrounded by all this stuff that didn't even belong to him.

Frank Bunce

The best centre I've ever seen play for New Zealand. Great skills, great trainer, great attitude; an awesome role model . . . well, that's enough about Sandra Edge. The beauty of Frank was that he was never on time. You couldn't trust him to turn up anywhere. If you wanted to get a hold of him you'd always know where he was – he'd be at home doing absolutely nothing. Frank was a real South Auckland boy. Nothing really mattered to him except his family, his mates and rugby. He was never interested in all the peripheral stuff. I remember coming home from the Uruguay Sevens once after we'd beaten the Australians in the final. The Aussies were sitting in a better class than we were and as Frank was walking to the back of the plane the Australian coach **Bob Dwyer said, "Nice trophy**

Normie Hewitt and Frank Bunce strike the European look . . . Frank's halfway there.

Frank." Frank offered to exchange it for his seat! Frank had a unique brand of humour. He was always looking to get one over his team-mates. One year he was named Player Of The Year for North Harbour and I was named runner-up. The prizes for the both of us were vouchers from an electrical appliance store. Because I was overseas at the time of the awards I never even knew I'd won anything. It took me three years to find out that he'd spent my voucher on a new vacuum cleaner and jug! **Of the times I've been drunk, which isn't that often, it always seems that Frank's been there.** After I played my first test – against Wales in the 1995 World Cup – he wanted to take me out on the town. I knew I was playing in the next game against Japan so I didn't really want to go, but Frank asked Lauire Mains if it would be okay and he said he didn't have a problem with it. We didn't get back until 8.30 the next morning. I was sitting in the back of this taxi van in between Frank, Walter Little and Jamie Joseph when one of the boys said that just because I'd played my first test didn't mean I could sit in the back seat. I ended up getting a pummelling. I staggered out of the van, my shirt was ripped and I was bleeding. Someone mentioned we had to be ready to get on the team bus to go to Blomfontein in 30 minutes. At the training later in the day, the other boys who'd been out were running around like nothing had happened but **I was dying. Frank kept saying, "You kept up with us last night but you're not doing it now, are yuh!"** Without a doubt, the funniest moments with Frank have been at North Harbour when he's shaped to kick the ball. These were some of the rare times the Harbour boys were 100 per cent focused because you never knew where the hell the ball was going to end up.

Adrian Cashmore

Only played a couple of years in the sevens before he got plucked out and became an All Black. He was always one of the favourites with the female fans in Hong Kong. He spends enough time in the gym getting that body of his into shape so I'm glad the hard work is paying off for him. We always said to

Cashie that those steroids were no good for him. We used to ask what he was going to do when – not if – he got caught. I think the only thing he was worried about was those tell-tail pimples all over his back.

Christian Cullen

The boys call him Cully but I call him Beer Bottle because he's empty from the neck up. One time in South Africa we got introduced to the Mayor of Cape Town. He was a pretty unique looking Indian fellow – short and bald. After the game all BB could talk about was meeting Nelson Mandela! BB is another example of how sevens can help launch an All Black career. He'd been groomed in age group rugby before joining the sevens team but it was his involvement with the sevens team at an international level that launched him on to the world stage. Jonah, Caleb, Glen Osborne . . . their All Black careers all took off after breaking through in sevens. One day I reminded BB how lucky he was because he probably hadn't had to work a whole day in his life. **"What do you mean? I've had a job. I used to do a paper round when I was at school!"** He's lucky he's a real good footballer . . . one of the best I've seen, actually. I don't like giving him too many compliments – but that's okay because he probably won't be able to read this far into the book.

Marc Ellis

Macca's favourite trick was pinching all the buses. The drivers would come in and watch training and when they went back out there would be no bus. **Macca is always good for a laugh with the boys.** We went out hunting in Africa with the All Blacks once and there were these three brothers who ran the farm we visited. They were the biggest men I'd ever seen. We were three hours out of Pretoria, hunting in the middle of nowhere. The boys were having a few beers and one of the brothers wanted to show us a trick. He poked a hole in the bottom of a can with a stick, shook it up, and pulled the lid off. Of course, it's just a 'shoddy', which every scarfie has done a hundred times. He

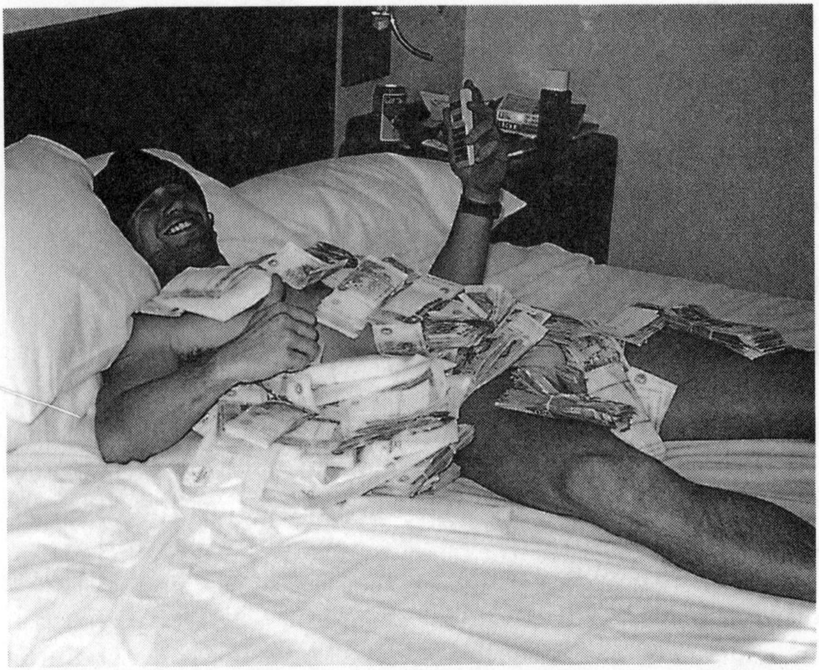

Not sure where this pic of Macca was taken . . . it could have been just after he signed his league contract.

asked if we could do it and Macca did it in about a quarter of the time it took the big fella. After that it was like a personal challenge between him and the three brothers. So Macca was taking them on, can for can. Every time Macca went for a leak he'd stick the old fingers down the throat so he was throwing it all up. **The three of them just couldn't believe how much beer this runt of a Kiwi could drink.** Macca decided he wanted to show them a few party tricks of his own. He found a condom in his toilet bag – he carried one especially for this trick – he decided to show the boys the "chimney sweep". So he pulled out the condom, wet it and stretched it out, stuck one end up his nose and sniffed it up his nose until it came out of his mouth. The big South African guys almost cried in horror. Macca's biggest claim to fame was that six-try effort against Japan at the '95 World Cup – a world record. But Lauire wasn't too impressed with Macca that day. Before the game he told Macca to make sure he fed his wings – because that's what a good centre does. So, on the day he set the world record for tries scored in tests, he was greeted by Laurie who absolutely tore strips off him as soon as he got into the changing-shed. To make things worse, two days later, after we'd been out with a few of the security guys, he'd been given a commando outfit. The morning of the test match against Scotland, Macca was running into everyone's room doing forward somersaults and pretending to shoot everyone . . . basically he was being the kid we all are at times. Anyway, he bowled into our room and then rolled out into the corridor. **He found himself lying at the feet of Laurie. I just shut my door and hoped Macca could talk his way out of it.**

Luke Erenavula
Another Fijian that played for New Zealand. He was one of our better players at the 1994 Hong Kong Sevens. He's a real nice guy who always calls up the team to wish us good luck. He's still good mates with all the guys. Woodsy called him The Shadow – because he was always in the background.

Sean Fitzpatrick
One of his main ambitions on each tour was to beat Zinzan at anything. He loved beating him. Fitzy didn't know the meaning of "touch" either. When we were playing touch football you could always rely on Fitzy putting the first tackle in. **He was a great captain, though. One of New Zealand's greatest ever players. You can't help but admire his courage.** I've got a tremendous amount of respect for him, as do all the guys.

Bradley Fleming
Like Dan Parkinson, he's probably one of the fastest rugby players in New Zealand. At the sevens squad's first training camp of 1998, with his rugby boots on, three of the boys went under 11 seconds for 100m – Brad, Dan and Todd Blythe. The boys call him Flash. People think we call him that because of

his speed, but it's actually because of a small problem he had in his younger days. Brad's a pretty reserved kind of a guy . . . something that was confirmed in Paris in 1998. At the players' dinner a stunning French model was dancing her way around all the different team tables. All the boys were loving it. But **when she got to our table, her provocative dance was interrupted by Brad. "Sit down, woman! You're embarrassing yourself."** Needless to say, she moved on to the next table pretty quickly.

Blair Foote

We call him 'Footy Baka' after the speedy Fijian winger Vunibaka. The boys call Footy that because he hasn't got much speed at all but I tell you what, he's still running at the same pace at the end of the game. Footy's the sort of player who would run through a brick wall if you asked him. Every team needs players like him. He's one of those hard grafters who does all the work and allows all the flash fellas out the back do the damage.

Stu Forster

I used to call him Gorse Pockets because his hands never went in them. He used to go on about how he had $80,000 in the bank. Well, it's pretty easy to save money when you've never bought your mates a drink! One time I went to stay with him in Dunedin. I was there to do a talk and the organisers were going to put me in a hotel, but I thought it would be better to stay with my mate. So I knocked on his door and told him I was going to spend the night and he said, "Look mate, you can stay, but it's $20 a night. When you leave a room, turn the lights out, don't shower and remember the heater stays off at all times." **He was a grumpy little bugger before games as well. He'd never say anything. He'd just frown and scowl.** But despite that, he's one of the funniest men I've come across and he's one of my best mates. We always used to have running conversations during games. When I was playing NPC the only person I used to worry about was Stu Forster. Whenever I made a mistake I knew that when I got home (probably the next day) I'd get a

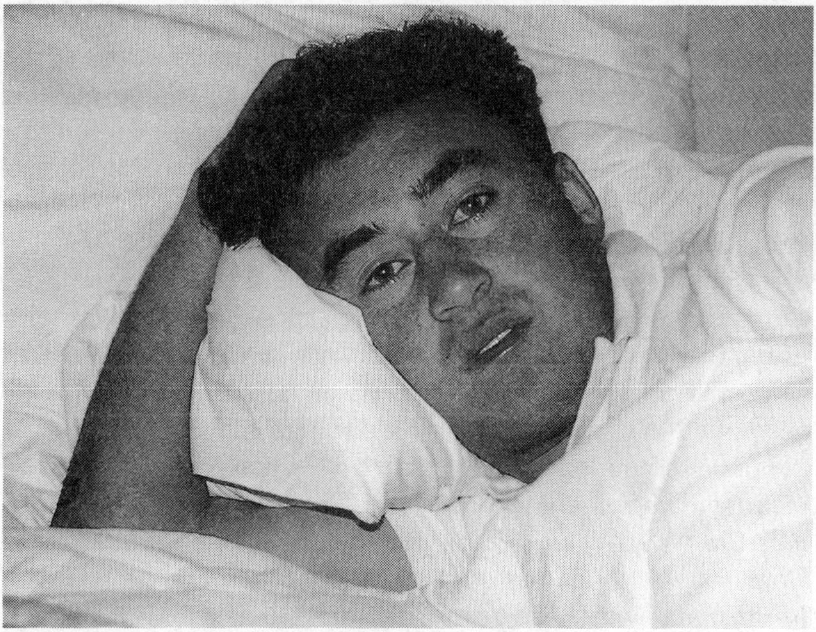

Stu Forster . . . the bear with a sore head.

phone call. If I dropped the ball, he'd call up and say, "Good hands, mate!" and then slam the phone down. One year we took him to the Rarotongan Sevens and I watched him closely. It was raining and it was muddy; he was playing with guys he didn't know and it was the worst display I'd ever seen in a seven-minute period. Everything he did went wrong. He dropped the ball, he missed tackles, he couldn't keep up . . . he was absolutely shocking. We called it the Seven Minutes of Hell. **Stu's also got a bad habit of ringing my place at three or four in the morning. But he never speaks to me. He just talks to my wife and tries to get her to leave me! You've just gotta love him.**

Grant Fox

Sought perfection in everything he did, and he expected similar attitudes from his halfbacks. I remember Brett Iti, who was a classy player, being on the end of a few choice words from Foxy. Foxy would always get to training an hour before anyone else and every now and then he'd nominate a young guy to catch the balls for him. He'd spend three quarters of the time practising his kicks and then he'd go to the corner flag and try to convert from there. He'd make four out of ten just about every time! Off the field, he was a hell of a nice guy.

Rico Gear

Most people probably wouldn't have heard of Rico before the Commonwealth Games. Rico is one of those young fellas with heaps of talent. **We call him Reaks . . . you can probably guess that he doesn't always smell too good.** When Jonah decided to give everyone No 1 haircuts after we won the gold medal, Reaks was the one who put up the biggest fight. He had a ponytail and he reckoned Mum – that's what he calls his girlfriend – liked his hair the way it was. We reminded him that he didn't win a Commonwealth Games gold medal too often and he relented. I noticed he wore head gear every time he played for Auckland in the NPC after that . . . I guess he wasn't too impressed with the way it looked. Reaks was a bit of a little Maori boy when he first came up the coast to Auckland, but the thing about Rico is that he only has to be told to do something (or not do something) once and he learns. He's got a good head on his shoulders. He missed out on being selected in the initial 1998 sevens squads, but by the end of the year Titch had voted him the best sevens player of the year. **I don't have any doubt that he can go all the way in New Zealand rugby if he puts his mind to it.**

Aaron Hamilton

Tama used to be a bit of a wild little man on the beers. We were in Uruguay once and I was talking to Titch. Anyway, Tama had been right behind us, but when Titch and I were done I turned around and he wasn't there. I looked for him on the team bus and he wasn't there either. Then, all of sudden, he was looking down at the driver through the windshield. He'd climbed on top of the bus while we were driving and had given the poor driver a hell of a fright.

Shane Howarth
He played in the sevens side in 1991. He played really well for Auckland for a number of years at fullback and went on to become an All Black. I really like Howie – his mum comes from Kaeo, the same place as mine – so we have some of the same ties. **For a guy who broke his neck when he was younger, he's done really well to get to where he has.** He plays for Wales now, and no doubt they're only just beginning to learn about his practical jokes. The best time he got me was when I was playing for Otahuhu and he was playing for the star-studded Marist team. After the game, which we won, he invited me into the Marist changing-room. As I walked in, the Marist coach was in the middle tearing strips off his team. He took one look at me and told me to "F--- off." Howie had set me up. He still reminds me about it every time I see him.

Alama Ieremia
One of my best mates so he won't mind me telling this story. We had to go and do a skit for a television show once and all he had to say was that he'd take this woman to a French restaurant. But he kept saying "fresh". It would have been about half an hour later when the director gave up and made him say "Italian restaurant". I also remember an incident on the All Black tour of '96 when we almost got strung up for singing the South African national anthem before the tests. We learnt the new anthem, Nkosi Sikelele Afrika, because it seemed no-one else in the stadiums ever sung it.

Ian Jones
The Kamo Kid. I introduced him in a speech once and said that in his spare time he was a surf lifeguard. **"He can't swim, but he wades out a hell of a long way!"** He wasn't too happy. He comes from the same town as Tony Monaghan, although Monza says he's the star up in Kamo, not Ian Jones. I played sevens with Kamo one year at the nationals and he wasn't too bad. He sets high standards for himself and those around him.

Ian Jones and Blair Larsen . . . Kamo can't swim and Lambie can't play sevens.

A lot of the younger fellas can learn much from him. He's a bit slow at times, though. When he first got into the All Blacks, Mike Brewer and Richard Loe gave him a bit of a hard time. **They told him to be initiated he had to play 'spoons'. This game involved putting a spoon between your teeth.** The guy who played with you sat opposite and when he put his head down you had to hit him as hard as you could. Of course, you could never get much power into it. Anyway, Kamo had a crack at Loey but couldn't really manage much of a hit at all. Then, as Ian put his head down to take his turn at being hit, Bruiser, who was standing behind him, took a spoon from behind his back and whacked him on the top of the head. Kamo took about five decent whacks before he finally worked out what was happening.

Martin Jones

Boogsie. Nice fella. His main job was to keep Joe Tauiwi out of trouble when we were on tour. It must be a Bay of Plenty thing, but they all collected as much gear as they could when we were on tour. **They used to get balls from every tournament we played at. I still don't know how they did it.** He could split open any game at any time – almost as quickly as he could nail a box of KFC.

Damian Karauna

Damian is one of those awesome team guys. We call him the Titanic because he carries as much freight as the Titanic did. Scrimmo reckons they call him Titanic because he's always going down. It was good to see all of Titanic's hard work pay off when he was rewarded with a Super 12 contract this year. We'll miss his great attitude in the sevens team.

John Kirwan

Legend. A real down to earth fella. He went to school in South Auckland so he couldn't have been anything else. It was a real privilege for me to play alongside him. Like Terry Wright, even though he was at the top of the rack, he always had time for the young guys. **Probably still my favourite All Black winger. He was strong, fast and had a great swerve but, like me, he couldn't kick to save his life.** My dream rugby match-up would be to see him go one-on-one with Jonah.

Josh Kronfeld

When you talk about putting your body on the line for your country, this guy is one of the first that comes to mind. He's changed the style of openside flanker from forager to ball winner at tackle time. He's the best in the business. Can't say anything bad about him because he's such a nice guy. I hate that.

Pat Lam

We dubbed him Patch after all the boils he used to get

whenever he went to Hong Kong. A real talented player. He was picked practically straight out of school for the New Zealand Sevens team by Peter Thorburn and he went on to become an All Black and the captain of Manu Samoa. He lived for the issue of the gear. At the start of each tour his motto was always, “Be the first one there, and the last to leave.” The thing I remember most about Pat was his tendency to buy heaps of clothes for himself . . . but most of them were real ugly. **I only remember seeing him buy something for his wife Stephanie once. I think it was an iron for those clothes!** Pat’s doing real well in the UK now. In 1997 he was voted Player of the Season. Last time I caught up with him his wardrobe had improved dramatically. I just wonder how Stephanie’s getting on.

Blair Larsen

Lambie got his break in sevens when he replaced an injured Ron Williams at the Rarotongan Sevens. I rang Lambie up in New Zealand and asked him if he wanted to come to the Cook Islands. He arrived just before the game the next morning. In the first few minutes of the game he tried to bowl over this little Raro guy. The little fella stood up as tall as he could when he came in for the tackle and his head hit Lambie straight on the nose and broke it. I was the water boy for the game and I hadn’t had a chance to see Lambie before the game – all I could say was, “Welcome to Raro, brother.” In between spitting out blood he replied, “Yeah mate, it’s good to be here.” That was Lambie’s introduction to sevens. I don’t think he’s played since. **Lambie and Liam Barry started a club called the Steers . . . because only players that had no calf muscles were allowed to join. Owen Scrimgeour would have been a bolter.**

Walter Little

Frank’s brother in arms – and that was usually where they’d find each other at four o’clock in the morning. He didn’t play too much sevens because he reckoned he couldn’t run fast enough, but I’m sure if he decided he wanted to have a go he would have been awesome. Walt always liked a drink (and then another one!) When the two of them got together to write *Midfield Liaison* with Bob Howitt the boys reckoned they should have called it *Drunk and Drunker* because Frank was always drunk, but Walt was always drunker. It didn't matter where in the world Walt was, there was nothing he liked better than walking into a pub and having a beer and a smoke with the locals. There were a few times when his drinking got the better of him. **I remember walking into his hotel room one time and there were beer bottles everywhere. It looked like he must have had a party the night before but he reckoned he had drunk them all himself.** He was fast asleep in a chair and as soon as we woke him up he started dancing. Poor fella had to be helped on to the bus after that. I'm sure he didn't know what country he was in. Frank and Walt drank hard and trained that way . . . well, sometimes. However, when it came to the games, it didn't feel the same if they weren't there beside you. They were without a doubt the best midfield combination I've seen. Both of them are the most capped All Blacks in their positions and you don't get a record like that unless you work hard at it.

Richard Loe
Had a bad reputation for his antics on the field. I must admit I'd been at the bottom of some of his treatment at times. But he was a great competitor and never took a backwards step to anyone. However, off the field he is one of the nicest blokes you could meet. I remember once the All Blacks were given a talk about fair play. After the session **I asked Loey if he believed in the fair play principles. He said, "Yeah, mate, when we're 40 points up and there are 10 minutes to go."**

Jonah Lomu
The most effective player on a sevens field . . . ever. So strong that it takes two or three players to bring him down. When he's fit, he's almost impossible to stop. His fame is huge. Until you've toured with him you can't begin to understand what it

must be like to be Jonah Lomu. He always gets the star treatment, but I know he'd prefer to be treated like everyone else. His biggest problem, though, is that he can't help spending money. He's an awesome shopper. So it's a good think he's got a big bank account. I don't want to upset the big fella by dishing up too much dirt on him . . . he's a lot bigger than me.

Willie Lose

The Mirror Man. He was such a funny guy because he always made a joke out of his own vanity. If anyone else had been that vain, they'd have been beaten up a long time ago. **The only man with a number one haircut who still uses gel.** The Mirror Man was as big as Jonah but he always wore small men's singlets and t-shirts. He tried to match Richard Turner's record for the most amount of deodorants in a bag at one time. Us uneducated fellas loved it because it meant more free stuff for us after the games. It was a far cry from my Otahuhu days when the players always brought roll-on deodorants so no one could hit you up for a free sample after they heard the "ppsssst" from the spray can.

Waisiki Masirewa

Another of the Fijian boys who has lived in New Zealand for a few years now and made a name for himself as a great sevens exponent. We called him Ski – I don't know why because there's not that much snow in Fiji. Nowadays he's playing fifteens for Fiji and hoping to get into their World Cup squad. He's a real good mate. It gives me great pleasure every time he pulls on a black jersey because the mana of it means a lot to him, even though he's proud of his Fijian heritage. When he puts on the black sweater, he's one of us. I always put the acid on the Fijian boys if there's any in the team when we play Fiji. I tell them they have to lead the way on defence. **"You hit them the hardest because they're your brothers."** When we play Tonga I say the same thing to Jonah. If there's Kiwis playing against us, we hit them harder than anyone else.

Tony Monaghan

Monza hails from Kamo – the same place that gave us Ian Jones. Monza could have easily have made the cut and got into the Commonwealth Games team. He only just missed out. Even though he was disappointed, being a good Northland boy he told me, "The kauri may bend, but it won't snap." He's one of the hardest trainers in the squad. He never stops running. Titch loves him. **He's got great skill and a heart as big as Frank Bunce's wallet, although he opens it as infrequently as Frank.**

Sam Nonoa

Another one of the Waikato boys. I don't know what it is about the Waikato but they seem to breed real hard workers down there. If hard work is a guarantee for success, then Sam is going to be a part of New Zealand sevens for a long time to come. Damian calls him Helmet because of his tight curly afro hair.

Junior Paramore

I played with Junior in the New Zealand Sevens team as well as with The Mongrels. He was always the good boy in the team. Like me, he hails from Otara but unlike me he never got into trouble. He didn't drink either, so we were always having to stop the other fellas from going over the top. He was a bit of hard case. **He was a real freshy – some days it was like he'd just stepped off the boat from Samoa – but on other days he'd try and be like a real educated pakeha.** Sometimes I think he got confused as to which one he was trying to be! But the thing I remember the most about him was that he was one of the greatest sevens players this country has produced. We called him Magic because some of the skills he had reminded us of Dream Team basketballer Magic Johnson.

Dan Parkinson

A real young talent. He's a pretty feisty young fella. He doesn't mind a bit of biffo if it starts on the paddock. Sometimes I think he looks forward to it. He came to my rescue when the Fijians were picking on me in the final of the Japan Sevens; he became an instant hero – and he loved it. They call him Ngapuhi. He's a bit of a smooth dude. He keeps going on to me how he likes my cousin but I know too much about him to let him anywhere near her . . . although it would make him eligible for my family team, Matangirau at Labour Weekends.

Scott Pierce

One of the unluckiest players not to play for the All Blacks. He had three All Black trials and broke his leg in two of them. In his prime he was one of the best sevens players in New Zealand. **He was also one of the most laid back players I've ever played with. If he was any more laid back he'd be horizontal!** But he always put his body on the line for his country. He loved baiting guys as well. On the field he was a real chatterbox and was always trying to upset the opposition. Most coaches struggle with Scottie because of his mischievous nature. Before my first game for North Harbour – a big occasion for me – Peter Thorburn was giving me a lecture in the changing-room. Behind him, Scottie was pulling down his shorts and pulling faces. It took all my concentration to keep a straight face.

Kevin Putt

One of those feisty little halfbacks that never knew when to shut up, and that was one of his strengths. He won a sevens tournament for us in Hong Kong one year when he scored two tries in the final. Another guy who made his mark in sevens before going on to to make a name for himself in fifteens – Putty did it with the Springboks. Another good halfback playing for us at the time was Taranaki's Alan Crowley. **We used to call him Smurf. He was a farm boy, nearly as dumb as Oz, but not quite.**

Lindsay Raki

There's too much about him in this book already!

The closest Scotty Pierce (right) ever got to Nelson Mandela was when he posed with him at Madame Tussaud's in London. With Scotty is former South African prop Guy Kebble.

Caleb Ralph

Caleb would be one of the fittest rugby players in New Zealand. We all reckon he's got three lungs. He does just under ten minutes for Titch's 3km time trial which is real good for a rugby player. **I call him 'Condom' because he doesn't really need to use them. He just uses his personality.** He's normally as quiet as a mouse until the aftermatch functions start.

Roger Randle

Rog should have been at least in the All Black training squad at the end of 1998. His form, both with the sevens team and with Waikato in the NPC, was outstanding. I'm sure it's that South African incident that is holding him back. People like to say that because he was cleared of any guilt it's all forgotten, but a few people obviously aren't prepared to give him a fair go. Anyone who knows Rog knows that he isn't capable of what they accused him of. When we heard the news from South Africa in 1997, all the boys knew it wasn't him. The funny thing about that incident is that it has made him a better person despite all the harm it has done to him emotionally and financially. I've never seen him more motivated than he was in 1998. It's a shame that mud sticks because Rog deserves to be talked about simply as a bloody good player. He's a good bloke . . . the chances are anyone that says anything different, probably doesn't even know him. His only problem is that he's a bit of a scrooge. Once, on the plane back from Dubai, we were told that if we paid $20 we could use the plane's phone for as long as we liked. **Rog ended up being on the phone for ten hours to his wife. At one point she needed to go up to the shops but, instead of calling her back, he hung on until she got back!** Peter Woods calls him Cacho – after a bus driver we had in South America whose backside was as big as his bus.

Taine Randell
In his first game as midweek All Black captain in South Africa he called the boys together for a pre-game talk. But he ran out of things to say pretty quickly so he offered, "Let's do it for the chicks!" It broke the tension quite nicely.

Bruce Reihana
Brucey was one of Titch's surprise selections for the Games. He'd seen him playing well for the Maori team and in other fifteens games in the middle of the year and it was an inspired decision to give Brucey a shot. **He's one of the those fellas who, when he has a go at something, he puts his whole heart into it.** I remember when he came to his first camp he was a little unsure of himself. I just told him to have a go. After the session Titch came up to me and said, "Did you see him? He had a go every time. That's the sort of player we want." He'd never played sevens at a high level before but he played his way into

the team. In the final against Fiji at Kuala Lumpur, Brucey, along with Jonah, was the best player on the paddock. I'm sure it took him three days to take his gold medal off.

John Schuster

Awesome guy. Real team man. As funny as they come. **It was a privilege to play with him. It was a laugh-a-minute touring with him.** In Hong Kong, one of the tournament sponsors took the team out on his launch and organised a cell phone for the boys. Schu called everyone he knew in New Zealand, Samoa and England. We never got a cell phone given to us again after that trip.

Owen Scrimgeour

He's a real good tourist as long as you can understand his brand of humour. I don't think I'd like to be a coach or manager of any tour he was on, though. He has a distinct problem with authority. He doesn't like being told what to do. He's one of those very intelligent fellas who gets bored really easily and likes to see how much he can get away with. Scrimmo's player profile in *Rugby News* gave away a bit of his personality. **When asked what the best advice his mother ever gave him was, he said, "Buck the system and party hard."** One time in South America, Titch had a team meeting in his room and when we'd left he realised one of his pillows was missing. He called us all back into the room and told us the pillow had better be back in his room by the time dinner was over. Without saying anything to Scrimmo, you knew Titch thought he was the guilty one. When Titch got back to his room he couldn't even see his door. Scrimmo had taken all the pillows he could find and piled them up in the corridor. Titch realised later on that the pillow never went missing . . . it had just fallen behind his bed! Scrimmo made a name for himself as the only man in world sevens to tape his ears up before every game. He's also the only player in world sevens that doesn't have any calf muscles. The standing joke when all the boys start their stretches, and begin with their calf muscles, is for Scrimmo to start on his hammies. A great player and a great tourist. Certainly would have enjoyed Mongrels' tours.

Dallas Seymour

My soul brother. I first met Seymour at the New Zealand Colts trials in 1986. He was doing all the drills with Laurie O'Reilly and the first thing I remember thinking was, "Who's this poncy prick?" The first time I played against him was at the sevens nationals in 1988 at Pukekohe. We both made the New Zealand team for the first time that year and we've been buddies ever since. I was one of the groomsmen at his wedding to Julie Dawson last year. He has such a big whanau that the guest list was so big I was his only team-mate to get an invite, so I had to carry the flag for rugby . . . something I didn't do too well, as I was outnumbered by all those netball girls. Dallas is THE favourite with all the girls up in Hong Kong. (Sorry Cashie!) **Whenever we're warming up you can always hear girls screaming out, "Dallas . . . I love you!" The worst part is that he pretends not to hear and then does a stretch right in front of them.** His other problem is that he likes getting his shirt off at every opportunity – not just for hakas – and makes all the skinny guys like me feel stink. I've been in a lot of battles with Dallas beside me over the years. Whenever the New Zealand team is overseas and we're in a tight situation with the crowd against us, it's always comforting to look across and see Dallas because you know that whatever happens he ain't gonna be backing down to anyone. If he hadn't been so injury prone he would have played a lot more than the three games he's notched up for the All Blacks. When I look at most of the flankers that have played for the All Blacks I believe he's right up there with them. We've had a lot of great times together over the years. **The biggest tribute I've paid him was when I named one of my sons after him.**

Wayne Shelford

Another legend. Awesome presence on the field. You always

New Zealand netball rep Julie Dawson and her husband Dallas someone before the opening ceremony at K.L.

gave 100 per cent when you were on the field with him in case he turned around and booted you up the backside. He wasn't scared of anyone, or anything. One time in France he took the Maori team to the sideline because the referee wasn't explaining his decisions. **Buck had such mana that they got an interpreter out of the stands to talk to the ref!** He was always very inspiring with his pre-game talks, although before the French Barbarians game on that tour he told us to remember that all of our "husbands and wives" would be watching. Thanks, Buck!

Carlos Spencer

Everyone calls him 'Los'. An awesome talent. Probably one of the most gifted players in the game since Frano. When he doesn't play well the boys call him Hope-Los or Dead-Los. One day in the Maori team we were going through our lineout calls. The move was called 'stack' but when the coach asked Los what it was called he didn't know. Glen Osborne leaned over and whispered into his ear and Los answered 'steak'. That was the last time he ever asked Oz for advice.

Joe Stanley

Smokin' Joe always looked after the young fellas in the Auckland team. **A great socialiser in the Frank Bunce mould.** His son, Jeremy, isn't a bad player either. He's a doctor, as well, which means all of his brains obviously came from his mum (I had to say that, otherwise she'd kill me.)

Arthur Stone

I first met him when I made the New Zealand Maori team in 1987. His first piece of advice to me was, "You have to learn how to dance because bros can usually dance and you've got a lot of learning to do."

Ant Strachan

We always gave Ant Strachan a hard time about getting up in the morning and wishing he was black because he was always acting like one of the bros. Once in Uruguay, as a part of The Mongrels, he got absolutely wasted and spent two days in bed recovering. **Lindsay Raki took one look at him and said, "This is the last time we bring a pakeha on one of these trips!"** He was a real good team man, but another of those halfbacks who talked too much. It didn't help that he was a schoolteacher either.

Joe Tauiwi

Awesome sevens player with an awesome vision on the field. After Jonah, he was one of the most influential players in the sevens team in the mid '90s. Both him and Peter Woods were a big part of the team, even though they were probably the least known players in the squad. Joe was always hiding away from Titch, trying to sneak a smoke. If he wasn't doing that he would be moaning about something ("it's too hot to train", "when's lunch?") or he was trying to scab your gears off you so he could give them to all his relations in Rotorua.

Karl Te Nana

Another of the younger guys with a huge future in rugby. He was also one of the guys who underestimated Titch on his first day at training. **He ended up throwing up all over the place. But he's a gutsy bugger.** When we played in last year's Hong Kong Sevens he left New Zealand with stitches still in his stomach following an operation. The only one in the team with legs skinnier than mine.

JT Thomas

One of the nicest guys you're ever likely to meet. He's a part of that Waikato Sevens team which has dominated in the last few years. He's a real hard worker and is as honest as the day is long. He's not the fastest player in the world but neither am I. He's one guy you like having in your team because 100 per cent is never enough for him.

John Timu

Sevens wasn't really his game but he backed himself to have a go at it and was rewarded with a place in the team in 1993. **Like Zinzan, he never lost sight of the fact that he was just a good ol' Maori boy.** One of the things the older All Blacks used to say to you when you made the team was "Never change". JT is still the same fella he was when he first played for the ABs in 1989. I wasn't surprised when he went on to have so much success in league – he had so much natural ability.

Rua Tipoki

Huge talent. He's got the best sidestep in the game. When he turned up at the sevens camp in 1997 he was just a wide-eyed little fella. After the camp he got a ride with Jonah and I back to Auckland. He sat in the back seat and didn't say a word. Now, you can't shut him up! He's cheeky to everyone these days. But the good thing is I know how to upset him. **All you have to do is say something bad about his Ngati Porou people and that's it . . . he's off.** He played for North Harbour in 1997 and, according to the *New Zealand Herald,* he had the second highest rate of turnovers in the whole of the NPC – we've started calling him Apple. Another player who could go a long way if he puts his mind to it, which he'll probably tell you himself if you give him half a chance.

Joe Tua

Joe wasn't even in the squad of 40 after the nationals in 1997. But he was working at the Waipuna Lodge Hotel when someone got injured. Titch invited him down to training to make up the numbers and he played out of his skin. When the selectors were picking a squad of 20, I was in on the discussion and they asked me what I thought about him. I told them I couldn't really say anything because he was my first cousin. I left the room when they were talking about Joe but Titch told me later on that he was in the team. Titch didn't want to release the team for another week, so everyday I had to deal with Joe coming up to my place to ask if I'd heard anything. **The day he got picked, he was over the moon. He was straight back up to my house and came in shouting, "I'm in! I'm in!" I said, "I know. I've known for the last week!"** Part of me wanted to tell him earlier but I could remember what it was like the first time I found out I was in the team. It is something he's going to remember for the rest of his life, so I thought it would be better coming from Titch.

Richard Turner

Pod was a legend. He could eat four or five pizzas by himself. The thing I liked about him was that he had no shoulders. He hit people so hard that all the nerves in his shoulders had been smashed and all the muscle had wasted away, so when he carried his bag he had to hold his arm straight out so it wouldn't slip off. He was a great captain at

Richard Turner, second from right, got the surprise of his life when he won a Blind Date competition in Bahrain.

North Harbour but he went off the field injured quite a lot. **That's why he got his other nickname, Yannice. That was the name of the captain of an ocean liner that sunk in South Africa a couple of years back. He left the ship by helicopter and left all the passengers behind.** Pod's also a walking pharmacy. He had all these different creams to help him look good for the ladies. His special beauty tip is to wear odourless deodorants to avoid a clash with aftershave. Everyone used to hassle him, but all us Maori boys knew where to line up after the game for some free smellies!

Simon Tremain

We called him Son Of because of his father Kel. I remember when Kel was the manager of the sevens team one year, we got taken into a little room to get our team talk from him and we were all real scared of him. He got up and said, "In my vocabulary there are two words that are very important. Honesty and discipline. Some of you might know my son. He doesn't know the meaning of either of those words." That summed Simon up. He was an awesome tourist. One time I went to South Africa for a Super 12 game. At the time he was a player with Eastern Province but he wasn't playing because he was injured. **That night I saw him in one of the local bars doing nude hand-stands on the bar . . . so much for the back injury!** Simon has kept his ties with the sevens team. He's been known to lead a tour group to Hong Kong. The group all wear t-shirts emblazoned with "The Shit Through The Eye Of The Needle Tour." Classy fellow, and a classy fella.

Amasio Valence

Without a doubt Mudgi was the find of 1998. He's the only schoolboy in New Zealand with a Commonwealth Games gold medal. He was discovered when the New Zealand Sevens team played a warm-up game against the Auckland Fijians. He absolutely cut us to bits. Titch invited him to our next camp and from there he made the Games squad. He's got a massive future ahead of him.

Joeli Vidiri

The first time I saw Joeli was in Hong Kong in 1994. He was playing for Fiji and he scored two tries against us. The following year he wasn't selected for the Fijian team and he ended up in New Zealand when Luke Erenavula organised for Joeli to replace him at Counties Manukau after he signed to play league at North Sydney. When he got to Pukekohe, Jonah convinced him to have a go at getting into the New Zealand Sevens team and the rest, as they say, is history. **He's big, he's fast, he's strong and he's Fijian . . . and that means he can play sevens.** He's so skilful. There's just so much to his game that you can't coach. He's a naturally gifted rugby player and Titch had no hesitation in putting him into the team straight away.

Jeff Wilson and Jamie Joseph . . . "come to the dark side, Jeff."

Jeff Wilson
When Goldie first came into the All Black scene he never used to drink or smoke . . . until he came across Frank. After every game he'd always have Frank in his ear, using his best Darth Vader voice: "Come to the dark side. It is useless to resist." In those days Goldie was a bit highly strung and a bit of a loner – probably a result of his cricket days when everything was more individualistic. Guys like Arran Pene, Jamie Joseph and Stu Forster probably helped chill him out a bit. **When Goldie got dropped from the All Blacks once, those three started calling him Bronzie!** He hated it. People always ask me what sort of sevens player Jeff Wilson would have been. I reckon he would, and still would be, a great sevens player. One day I asked him why he doesn't play sevens and he said, "Because no one has asked me. Just because I'm white doesn't mean I can't play."

A toothy smile from Peter Woods, posing here with David Campese.

Peter Woods

I call him poto – which in Maori means 'short', but in Rushy means 'short arse'. Some of the other boys call him 64 because he's thinning on top and they reckon he's got about 64 parts in his hair. He's got a cap in one of his teeth, as well, and **one year in Hong Kong we were in the bar talking to a women's rugby team and right in the middle of the conversation his tooth popped out.** I made the DJ stop playing music and I got on the mike and told everyone to "freeze". Within seconds everyone in the nightclub was on the floor looking for his tooth. I've never seen him so embarrassed in all my life. Poto was one of the best team men around. Whenever a new fella came into the sevens team we'd always room him with Poto. Within 30 minutes of being in the squad, Poto would be getting smart to them. Roger Randle had to put up with jibes about his big bum; Joe Tauiwi's smoker's breath came in for some fire and Seymour's vanity was always a source for a good laugh.

Terry Wright

TJ was one of the best guys I've played with. He never made mistakes, he worked hard, he was fit and, for a skinny bugger, he was as tough as they come. You don't play 30 tests for New Zealand if you're not tough. I learnt a lot from watching TJ. He was always willing to help the younger fellas. He helped me a lot when I started playing on the wing. **He's a good bloke . . . as far as skinny white buggers go.**

Andrew Blowers, Eroni Clarke, Michael Jones, Timo Tagaloa and Inga Tuigamala

I call these guys The God Squad for obvious reasons. I've put them all together because, at every chance they get, they're always together. The most important thing to them is their faith which means the only thing wrong with them, in terms of this book, is that I've got no dirt on them. **The only time I've seen Ice (Michael Jones) a little angry was when Zinzan started calling him Rat because his eyes are so close together.** People will be shocked to know that Ice nearly floored an old lady at an Auckland aftermatch function. The big thing in the team those days was to tap a team-mate on the shoulder and stick your finger in their cheek as they turned around. After a while some of the boys knew what was up so they'd try and slap the other fella's hand instead of turning around. This poor old lady wanted to talk to Ice, tapped him on the shoulder and he smacked her hand as hard as he could. I've never seen him so upset. Me and Zinny thought it was great.

Norm Hewitt and Bull Allen

Great mates on and off the field. Norm was the aggressor and Bull was the peacemaker. Norm could kill with some of his looks, while Bull wouldn't say a bad word about anyone. They were the backbone of the midweek All Black team for a long time and it will be a shame if Bull never plays rugby again. The game needs characters like him.

Scott McLeod and Matthew Cooper

Two of my best mates. Scottie's a bit of a perfectionist. Everything has to be perfect with him – his clothes, his hair. He has to look good all the time so I call him 'Nobody' . . . because **Nobody is perfect. I call Coops 'Jelly' because that's what his passes were like when they were coming out to the wing.** Their other claim to fame is that they are both vying for the biggest nose in New Zealand rugby. They need a tube of suntan lotion each, just to cover their honks in the summer. Joking aside, two of the nicest blokes in New Zealand rugby. (Can't believe I said that.)

Andrew Mehrtens, Justin Marshall, Tabai Matson, Bubs Mayerhofler (The Four Ms)

I don't understand any of their humour. Mehrts is as quick witted as they come so a few of the Maori boys struggle to keep up with him. Normally he'll tell a joke and a minute later the bros still haven't caught on. **They're a good bunch, those Canterbury boys, but sometimes you listen to them and it's like they're talking another language.**

Hika Reid and Steve McDowell

I used to be their guinea pig when they were showing each other their judo moves. It was on the Maori tour in 1988 and I was brand new to the team. I must admit I started locking myself in my room and not answering the phone in case they summoned me again.

Jamie Joseph and Arran 'Tupapa' Pene

Two of the hardest men in New Zealand rugby – to get a drink out of, that is! Jamie's nickname was 'fly' because of all the hair over his back and arms. Most of us, though, called him Jake the Muss. As far as Arran goes, I've never met anyone with a bad word for him (except his wife!)

The Oz Files

IN THE COURSE OF any rugby career there will be plenty of players that you'll admire for their talent. Many will make you laugh. Some will inspire. Others will act as sources of motivation. If you're lucky, really lucky, you'll come across a player that is all those things and more. For me, that man is the one and only Glen Matthew Osborne.

Since the first day I met him, back in 1992, he has been at the centre of some of the funniest incidents of my career. I should have been able to guess that would be the case when he arrived at his first North Harbour training. All the players were sitting in the changing shed and I saw this guy getting autographs from all the players. **I said to Walter Little "I didn't know that they let fans in the changing-rooms to get autographs at trainings." Walt said, "He's not a fan . . . he's in the team. His name is Glen something."**

At the next training run the management handed out some boots to the All Blacks in the team. Frank Bunce got a couple of pairs. Oz was sitting beside me and he goes, "Cuz, look at those flash boots, bro." I told him he should ask Frank for a pair because he had heaps of boots. Oz was like, "Oh nah, shame man, shame." So I asked Frank myself and he threw a pair across the room. Oz didn't want to take them unless he could pay Frank for them "cos that's the way I was brought

Oz and Peter Woods after another triumph in Hong Kong. Woodsy and Oz were flatmates in the early days.

up". Frank said he didn't want anything for them but at the next training Oz comes walking in with his gumboots on with a bag full of lambs' tails and three eels on a hook! Geez they smelt bad. Oz was quite offended when Frank wouldn't take them off him.

That year we went to the national sevens and Oz, born and bred in Wanganui, was green as hell. A couple of the well-travelled North Harbour boys always travel with passports. I pretended that I was collecting them and I got to Oz to get his and he was like, "What do I need that for?" I told him you needed a passport every time you travel on a plane. "Oh shit, cuz, I don't even have one of those!" By the time we got to Palmerston North he was going to make a run for it and jump over the fence and run up the road!

A couple of weeks after leaving Wanganui for North

Harbour he started flatting with Peter Woods. He came to training one day and said, "Boys, I got a job. I'm going to be selling insurance. I have to do a six week course and then I can sell insurance to all you guys." We were all a little surprised because Oz had trouble speaking English in those days and none of us could imagine him selling anything. **Woodsy asked Oz what insurance was. "I've got six weeks to learn that, bro," he said.**

We thought we'd better try and help him out by increasing his vocabulary a bit as he didn't really have one. We got him into crosswords. Walt and I bought him a book and all the clues through the whole book were three letters long. He was sitting there happy as Larry because he was flying through them, and then he got stuck so we had a look over his shoulder. **The clue was a three letter word for taxi. He knew the first letter was 'C' and we could see him sitting there struggling to work it out.** After a bit of encouragement the lights obviously came on in his head and he wrote 'car'! We didn't have the heart to tell him he'd got it wrong, so we thought we'd buy him a thesaurus. We stopped at a bookstore and were listening to Oz ask the lady for the thesaurus. He was asking for "one of those books, like a dictionary". The lady asked whether he meant the Oxford Dictionary. "Nah, nah, nah. It's got something to do with dinosaurs." Walt and I were just pissing ourselves behind the bookshelves.

One day I was in the bathroom at his flat and I saw a bottle of Sunlight soap in there, so I came out and asked him what it was doing in there. He wouldn't tell me and even his girlfriend quickly looked away. Later on she confessed that Oz had a bubble bath the night before. No wonder he's so slippery on the field!

At one of the All Black camps in Christchurch we all went up the river to go white water rafting, and he found this white rock. It was just a regular rock but he keep saying "choice rock". We couldn't take it back down in the raft. At the time most of us were shit-scared of Laurie Mains but Oz just walked up to him and asked Laurie to carry his rock back to the hotel. So Laurie took it back with him in the bus! I think the rock is in Oz's house now.

Oz caused just as much trouble on tours. One morning we had to get up real early and we had to wear our All Black No 1s, white dress shirts, the works. We got on the plane and Frank found Oz's passport on the floor. **Oz, still a bit tired, opened up his shirt but couldn't fit the thing in his pocket. Frank had a closer look and he had his shirt on inside out!** The worst part was he had all the buttons done up and a tie on as well. I've tried to sit down and do that and I haven't managed it yet. He told Frank not to tell anyone. Sorry, Oz, he told everyone!

Another time when we were in Queensland for a Super 12 game we arrived back to the hotel to find a whole bunch of Japanese tourists in the lobby. It turned out it was Japan Day and all the ladies had kimonos on and all the men had their traditional robes on. They recognised a lot of our team and we were all standing around signing autographs. Then they asked to get a photo with us in front of their flag. **Oz was up the back and the next thing we heard was, "So, where are all you people from?"**

Oz has a habit of buying really ugly clothes, too. He bought some bright red shoes in Scotland once and when we were in Argentina he bought some overalls because he thought they'd match the shoes. I was sitting with Junior Paramore waiting for him while he was trying them on. We were getting a bit annoyed because he was taking so long. Oz said he was having trouble doing up the straps. We told him to come out and we'd help him. So he comes out and he had them on back to front!

Like a few of the boys, Oz is a bit paranoid about his weight – he's always trying to put some on because we give him a hard time about being skinny. One day we were at the airport and I jumped on the scales to see how much I weighed. Then he jumped on but I was still heavier. But then he had an idea. He jumped on again, grabbed his wallet from his back pocket and threw it on the scales as if it was going to make a difference. "It went up! It went up!" Whatever, Oz.

Oz used to have an annoying habit which involved his little finger and his nose. I'm proud of my part in curing this habit.

Another time I was sitting next to him on a plane trip and he told me that every time he goes on a plane his ankles swell up, but it only ever happened when he was leaving New Zealand and never when he was coming home. "That's because we're going downhill, bro." He didn't bat an eyelid.

Oz, if nothing else, is honest . . . but sometimes it's the kind of honesty that we can do without. I remember being in London once with Oz, Peter Woods and Nigel Ward on our way back from the Portugal Sevens. We were flying United Airlines and we had to go through their security check before boarding the plane. The guy at the check-in desk asked us if we'd packed our own bags. "Ya. Ya. Ya. Yes." Have you had your bags with you at all times? "Ya. Ya. Ya. Yes." Could anyone have

Ian Jones and me with Dame Kiri Te Kanawa. When Oz met her he was, as usual, straight up front.

interfered with your bags? "Na. Na. Na. Hang on! The bus driver! Remember we put our bags underneath the bus!" The security guy spent the next hour going through all of our stuff! We could have killed Oz. All he could say was, "Well, he could have!"

One of the most nervous times to be around Oz is when there are celebrities around because you never know what he's going to say. When we were in South Africa we had the chance to attend a concert by Dame Kiri Te Kanawa. Nelson Mandela was also in attendance. After the concert we were invited to the back room. Oz looked at me and started going on about what stink music opera is when **Dame Kiri comes over and starts talking to us. Oz, who'd never heard of her, realises something and says, "Are you Maori?"** A surprised Dame Kiri confirmed she was and all Oz could say was "Oh yeah. This place is a bit different than when the guitars are out on the marae, aye!"

Then Nelson Mandela comes into the room. All the boys were in awe of him. I told Oz a little bit about him. "He was brought up in a mud hut, and was in jail for 27 years, but look at him now . . . he's running the country." As Mandela comes down the line Oz greets him by saying, "Kia ora, bro. Does your family still own that mud hut?"

A great thing about Oz is that he can unknowingly relax a tense situation in a heartbeat with some of his antics. When the All Blacks were playing the Springboks at Newlands in 1996 the backline came out of the tunnel in hysterics. **Oz got a bit thirsty just before heading out on to the field and he decided he needed a drink of water. The only trouble was he grabbed the liniment bottle!**

On the tour to Italy and France the year before, Oz wasn't playing that well and he'd lost his test spot. In the second to last game of the tour the All Blacks were set to play France 'B'. Oz was down to play but he couldn't sleep so he took a sleeping pill. The game started at 2pm and Oz woke up at 10am. He thought he should get a bit more rest so he had another sleeping pill. **A few us were sent to wake him up but he was in fantasyland. When we got him into the changing shed he was walking around in a daze.** There was a big mirror on the wall but poor old Oz thought it was another changing-room and walked right into it. Laurie stared at him with a bemused look on his face. The ironic thing was that Oz had a stormer and three days later he was in the test team. The boys wanted to give him another sleeping pill before the test!

Another memorable changing room incident came in his early days at Harbour. We were getting ready for our game at Onewa Domain against Transvaal when someone walked in 20 minutes before kick-off and told us it had started to rain. All the forwards took out their short sprigs and put in the long ones. It was a big game and all the fellas were real serious. Five minutes before kick-off one of our props, Ron Williams, taps me on the shoulder and says "What the hell is Oz doing!" I looked across the room and all I could see was Oz's arse. I asked him what he was doing. "Bloody hell, cuz," he said as he was picking sprigs up out of the garbage. "They're still good. I can't believe they're throwing them out!"

Oz has come a long way since 1992. He's grown up a lot in the last few years but he's never got carried away with his success. He's still the same old country boy just looking to enjoy life. Oh, and by the way, in 1998 he sold his insurance business for a six figure sum. Primo, Cuz!

The Right Of Reply

No doubt a few of the boys I've played with down the years have collected a few stories about yours truly so I've decided to give them the right of reply. I'll let you decide which ones are telling the truth and which ones are just trying to do what they're always trying to do . . . jerk me!

Errol Brain

Rushy's one of those guys that absolutely thrives on touring. He's been on lots of trips and he's always got heaps of stories to tell about a hotel we're going to, a team we're playing against or a restaurant we're eating in. The one thing about Eric is that he goes at everything at 100 per cent. He plays hard, he trains hard and he knows how to party hard. I must admit that because he's such a likeable character I've often used him to help with the younger guys in the Maori team. **He's a great role model . . . until he takes out his front tooth. Geez, he's an ugly bugger when it's out.** One of his party tricks is to slip it in one of the boy's drinks at a restaurant. The victim will come back from the buffet, start sipping on his drink, and by the time he gets to the bottom of the glass he'll find a rotten old tooth floating around. I saw Rushy do it to Norman Berryman once and I warned him then if he ever did it to me I would take it out of the glass and stand on it!

Ross Cooper

Over the years Rushy, being the professional sort of person he is, has learnt how to play and train exceptionally hard, but he also knows how to switch off from rugby. He would be one of the best balanced tourists I've come across. **A lot of players would do well to model themselves on Rushy because he's got the balance between playing and relaxing absolutely right.**

Matthew Cooper

I used to get a bit of stick from Rushy about my passing. He used to joke that he'd need one of his mother's washing baskets to carry around on the paddock to give himself a better chance at catching one of my passes. Eric's one of those guys you never strike in a bad mood. One rule you learned very quickly when you were touring with him was that when things were getting a bit tough you hung around him because you knew he'd have a smile on your face pretty quickly. **He's always positive, always happy and always making fun out of people . . . but not in a nasty way.** He makes everyone relaxed which obviously means the guys are more comfortable with each other. But probably more important than all that is that he's a huge competitor. I don't think people recognise how difficult it must have been for him when the All Black selectors decided in 1992 to change him from a flanker into a winger. It was a huge ask but you never heard Rushy complain. He was keen to learn as much as he could as quickly as he could. For me, that summed up his professional approach to rugby. At first class level it was a remarkable transition. It says something about his commitment and attitude. Rushy would always put the team first. That's not the most common thing in rugby these days.

Brad Fleming

I've only known Rushy since 1995 so I'm still working on

my dossier of stories about him. What I know already is that he can't handle a drink. After we won Hong Kong in '95 we all had a glass or two at the official dinner. It was only the second time in his life that Rushy had taken a drink and after two beers he was written off. **He didn't make it to the nightclubs that night – he was last seen crawling under a table at the dinner venue.**

Rico Gear

The first time I met Rushy was at the 40-man sevens camp in 1997. He was really good to me. He always has a lot of time for the younger guys. I was real nervous about meeting him but he was giving me lip before I ever really knew him. But that's a good thing because it puts all the boys at ease. With all of his success he could be a bit stuck up, but that's not Rushy .

Earle Kirton

The decision to turn Rushy into a winger was a pretty straight forward one, although by the reaction of some sections of the media you wouldn't have thought so. I knew he had a fair bit of pace. We didn't have a whole lot of wings that were going well at the time. It certainly wasn't the same situation as we have now where there are dozens of good wingers throughout the country. I suggested to the gang (coach Laurie Mains and fellow selector Peter Thorburn) that we give him a go. **When we approached him he told Laurie he didn't give a damn where he played if it meant he could be an All Black.** There was lots of rage, mainly coming out of Auckland, that we were playing too many players out of position and a lot of the times it was Rushy they focused on. It's interesting that the harshest critic of the move – namely the current All Black coach – turned around and played Rushy on the wing when he took over in 1996. To this day I don't believe that we played Rushy out of position, we simply played him in his rightful position – the position that

After all the nice things Earle Kirton has said about me I really feel bad about putting this photo in the book.

he should have been playing from day one. We told him that he was never going to make it as a flanker. We had enough flankers at the time, anyway. In my view Eric Rush wasn't a flanker, he was a sevens player. It was what he did on the sevens field that interested me.

There's little doubt that Rushy played a key part in helping Jonah become comfortable at the All Black level. **I remember Rushy coming to me one day and telling me that to get the best out of Jonah you couldn't give him too much aerobic stuff.** You hear people say Jonah could play No 8 or on the blindside flank but it's all crap. Jonah couldn't play there any more than fly because Jonah would never get the aerobic capacity to do the miles that a player in those positions is expected to do during a game. Rushy knew that. In those early days of Jonah's career, he often struggled with his fitness. Rushy was great with the big boy because he'd go out of his way to help him. Jonah, to my knowledge, has never said it, but it was clear to me that Rushy was very much a mentor to him.

From a managerial point of view, Rushy was worth his weight in gold because he was tremendous with Jonah. Rushy wouldn't give Jonah an easy ride, though. He'd give him a bit of attitude every now and again but the difference was Jonah would take it from him. Jonah wasn't always receptive to criticism but he never had a problem with Rushy telling him to pull his finger out. When you have a player like Rushy – with all of his influence – management shouldn't be afraid of letting him be a leader.

Rushy was always very good natured. Even when he used to tell off Glen Osborne he did it with a smile on his face. He used to call him Blinkers because he reckoned Oz must have been wearing blinkers whenever he ran to his left because he'd never pass the ball. The poor boy couldn't pass left so he'd run towards Rushy on the left wing and just bowl into whoever was in front of him. Rushy used to say to him, "Once, just once, pass the ball to your bro." Rushy's a great character, but never forget his talent. That is what saw him become an All Black.

Walter Little, flanked by me and Jeff Wilson. If Walt hadn't used the elephants story, I wouldn't have mentioned his drinking.

Walter Little

Rushy always likes being the centre of attention. **If he's not telling stories about his times as a sevens player, he's playing practical jokes on us.** His high pitched laugh can get a bit annoying at times but every rugby team needs a fella like Rushy . He's always good for a laugh . . . sometimes at his own expense. When we were on safari in South Africa once Rushy reckoned he'd seen some elephants. None of us believed him and then, as he pointed to them, he said, "Over there . . . grey elephants." What other colour were they ever going to be, Rushy?

Colin Meads

Rushy is one of the great characters of New Zealand rugby. He's a marvellous guy and a sensational team man. When I was ever lucky enough to be a manager of a side he was involved in, I always knew I'd be in for a bit of a tough time because he'd always have me in stitches. He was a fun character, always playing jokes on his team-mates. Teams need guys like Rushy to keep the balance right when you're on the road touring. But **along with the laughter he knew when he needed to switch on. He was a front-runner at training and a game breaker on the paddock.** When I think about the transition he made from being a flanker to a world class winger it still impresses me. Not too many players could have made that transition, and the fact that he's been successful at it is a measure of the talent and commitment he brings to the game.

Glen Osborne

I'd seen Mr Rush playing at the national sevens championships when I was playing for the mighty Wanganui team, but the first time I met him was at Rosmini College in Auckland at a North Harbour training. I remember thinking

Mr Osborne makes another fashion statement with his head.

what an awesome guy he was. He was so fit. He was like a machine. I remember thinking this guy was the greatest player on earth . . . until I actually got to know him. Actually, I must admit that Mr Rush has been a great mentor to me. In that way he's a lot like Zinzan Brooke because he's always looking after the younger guys, he's always getting a laugh and he's the guy that the whole touring environment revolves around. I must say I'm a little disappointed that Mr Rush finds it so amusing to tell so many stories about me. **I always thought that what went on tour, stayed on tour. Obviously Mr Rush has failed to grasp that concept.** I would like to tell some stories about Mr Rush to balance the score but he's just too much of a nice guy. He's never done anything he shouldn't have done on tour. In fact, he's the closest All Black to a Boy Scout that I know.

Lindsay Raki

There's nothing better in rugby than getting one over Rushy. He's not the easiest bugger to get, either, because he's generally a bit cleverer than the rest of us. It doesn't help that most of his team-mates like a drink and Rushy doesn't touch the stuff – so he's got an unfair advantage right there. He's always playing practical jokes on the boys, but one day in Europe I got my revenge. We'd been playing a sevens tournament in Portugal when we were invited to Switzerland for a bit of a holiday. We were at a bar talking to a couple of ladies. One of them was getting married and they were organising a hen party, but the strippers they'd organised pulled out at the last minute. So Eric and I agreed to do it. We showed up at the apartment and we were both quite nervous, so I convinced Eric to have a drink with me to get a bit of Dutch courage up. **We'd bought a couple of rubber flotation tubes and put them down the front our jockeys so it looked like we were well endowed. Actually, I didn't need one so I gave Eric mine to use as well.** After a couple of shots of alcohol Eric was feeling a little brave so we decided to walk in doing our best impersonation of the famous Kiwi wrestlers The Bushwhackers – arms pumping up and

Lindsay Raki gives the thumbs up sign. I doubt I'll see that again after he's read this book.

down in unison with our legs. So off we went, down the hallway. Eric was leading the way and once he stepped inside the room I slammed the door shut and locked him in there. Apparently he just stepped up on to the makeshift stage and started dancing. When he realised I wasn't there he went into a state of shock but the 30 women that were watching soon got his attention when they mobbed him.

Caleb Ralph

I think Rushy must be on Titch's payroll. Titch is a real disciplinarian and one of his rules is to always eat healthily. Rushy has a good way of making sure the boys lose their appetites. **Every time we sit down in a restaurant he takes his false front tooth out and puts it on the table!**

Bruce Reihana

The thing that stood out about Rushy when we first played together in the Chiefs in 1996 was how down to earth he was. For a guy who had been an All Black and such a legend at sevens I was expecting to be quite intimidated by him. But he was great. He helped me a lot. He was always offering advice and when I look back he's had a big influence on me. One of his strengths is that he knows how to relax. When it comes to down time Rushy is the master, but when it comes to stepping it up he switches on.

Owen Scrimgeour

The thing about Rushy is that he doesn't have too many enemies. In fact, he's probably one of the most well liked people within rugby. When Rushy retires it's going to leave a huge hole in New Zealand sevens. **When we went to Dubai at the end of 1998, Rushy couldn't travel with us because of a calf injury – it just wasn't the same without him.** Something was missing. It's the same when Dallas Seymour isn't with us . . . they both carry a lot of influence with all of the boys. Rushy's a great captain. He doesn't rely on talking too much, he leads by

Bruce Reihana, who was almost arrested in Kuala Lumpur for molesting his gold medal.

example. He's the sort of bloke that, if the team is in trouble, he'll demand the ball and try and win the thing for us. I'll always have a lot of time for him. When I missed out on being selected for the Commonwealth Games team, Brad Fleming, Tony Monaghan and myself were sitting in a room in the hotel and Rushy came and sat with us for 20 minutes. There wasn't much he could say . . . he tried, but we didn't want to hear anything from anyone. But looking back, the fact he made the effort meant a lot to me. We were all pretty devastated. The three of us and the other unlucky player, Dan Parkinson, got smashed on the flight home. If you mentioned the name Gordon Tietjens you had to skull your drink. We basically got drunk and disorderly. We were four angry young men . . . if anyone looked at us the wrong way they soon got it in the ear! Rushy's a good laugh, too. **He's always telling stories about some of the fellas he's toured with. I've heard him tell the story about Woodsy losing one of the caps off his teeth at a Hong Kong nightclub but Rushy did the same thing in Jerusalem.** We'd been asked to do that haka near the Wailing Wall and in the middle of it, one of Rushy's false front teeth fell out. As usual, he didn't panic, he just caught it before it hit the ground and continued the haka. If you watch the video of the haka that appeared on CNN, you can see Rushy's quick hands in motion.

Dallas Seymour

Sometimes you hear about those rugby relationships that last for a lifetime. Well, that's the way it will be for Rushy and me. He's like a brother to me. I feel like a part of his family and he's definitely a part of my family. And, like any set of brothers, we've had a few run-ins over the years. It's always great playing against him because you can always be sure there will be a few cheap shots going in. **Fingers up noses and rubbing faces in the dirt are both in the rules.** I remember once being tackled and not realising it was Rushy. I was lying on the ground, trying to get up but this guy kept holding me down. The next thing I knew this fella started chucking dirt in my face. I got up and gave

Dallas Seymour's eyes tell it all. The man should never be let loose with a firearm.

him a bit of a slap, and then realised it was Rushy. We had a chuckle and got on with the game.

We've had few laughs over the years. One of the more memorable was during a Mongrels trip to Uruguay in 1992. We'd had a hell of a journey getting to Uruguay and by the time we got to our hotel the boys were a bit tired but we figured we'd go out on the town, anyway. Rushy decided to head home early. That was a bit unlike him because, even though he doesn't drink, he usually enjoys hanging with the boys. A couple of hours later I headed back to the hotel with Richard Turner and Ant Strachan. We'd had pizza early on and started hooking into the leftovers when we decided we'd wake up Rushy. It took us half an hour of banging and yelling to get him to come to the door. **"For heaven's sake, fellas, if you can't handle your piss without annoying me, bugger off." With that, the three of us hammered him with pizza.** Rushy just stood there, trying to look serious, with pizza all over his face!

You couldn't help but be inspired by Rushy's captaincy. He's the sort of player that leads by example. He's not a really big talker . . . he chooses his words carefully. It's what he does on the paddock that has the most effect on his team-mates. You can never play in second gear with Rushy because he demands 100 per cent effort all the time. And you don't mind giving it, either, because you'll never see him in cruise mode. I have a tremendous respect for him. **Look at what he did at the Commonwealth Games. He went to the Games with a broken hand, re-broke it during the Games but still led us to the gold medal.** The fact that he was able to remain focused on the job in Kuala Lumpur, despite the injury and despite the aftermath of the traffic accident he was involved in before he left, is a tribute to the high professional standards he sets himself.

Matt Te Pou

The biggest compliment I can pay to Eric Rush is that he has been at the heart of the resurgence of Maori rugby. It wasn't that long ago that the only games the Maori side played were internal games within New Zealand. At the time a lot of people were pointing the finger at the NZRFU demanding better games for the Maori team, but the fact was that a blame mentality wasn't going to get us anywhere. The team needed to achieve to be recognised and Eric, along with Errol Brain, Phil Coffin, Kevin Nepia and Jim Coe recognised that.

Players want to be a part of Maori rugby now but during the 'dark days' when a New Zealand trial was on, a lot of the top players didn't bother showing up. But Eric always found time to come, no matter what other demands he had on his time. It was a key to the improved status of Maori rugby because Eric's like a magnet. **His mana within the game means that other players are prepared to follow him. He's a leader but not the sort who pushes himself on people.** He was never one of those untouchable All Blacks. He leads from within and other players are drawn to him.

Gordon Tietjens

Mana. It's a word that is used a lot these days . . . probably more than it should be. But when it comes to describing Eric Rush there's no other single word to use. There was an incident at the Commonwealth Games that summed him up for me. He was on the verge of playing in the most important sevens event of his career. It was an event he'd been dreaming about for a year. It was an event that he hadn't been able to stop talking about for months. But two days before the Commonwealth Games started Rushy came to me and told me that he should drop out of the team. He believed that his broken hand wasn't coming right and he suggested I put Rua Tipoki in the team instead. **Rushy had, of course, been struggling with his hand since the fatal road accident he was involved in a month before the Games. It was a heartbreaking thing for Rushy to be involved in and, to be honest, I wasn't even sure at that stage if he'd make it to the Games.** I was very concerned about him and worried about how he was coping with everything. In terms of the sevens team it was devastating. The last thing I wanted to do was go to the Commonwealth Games without him. It would have been completely disruptive. It would have meant that I would have had to have found a new leader and it would have meant that we would have been without the best sevens exponent in the world.

There wasn't a night that went by that I didn't worry whether Rushy would make it or not. Even when we went to Singapore to build up for the Games there was still no guarantee he'd make it onto the field in Kuala Lumpur. **He couldn't take part in any physical work, so I demanded that he visit a local doctor to get an update. We were advised that there was no way he'd be able to play for a couple of weeks.** At that time, I knew I had to pick guys that were 100 per cent fit and I honestly didn't think he'd make the Games team.

I asked the NZRFU for permission to take an extra player to KL in case Rushy couldn't play. That player was Rua Tipoki. The team hadn't trained well in Singapore, or in our early days in Kuala Lumpur. Rushy was obviously concerned about his injury, and his subsequent inability to train was proving to be too much of a distraction. That's when he offered to pull out. I told him to wait until he had sat his final fitness test. I had Christian Cullen and Dallas Seymour tackling him and ripping the ball out of his hands and, remarkably, Rushy came through it. We waited until the next morning to see how the hand was and he told me it felt fine. Well, that was enough for me. Rushy was in the Games team.

The young guys love Rushy because he's the ultimate professional. He's in his 30s now but none of the younger fellows can beat him or Dallas in the beep tests. People like to talk about this debate about who the No 1 player in the world is. **Some people say it's Rushy, others say it's Fiji's Waisale Serevi. To me, there's no contest. Rushy has won three Hong Kongs and a Commonwealth Games gold medal since I've been with him.** He's been playing on the sevens world stage for the past 11 years. No one, not Serevi or anyone else, can compete with that. When I first took charge of the team in 1994 there was never

I've always had a lot of time for Gordon Tietjens (well, certainly since he became national sevens coach.)

any doubt that Rushy was going to be my captain. The team had struggled in 1993 but I could see straight away how much respect the guys had for Rushy.

I think he got a bit of shock when I first came in and introduced a pretty disciplined set-up. The first thing that Rushy had to change was his diet. **He was very much a burger freak but he accepted my ideas without too much of a fuss. It took me a while to get used to some of his off-field antics but the thing with Rushy is that he can enjoy himself without ever jeopardising his rugby.** He can be acting the clown with guys like Dallas and Glen Osborne but, when 30 minutes to game time comes, he has a saying for the boys – "Time To Front" – and everyone switches on.

His sense of humour is a source of great fun within the team. He's tremendous when he has to address an audience. A lot of times he will give the fellas nicknames as he introduces them. Two of my favourites involve Christian and Oz. In 1996 he introduced Christian at a function and said his nickname was Chester. Christian got up shaking his said, wondering how the hell he ended up with the name Chester. Rushy explained, "A couple of years ago when South Africa toured New Zealand, Chester Williams was their only black player. Christian's our only white player!" And one of his favourite lines about Oz is, "His best three years at High School were in the fifth form!"

Despite all the success that has come Rushy's way, he has remained humble and still has the ability to laugh at himself. People often say the thing that stands out from the sevens team is that we're a team of no 'stars'. That's not entirely true. **We have many world class players - Rushy's the best of them - but none of them act like stars and a lot of that is down to Rushy.** He encourages everyone to participate, and he has the ability to treat everyone the same – whether you're Jonah Lomu or the guy just trying to make the squad. It's a unique ability, but then Rushy's a pretty unique character.

Maori Rugby – The Soul Game

BEFORE YOU ADDRESS ANYONE it is a Maori custom to establish who you are by reciting your whakapapa (family history). My Maori blood comes from my mum. This is the whakapapa of her parents and, therefore, of me.

Henare Tua (Grandfather)		Hikiora Tupe (Grandmother)
Matangirau	Maunga (Mountain)	Matangirau
Te Touwai	Awa (River)	Te Touwai
Whangaroa	Moana (Sea)	Whangaroa
Karangahape	Marae	Karangahape
Kaitangata	Hapu (Sub-tribe)	Whanau Pani/Ngati Kawau
Ngati Kahu	Iwi (Tribe)	Ngapuhi
Mamari	Waka (Canoe)	Mataatua

When I was growing up in Matangirau it was the Maori All Blacks that inspired me. When I saw them play I was looking at men that looked like me. All of the impossible dreams that kids have – wanting to play for North Auckland, wanting to play for the Maori and wanting to be an All Black – seemed one step closer. I used to think to myself, "If that Maori fella can do it, then so can I."

I've been lucky enough to have played for both the Maori All Blacks and the All Blacks and it's impossible to separate the two in terms of their significance. The All Blacks are obviously the pinnacle team. It's the team that every New Zealand kid playing rugby wants to play for. **But the Maori team is something special, too. The passion that Maori have for rugby is immense and when you graduate to the Maori All Blacks that passion overflows.** There is a real sense of togetherness. A real sense of playing the game knowing that you are playing for every Maori in New Zealand. In that sense it's a bit like playing for the All Blacks . . . but somehow it seems more personal.

Unfortunately every time a Maori All Black team runs out for a game, a certain section of the New Zealand rugby public will brand the team as racist. Why, they ask, should Maori have their own team?

I honestly don't see the difference between picking a Maori team and picking a New Zealand University or New Zealand Marist team.

Maori will always have a rugby team whether it's sanctioned by the NZRFU or not. We are proud of our heritage, our culture and who we are. **Rugby is one way in which we can celebrate that pride, just as it is for our Polynesian brothers from Samoa, Tonga and Fiji.**

To label the Maori team as a racist concept is, I believe, naive.

Matt Te Pou – the current Maori coach – hit the nail on the head when he said that these same people said not a word when the greatest Maori team to ever go overseas from these shores – the 28th Maori Battalion – left to fight in World War II. The mana of these men is so great I hesitate to even mention them in a book like this.

Rugby is a positive for our people in every way. Why try to

limit something that can do only good?

If there is anything else that is certain when the Maori All Blacks run on to a paddock, it's that you are about to be entertained. There is an unwritten rule in Maori rugby that you run the ball at every opportunity. People like to talk about how exciting the Super 12 competition is with its open, expansive style, but anyone who knows anything about the history of Maori rugby knows they've been playing that way since the first official New Zealand Maori game back in the early 1900s.

Every rugby team I've played for has had a special atmosphere. East Tamaki, Otahuhu, Takapuna and all the rep teams. However, the one team which I really love playing for is my marae. **The Matangirau team has one ingredient that none of the others have. We're all whanau which is a bond that can't be explained.** Most of the guys don't play any rugby all year, yet at the Labour Weekend Pa Wars in our little county of Whangaroa, you'd think it was test match time, such is the feeling and intensity of the rugby. I've learnt a lot about rugby and a lot about having pride in who you are and where you come from from playing in those games.

It's that sort of feeling that exists in the New Zealand Maori team.

My first experience with representative Maori rugby came in 1985 when my East Tamaki under 19 coach Ron Reti convinced me to go to the Auckland Maori Colts trials. I wasn't too keen because I was sure that I wasn't good enough and when I got to the venue I was even more convinced I was out of place. All the guys looked so much older than me. After the game Ron let on that it was actually the Auckland Maori senior trials. **The next thing I knew I was in Tony Andrews' Auckland team. After a couple of seasons for them I was selected in the North Island's Prince Of Wales Cup side.**

When I got to Wanganui for the game against the South Island I was a nervous wreck. I kept wondering what I was doing there. If I could have got on the next plane to Auckland I probably would have caught it because I was shit-scared of half of my team. When I looked around the changing-room I was surrounded by guys like Buck Shelford, Hika Reid, Steve McDowell, Arthur Stone, Ian Dunn and the Brooke brothers Marty, Robin and Zinzan. Being a flanker in those days I remember just being happy that Buck was on my side. He was at his prime in those days and the thought of going up against him wasn't too appealing.

I must have played okay because I was named in the Maori All Black team for it's one off game against Wanganui. It was my first black jersey. Geez I was proud – not of myself – just proud to be in the Maori team.

The next year the Maori team toured France, Italy, Spain and Argentina and to this day, it still stands out as one of the best tours I've been on. The team was full of characters. I don't know how the coach Mattie Blackburn put up with us. The team was made up of the players of the calibre of Buck, Hika Reid, Ian Dunn, Arthur Stone, John Timu, Kawhena Woodman, Frano Botica, Bruce Hemara, Dean Kenny, Wiremu Maunsell, Brett Iti, Chris Kapene, Paul Simonsson, Rhys Ellison, Steve Hotton, Jasin Goldsmith, Len Mason, Mike Te Paa, Paul Leonard, Liston Heke, Arthur McLean, the Brooke brothers and a fella called Lindsay Raki.

Our playing record was good. We played 12 games and our only loss was against a Languedoc Selection at Narbonne. If there was a problem on the tour it was discipline, or lack if it, from some of our opponents.

Before our game against a Littoral Selection at Toulon, Buck had warned us to expect a bit of biffo. He'd played in France and he knew a couple of the characters in their side were going to be looking for trouble. **At the team meeting he told us that we couldn't afford to fight back. "Take all their shit, play rugby and we'll win the game."** All the way through the first half they were kicking, punching and even eye-gouging us. Then one of our props, Chris Kapene, got kicked in the head and was stretchered off. It was a vicious attack that ended Chris' playing time on the tour. Buck called us all together. "There's

The 1988 New Zealand Maori team to France, Italy, Spain and Argentina. I'm in the third row, third from left.

going to be a fight in the next couple of minutes and if I see any of you bastards hanging back you're in trouble!" At the next lineout Zinny didn't even wait for the ball to be thrown in. He just turned around and smacked the guy opposite him. It was all on.

Buck was the kind of guy you followed no matter what the circumstances. He had my total loyalty. To this day I remember the talk he had with me after my first Prince Of Wales game. He sat me down and told me not to waste any of the opportunities I had. **They were simple words but when they came from Buck they carried special significance.**

Despite the on-field problems the tour was one long laugh. Everyone, except Robin and Zinny, could play the guitar so there was lots of singing and lots of hakas. And with Raki there, you knew you had to have your wits about you. When we got to Spain a local rugby club had put on a bit of a night for us. Raki took it upon himself to introduce the boys to the crowd whose only real knowledge of rugby was the names of New Zealand's 1987 World Cup squad. They didn't know who the players were, but they recognised the names. Raki introduced Buck and there was a big roar. Then it was Zinny's turn . . . another big roar. Then he introduced David Kirk . . . Alan Whetton . . . Grant Fox. **With each name another Maori boy would walk out and take the applause. Raki even threw in "Elvis Presley" when our physiotherapist Neil Familton entered the room.**

Any joviality in the team had long but disappeared by the time kick-off came in our last tour match, against Argentina's Tucuman. They had already claimed scalps like Australia, France and England and we knew we were in for a bit of a tough match when they all emerged from the changing shed in tears. The crowd had whipped them up into a frenzy. Sure enough, they were throwing punches from the first whistle. The whole game was a running scrap. I had the misfortune to be the one who started the last fight that saw the game eventually called off ten minutes early. Someone had hit me from behind and when I turned around a little winger was

Another game, another shower on the '88 NZ Maori tour. I'm here with Buck, Paul Leonard, Zinny and Brett Iti.

Jasin Goldsmith, Paul Simonsson and me in party mode on the 1988 NZ Maori tour.

running away from me so I chased him. We ended up having to retreat to the middle of the field because the crowd started throwing things at us. Eventually the Tucuman players surrounded us and led us off the field. But we had to fight our way through thousands of people. Jasin Goldsmith got a bottle smashed across his face. Meanwhile, the Brooke's were in their element, swatting as many people as they could. Raki was doing his best to encourage the locals by giving them the finger at every chance. **We had to stay in the changing-room for three hours while the police cleared the crowd, so the boys organised a couple of dozen beers and the guitars came out.**

Eventually we were led to a new bus – the Tucuman fans had destroyed the other one – and were driven back into the city. The local Chief of Police was travelling with us and, as we came up to a garden bar, he told us to ignore any abuse that may be given to us as we passed the rugby supporters who were in the bar. Without a word being said the whole team went to the side of the bus closest to the bar and started shouting. Talk about inciting a riot!

I don't know why, but us Maori boys seem to act in a pack a lot of times. When we were on tour in Samoa in 1992, our manager Colin 'Pinetree' Meads was a bit upset with the team the day after an aftermatch function. "I'm not happy boys. One of you guys was seen urinating in public last night. **I'm asking for an honesty call. I want that guy to stand up and make an apology to the team." Three-quarters of the team stood up!**

Billy Bush was our coach on that tour – one of the toughest tours I've been on because it was always so hard playing the Samoans, Fijians and Tongans in their own backyard. We were humbled by the generosity of the Islanders. In Samoa one of the villages presented us with a whole cooked pig. We had nowhere to put it except on the top of the bus. It was three days later when the boys noticed a strange smell . . . it was still up there!

At that time a few people were upset that Pinetree was the Maori manager. Some people thought we should have had a

Hika Reid and Arthur Stone (with guitar) lead another sing-along on the '88 Maori tour.

Maori manager but, for the boys on that tour, we couldn't have had a better guy than Pinetree. He had huge mana wherever he went. He wasn't a Maori, but he had rugby in his blood and he had Maori people in his heart. He was the best manager we ever had.

Pinetree was inspirational on that tour. We'd lost to a Tongan President's XV a few days before our test at Nuku'alofa and Pinetree took it upon himself to help Billy get us ready. In those days no one was sure what future Maori rugby had. There were some who wanted the concept brought to an end and Pinetree reminded us of that. **"If you want any added motivation, remember that Maori rugby is on the line. If you don't want to play for yourselves, play for all the kids. If you want your kid to play for the New Zealand Maori, you'll work hard for them."** It was an awesome speech. We went out there and whipped them 33-10.

Maori rugby was in good hands on that day and now – with Matt Te Pou following the footsteps of Chas Ferris – Maori rugby has continued to go from strength to strength. He has instilled pride, discipline and an awareness that results on the paddock will lead to more recognition for individuals, the team and our people as a whole. I believe Maori rugby has got a part to play in New Zealand rugby. It inspired me to believe in myself and believe that maybe, just maybe, one day I could be an All Black. I hope that dream is never taken away from today's kids.

Sevens Heaven

THERE'S BEEN A BIT of speculation about what I will do after I stop playing rugby in New Zealand. Depending on which Sunday newspaper you read, I will be coaching the New Zealand Sevens team or playing out my career in France.

To be honest I am undecided but I thought I'd have a go at practising my selectorial skills just in case I decide to turn to coaching.

I have selected three sevens teams – a World team, an all-time New Zealand team and the 1999 version of The Mongrels.

The first team I selected was the World team. Predictably, Fijians feature strongly.

Mesake Rasari

Rasari had to be in the team. A big Fijian forward. He was about 6ft 7in and he could run like Terry Wright. **When he ran the only thing you could see were his teeth.** He played in five Hong Kong tournaments and, between 1990 and 1992 when Fiji won three consecutive finals, he was unstoppable. He was named Player of the Tournament in 1992.

Vesi Rauluni

To me, he was the reason why Fiji were so dominant in the

early '90s. He was a great leader. He had the total respect of his team-mates. A real hard man who would add a bit of steel up front.

Simon Poidevin

A real hard-nosed loose forward. He gets into the team because he's as tough as they come but he's also got a good footballer's brain on him. He reads the game as well as anyone. He's a good man to have around after the game as well because he knows how to have fun.

Waisale Serevi

The best sevens player in the world. The thing that continues to amaze me about him is his ability to beat guys so easily one-on-one. There have been a few times when I've played against him when **I couldn't help but admire what he was doing . . . I almost wanted to start clapping a couple of times! He's a cheeky little bugger, though. When Fiji was dominating in Hong Kong a few years ago, when he knew they had the final won, he'd start winking at us.** But in 1994, after Fiji had won three in a row, we played each other in a semi-final. At halftime he winked at me and I said, "It's a bit too early for that nonsense, boy." We ended up beating them 28-14 and as soon as the final whistle went the whole team started winking at him! Serevi's been playing Hong Kong since 1989 and he's still not 30 years old. He's got a lot of sevens ahead of him and, as long as he's still in the Fijian team, they'll continue to be New Zealand's toughest opponents on the world stage.

David Campese

There's no way Campo couldn't be in this team. Like Serevi, when Campo was in his prime, he could beat anyone. His great value in sevens – apart from his ball skills and his great vision – was his unpredictability. You never knew what he was going to do. To me Campo sums up what rugby is all about. He played for the sheer fun of it. He always had a go and was

Photo: PETER BUSH

Waisale Serevi . . . the best sevens player in the world.

never afraid of making any mistakes. He was a good fella, too. He made a point of saying gidday to everyone and he wasn't too big to talk to the younger guys, even though he was held in great awe. He'd always talk to you during a game but never used the nasty stuff.

Campo's style was much more refreshing. He'd always have a few well-timed quips for the opposition – sometimes you'd have to remind yourself not to listen to him and just concentrate on the game. **Campo had one of the best rugby brains in world football. He knew exactly what has happening anywhere on the field and he had the ability to take any opportunities that came his way.**

It was quite amazing to watch the Australian Sevens team in 1998 when Campo was playing. At times he was three steps ahead of his team-mates. His legs have slowed down a bit in recent years but not enough to stop him from embarrassing us. One time in the Sydney Sevens I remember watching him turn Peter Woods inside out. Then he did the same to me in the final at Paris in 1998 when he led Australia to its first win against New Zealand since the final in Hong Kong in 1988.

The boys were all pretty subdued in the changing shed after the game and, as usual, Campo was the first in the door. He took one look around and said, **"Typical bloody Kiwis. You can't even let us enjoy one win in 10 years!" The boys lightened up after that.**

At that time Campo reminded me that rugby was just a game and told me to be proud of what New Zealand had done over the previous 10 years. It was a nice gesture, but Kiwis don't like losing to Australians at the best of times so the boys decided to get a little bit of revenge. During the after match celebrations, whenever Campo was dancing with a woman – he's still single because he says guys are the only people who talk to him – one of the Kiwi boys would cut in on him without looking at him or saying a word. Eventually he realised what was going on. "Bloody Kiwis. Go and find some sheep!"

Noa Nadruku

I only played against him once but he did enough in that game

David Campese . . . always reminded me that rugby was just a game.

to warrant selection for any World team. He was the difference between Fiji and New Zealand that day. He thrived playing outside Serevi. He was strong, fast and he had a great step. He went on to play league at the Canberra Raiders.

Andy Harriman
He wins selection because of what he did at the World Cup in Scotland in 1993. He had good forwards who won a lot of ball for him but once Andy got it, he just ran around everyone – Australia, Fiji, even New Zealand, couldn't stop him. He virtually won the Cup for England on his own.

Reserves
Marika Vunibaka
Another Fijian speedster. A real quiet fella on and off the field. **The only time I have ever seen him smile was when he won the Player of the Tournament award in Uruguay in 1997. He's got a good punch on him, too . . . something I found out in Japan.** Fiji had thrashed us in Hong Kong so I thought I'd try and upset them a little in the rematch to help fire the boys up. I was having a tussle with one of the big boys. I was on top of him giving him a few friendly taps when Vunibaka came running in from the wing and clocked me. I didn't see it coming . . . the only thing I could see were stars.

Andre Venter
Like Rasari, he's got the size of a forward and the speed of a back. He's South African and you have got to have at least one of them in the team.

I didn't consider any New Zealand players for the World team . . . I wanted to save them for my all-time New Zealand selection. There is so much sevens talent in New Zealand it's impossible to pick a team that everyone will agree with. I have chosen a team from players I played with – ones I think would do the most damage on the field. You have already read all about them . . . here's the list: Jonah Lomu, Dallas Seymour, Zinzan Brooke,

Four All Blacks . . . and four players who each won the Player of the Tournament trophy at Hong Kong. From left: Christian Cullen, Jonah Lomu, Glen Osborne and me.

Joe Tauiwi, Frano Botica, Christian Cullen and Glen Osborne. Bench: Joeli Vidiri and Waisake Masirewa.

The last team selected was the 1999 Mongrels – a collection of players who can play a bit but only qualify for selection because of their off-field antics. By this stage of the book, you've heard all the stories about the fellas I've come across during my years in sevens. The only real headache picking this team was the halfback position. Graeme Bachop and Ant Strachan both put up a good fight but, in the end the nod, went to Stu Forster. **(Anyway, Bash is too busy ripping off his Japanese employers while Ant didn't help his chances by wetting his bed in Uruguay . . . there's funny and then there's sick, aye!)**

So, if there was a Mongrels reunion tour to all the old hangout spots, this is the team I'd select: Richard Turner, Pat Lam, Simon Tremain, Stu Forster, Lindsay Raki, Frank Bunce and Glen Osborne. Bench: Peter Woods and Scott Pierce.

To help the boys on their way I've selected back-up staff for The Mongrels. The coach would be Henry Peevers – the main money man for The Warblers. He'd ensure there were plenty of healthy cheques for the boys at the end of the tour. In fact, he's got so much money I'm not sure if he knows what to do with it. One time in Bahrain he bet Raki $2000 that he couldn't skull a jug of beer. Raki won the bet (and Raki being Raki, he still talks about it today!)

The manager's duties would go to Pedro Bordaberry. He's the guy that runs the Uruguay Sevens. He was always popular with the players because he'd do anything for you.

Liz Goldenberg, an American photo-journalist, would be the team's official photographer. One year she invited Oz and I to the New York Sevens, which she organises. **Typical Oz. We were going to go and see the Statue of Liberty and I asked Oz if he wanted to go. "Oh, nah. There's a good video on."** There he was, in the city that never sleeps, and he spent the whole trip in his room!

Simon Davies, the European agent for The Warblers, would

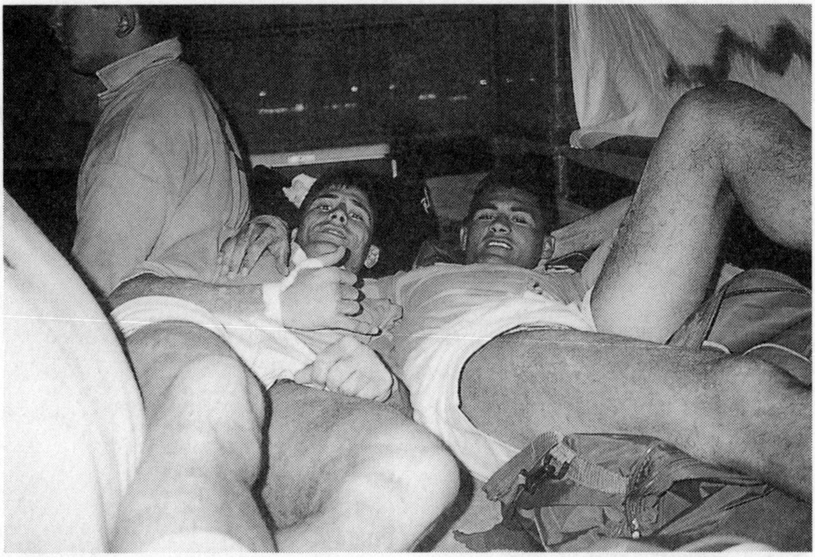

Above: Dallas and me after another hard day's grind on the sevens' circuit. Below: Several candidates pictured here for a potential Mongrels' reunion tour. Back row: Chris Caro (manager/sponsor), Lindsay Raki, Richard Turner, Junior Paramore, Frank Bunce, Glen Osborne, me and Ant Strachan.

Mark Thompson . . . one of the funniest fellas in the game.

take charge of entertainment. He's another fella with a big chequebook so the boys would love him.

And, as with every team, we'd need a couple of hangers on. The lucky two are Mark Thompson and John Gilmer. They're two of the funniest fellas I know. We could rely on these two jokers to get into more trouble than any others in the team – with the exception of Raki!

I couldn't write a rugby book without mentioning my

favourite team of all. The Saintz is my touch team which is made up of fellas from in and around Otara. We've had the same team now for 13 years. They're all longtime mates from school, plus cousins and brothers. In fact, we've been together for so long that the boys are as much a part of my family as my blood relatives. And, like my own family, they were there before I started playing footy and they'll be there after I stop.

I don't know how they have put up with all my abuse and swearing over the years and that also goes for some of the refs that I've encountered. (That was my public apology fellas!)

I am so used to playing with All Blacks and top NPC guys that I expected the same standards from them. There are only a few players left in the team who are under 30, but we still keep trying to hang in there with the young teams in the Open grades.

So this is my tribute to them – the boys who continued to remind me that after all the things that I have achieved in rugby, I'm still just one of the boys from Otara.

Willie Bates
The FOB of the team. More sinbins than anyone else. (Tongan)

John Kani
NZ Touch selector. He had the first car out of all of us. We used to fit the whole team into his little Austin. (Maori)

Richard Tavai
The leader of the Dark Siders. Whenever we won prize money, Rich was the first to put it straight on the bar. (Rarotongan)

Manuel Hohua
The yardage man. He kept getting speed injuries, i.e.

hamstrings strains. I guess it's hard to stop 18 stone! (Maori)

Rob Tito
The oldest, along with my brother Putti. Almost time to move to the managerial side. (Rarotongan/Maori . . . we can't work it out!)

Kopa Kopa
Our touch pro. Plays better after a few smokes. (Rarotongan)

Quentin and Gabriel Hoete
Quentin married my cousin Bett – Gabriel is their son. Quentin played table tennis up to the very top New Zealand standard . . . didn't in touch. (Maori)

Joe Tua
My cousin, Bett's brother. When he first made the Auckland touch team he got himself a hat made up. The words on the hat read: "Joe Tua – Auckland Touch". A real modest fella is our Joe. (Maori)

Rock
Went out with my sister and I don't even know his last name – or his proper first name! (Rarotongan)

Kasey King
He has a black belt and he's The Saintz' version of Oz. What a lethal combination. (Maori)

Tony Makai
Fattest halfback in Auckland club rugby. (Rarotongan)

George Pamatatau and Heta Pamatatau
Relations of our manager Tara. Good party boys but, let's face it, which Rarotongans aren't? (Rarotongan)

The Saintz touch team of 1990-91 – I don't know how they put up with all my abuse.

Putti, Beru and Honky
My three brothers. We've all graduated from our backyard scraps to be able to play together now without having a go at each other. Mum would be proud. (Maori)

Tara Paitai
Best manager we've had since Bett. Mind you, he's the only one who would do it. Tara is also the team's DJ. Awesome sounds.(Rarotongan)

THE ACCIDENT

AUGUST 10, 1998 – THE darkest hour of my life –the day I killed a young man, Brendan Malcolm

I have agonised for months over whether or not to talk about the accident in this book. Do I leave it out and get slammed for forgetting it ever happened or put it in and get slammed for being insensitive to the Malcolm family?

The publishers and I had agreed to do the book at the start of 1998 and had a lot of it planned. It was always going to be light-hearted in nature – a good reason for not talking about the accident. However, I decided it had to go in and this is the reason: I can't change what happened in the past but, by talking about the accident, if I can convince just one person to drive more carefully, then writing this chapter would have been worth it.

The New Zealand Sevens team were at camp in Rotorua

as part of our preparation for Kuala Lumpur. After training I had to do a speaking engagement back in Auckland and left while the guys where in the hot pool. I borrowed Glen Osborne's car.

I stopped at Tirau to get gas where the police logged the time of my departure on video. The corner where the accident occurred is one I have driven around more times than I care to remember. One moment everything was fine, the next I was skidding. I remember seeing some lights and the next thing I knew I was waking up on the road.

To this day I don't know what went wrong. I know that I wasn't being an idiot on the road but I also know that cars don't lose control and fall off the road by themselves, either.

The first cellphone call for help was made moments after my car rolled to a stop. This allowed the police to calculate the exact time I took to get to where the accident happened. One hour and nine minutes. The police then went back and timed themselves doing it at 100 kilometres an hour. It took them one hour and 15 minutes. They then did it at 120 kilometres an hour, it took him one hour and five minutes.

That tells me that I was driving between one hundred and one hundred and twenty kilometres per hour which, when I'm totally honest with myself, is the speed I usually drive at on the open road. I remember slowing down for the corner, but obviously not enough. It was raining that night and this combined with the speed, an unfamiliar car and bad judgment made for a deadly combination.

I ask myself all the time what would have happened if I was going 10km slower. I know the answer . . . everyone would have been safe.

There is nothing I can do to bring back that young man and that is the part I can't handle. His wife and best friend who were in the car also suffered serious injuries. To know that I shattered the lives of two innocent families through one second's inattention, and knowing that there is a wound I can never hope to heal, is something I will have to live with for the rest of my life. I can't ask them for forgiveness because I can't even forgive myself.

All through this tragedy I have been concerned only about one thing and that has been their pain.

The media certainly haven't helped. At first they only reported about me as a rugby player being hurt and my chances about getting to the Games; not about the two injured people and the one dead person which I know caused the Malcolm and Casey families even more grief.

At the time, I was a mess physically and emotionally but the whole time I could think only of the greater pain that the other families were suffering.

At the hospital the doctors wanted to put a metal pin in my hand which I'd broken and would take about six weeks to heal. My brothers Beru and Honky told them not to because I had to play rugby in three weeks. To be honest, the Commonwealth Games were the last thing on my mind.

My family, friends and counsellor encouraged me to go to the Games. They said I couldn't just give up living. If I did, they said I would destroy another family in the process.

I decided to treat the Games as an attempt to get back on track but, as it happened, I decided to pull out of the Games because I didn't want the Malcolm and Casey families to turn on the TV and see me carrying on my life as though nothing had happened.

Gordon Tietjens wanted me to go. I really respect Titch. My counsellor also said I would be letting down my team-mates and a lot of other people if I didn't. I decided then I would only go if the victim's families didn't mind.

My lawyer then asked the police if they would make enquiries. The message that came back was that I should carry on with my life. I felt a huge load lift from my shoulders. Therefore, it came as a huge shock after we won gold, to learn that they were upset at my going to the Games. It was later I learnt the police hadn't actually spoken to them at all.

I saw another headline that said I had dedicated my medal to Brendan. I couldn't remember doing that, although in the euphoria after we had won, I wasn't sure exactly what I'd said. I tracked down the TV footage and recalled being asked about Richard Crawshaw – our manager who had died just before the Games. Then another reporter asked if I had thought about the man killed in the accident. It was a question which took me by surprise. I said a day didn't pass when I didn't think about him. But on TV they never showed the question which was asked and they made it look like I had elicited the whole conversation.

I never dedicated my gold medal to Brendan. His wife was on TV saying that was an insult – I agree with her, which is why I know I would never have said that. I'd never do something like that because it could only make matters worse, and that was the last thing I wanted.

Certain sections of the media have been quite grubby in their exploitation of the matter, I believe, but I guess they have a job to do. I have had plenty of positive headlines in the past so it's a little bit of taking the good with the bad. It's part of the territory when you're in the public spotlight, I suppose.

There are two events which stick in my mind as the hardest things I've done in my life. One was to watch while they turned off the life support machines which were keeping alive my cousin Bett, whom I had grown up with. The second was meeting Claire Malcolm, the widow of the young man I killed.

I can't explain the emotions in the room that day. All I know is that she handled it a lot better than I did. I don't know if I'll ever meet with Brendan's family, or the Casey family, as apparently they are too angry to have anything to do with me, and I can't say I blame them. If I were in their situation I'd probably feel exactly the same.

To live with the knowledge that you have ended a young person's life is not an easy thing to deal with. I still wake up at night with all the images burned into my brain. I can only hope that the passage of time will ease the pain for everyone. It will never be completely over for me or the families involved

There is one person who can forgive me for all I have done and I pray every night for that forgiveness.

My only hope is that when you finish reading this chapter you don't say, "It won't happen to me." I used to think like that, too. Back off the pedal just a little bit and you'll never have to live through your own private hell.

You're Nicked (And Named)

MAGNIFICENT SEVENS
Graeme Bachop – *Grim*
Todd Blackadder – *Blacky*
Norm Berryman – *Stormin*
Frano Botica – *Bots*
Robin Brooke – *Moose*
Zinzan Brooke – *Zinny or Murray*
Olo Brown – *O.B. or Max*
Frank Bunce – *Buncey or Senor*
Adrian Cashmore – *Cash*
Christian Cullen – *Cully, Kini or Beer Bottle*
Marc Ellis – *Macca*
Luke Erenavula – *Shadow*
Bradley Fleming – *Flash*
Blair Foote – *Footy Baka*
Stu Forster – *Bear*
Rico Gear – *Reaks*
Aaron Hamilton – *Tama*
Shane Howarth – *Howie*
Alama Ieremia – *April*
Ian Jones – *Kamo*
Martin Jones – *Boogsie*
Damian Karauna – *Titanic*
John Kirwan – *JK*
Pat Lam – *Patch*

Blair Larsen – *Lambie*
Jonah Lomu – *Jo*
Waisake Masirewa – *Ski*
Tony Monaghan – *Monza*
Sam Nonoa – *Helmet*
Glen Osborne – *Oz*
Junior Paramore – *Magic*
Dan Parkinson – *Ngapuhi*
Scott Pierce – *Basil*
Kevin Putt – *Putty*
Lindsay Raki – *Croc*
Caleb Ralph – *Snake*
Taine Randell – *Teapot*
Roger Randle – *Cacho*
Bruce Reihana – *Brusier or Hopsing*
John Schuster – *Shu*
Owen Scrimgeour – *Scrimmo*
Dallas Seymour – *Nails or Glass Body*
Wayne Shelford – *Buck*
Carlos Spencer – *Los*
Arthur Stone – *Stoney*
Ant Strachan – *Strakan*
Joe Tauiwi – *Kutu*
Karl Te Nana – *Nana*
JT Thomas – *JT*
Rua Tipoki – *Apple*
Joe Tua – *Joe Tua Auckland Touch*
Richard Turner – *Pod or Yannice*
Simon Tremain – *Son Of*
Amasio Valence – *Mudgi*
Joeli Vidiri – *Joey*
Peter Woods – *Poto*
Terry Wright – *TJ*
SUPPORTING CAST
Mark Allen – *Bull*
Mattie Blackburn – *Mattie*
Andrew Blowers – *AB*

YOU'RE NICKED (AND NAMED)

Mike Brewer – *Bruiser*
Billy Bush – *Bushy*
David Campese – *Campo*
Matthew Cooper – *Coops*
Eroni Clarke – *Roni*
Chas Ferris – *Chas*
Sean Fitzpatrick – *Fitzy*
Grant Fox – *Foxy*
Paul Henderson – *Ginge*
Norm Hewitt – *Normie*
John Jeffrey – *The Shark*
Michael Jones – *Ice*
Jamie Joseph – *JR or Fly*
Earle Kirton – *Ernie*
Josh Kronfeld – *Crusher*
Walter Little – *Walt or Laulau*
Richard Loe – *Loey or Dick*
Willie Lose – *Mirror Man*
Steve McDowell – *Stevie*
Scott McLeod – *Stormy*
Laurie Mains – *Lemons or Sir*
Justin Marshall – *Marshy*
Andrew Mehrtens – *Mehrts*
Tabai Matson – *Tabs*
Arran Pene – *Rewi*
Simon Poidevin – *Poido*
Hika Reid – *Hik*
Wayne Smith – *Smithy*
Joe Stanley – *Bullet*
Timo Tagaloa – *Tags*
Matt Te Pou – *Sir*
Peter Thorburn – *Thorbs*
Gordon Teitjens –*Titch*
Inga Tuigamala – *Big Bus*
Jeff Wilson – *Goldie or Bronzie*

ABOUT THE AUTHOR

This is John Matheson's sixth book. In 1999 he collaborated with Eric Rush on his best-selling book *Gold Rush*; in 2002 he penned the critically acclaimed *Black Days*; in 2002 he wrote Stacey Jones' book *Keeping the Faith* and another best-seller with Rush, *Rushie*; and in 2003 he wrote Christian Cullen's best-selling biography *Life On The Run*.

Throughout his 18 years in journalism he has been based in Auckland, London and San Diego and has covered such diverse sporting events as the Rugby World Cup, English soccer, Grand Slam tennis, the NBA and the America's Cup. While in New Zealand he has worked for the *Auckland Star* and *Sunday Star* and is the longest-serving editor of *NZ Rugby World*.

He is currently a senior journalist at *Sunday News*. Matheson — a four-time recipient at the Qantas Awards — directed the Sky TV rugby show *Offside* and lists completing the Ironman as one of his proudest achievements. He wishes to thank Hodder Moa Beckett's Kevin Chapman and Warren Adler for their continued support. He would also like to thank Jessica May Galu for her continued support and inspiration.